MW00851675

PATHS OF ARMOR

The Fifth Armored Division in World War II

THE BATTERY PRESS
Nashville

Originally Published 1950

The Battery Press
P.O. Box 3107, Uptown Station
Nashville, Tennessee 37219

Twenty-Seventh in the Divisional Series

1985

ISBN: 0-89839-084-2

Printed in the United States of America

DEDICATION

To all those, the living and the dead, who fought with the Fifth and faced each day new and unknown but common perils, this book is respectfully and humbly dedicated.

FOREWORD

THE FIFTH ARMORED DIVISION'S record of achievement is unsurpassed by that of any other division. And the ratio of its casualties to such achievement is the lowest in the entire United States Army.

It was the Fifth Armored which devised the married formation of tanks and infantry; it led the Normandy break through; it sprang the Falaise trap which meant the death of the Seventh German Army and the Field Marshal who commanded it. The Fifth Armored was the first division to reach the Eure River, the Seine, and the Our; it cut off near Mons thousands of Germans, later taken by the 1st Infantry Division. In one incredible day, it crossed the stubborn battlefields of World War I and outraced fleeing Germans from Nyon to the Belgian frontier. Throughout that day the route of its advance was a roll call of past battles: Cambrai, Le Cateau, St. Quentin, Vimy Ridge, Valenciennes.

The Victory Division was the first to enter Germany. It breached the Siegfried Line early in September, while other parts of our armies were still demonstrating before it, or skirmishing within it. The Fifth Armored cleared the Hurtgen Forest, after the job had been begun by five infantry divisions. In four days it overran its given area of the Rhineland. Three weeks later, within a few hours after crossing the Rhine, its engineers were maintaining bridges at Hamelin where:

The River Weser, deep and wide,
Washes its wall on
The southern side;

A few days later the division was on the Elbe, with bridge sites chosen and reconnaissance parties in boats—nearer to Berlin than any combat group in the American Army.

While the Fifth Armored was accomplishing these feats, the American public heard little about the division because of the tight censorship under which it operated and because it did not possess an elaborate public relations staff.

This history is now published to cast some light on these outstanding achievements. It tells how they were accomplished. It is also published as a tribute to the division's Commanding General, Major-General Lunsford E. Oliver (now retired). The record of the division, we all agree, merely reflects his wise, patient, intelligent and always aggressive leadership. It is only borrowing a phrase from the greatest of Books to say that General Oliver created the division in his own image.

No foreword would be complete without a word of appreciation; first and foremost to Vic Hillery and Major Emerson F. Hurley, without whose efforts, over 30 months' time, this history could not have been written at all. Lon MacFarland, Dave Batey, Bill Daniel all spent a great deal of time getting it published. Lt. Col. Fred E. Ressegieu and Harry Entrekin helped very much and Erling Foss took many of the photographs used. And probably most harassed of all was Lou Filas, our Association Secretary, who had to type, retype, edit, and re-edit the script, to decipher strange hands, and never once lost his good humor in doing so.

In the name of and on behalf of the Fifth Armored Division Association we thank them all; and we thank all of you who contributed source material in the form of letters, stories and whose actions we have been writing about.

We hope you like the book.

MARTIN PHILIPSBORN, JR.
(President, 5th Armored Division Association 1948-1949)

CONTENTS

5

A Message from General Oliver

THIS IS THE STORY of the Fifth Armored Division; the division which led in the drive that created the Falaise pocket, which was the first of all the Allied units to set foot on German soil and to pierce the Siegfried Line, which in the closing days of the war went out a hundred miles in front of the supporting infantry and fought its way to the Elbe River, closer to Berlin than any other Allied unit, and which was stopped there, not by the Germans, but by order from Ninth Army. Necessarily there can be mentioned in this story only a few of the many acts of heroism which made this record possible. The long months of training for the task ahead, the drudgery, the endurance of cold and wet and fatigue, that contributed to this record could not possibly be adequately portrayed. To have participated with you, men of the Fifth Armored Division, in all these things has been the greatest privilege of my life.

It is my hope that in the years to come the same spirit which drove you onward to your achievements in this war will cause you to take the lead in your communities in doing everything possible to make our country a better place in which to live, and to improve our international relations and prevent future wars, so that our heroic dead shall not have died in vain.

Lunsford E. Oliver

Mayor General, Commanding

PATHS OF ARMOR

I

A STAR IS BORN

It was 1 October 1941.

On Europe's Eastern Front Wehrmacht forces under Field Marshal Gerd von Runstedt broke through the Red Army's primary defenses as the Germans concluded the first week of their offensive against the Crimea. North and east of Dniepropetrovak, on the line toward the industrial Donets River basin, German armored divisions captured several Russian batteries, destroyed 45 of their tanks and encircled four Soviet infantry divisions.

In England inhabitants of Newcastle dug the dead and wounded from the rubble of the still-smouldering buildings that has been crushed and burned by a devastating Luftwaffe attach during the previous night.

On the red clay wasteland of Kentucky's Fort Knox, far from all this clash and smoke of battle, a group of soldiers lined up and came to attention. Some were regular U. S. Army men, others 12-month selectees, others active-duty reserve officers. They had been gathering here in tent city all during the previous month of September. Now their numbers were sufficiently great officially to form the nucleus of an army division.

This was activation day of the Fifth Armored Division. Appointed to command the new group was an officer from the Armored Force Replacement Center. He was Brig. Gen. Jack W. Heard (later promoted to Major General).

In his address to these assembled soldiers General Heard declared that this division would have a brilliant future. It seemed a rather rash and optimistic prediction. For if this division ever did come to grips with the enemy its battle opponents would be these Wehrmacht units which even then were already battle-seasoned and were winning brilliant engagements on the Eastern Front. Certainly it would be an exceptional accomplishment if this Fifth Armored Division even succeeded in holding its ground in any future encounter with any one of these German units.

But the Fifth Armored Division *was* destined to have a brilliant future. It was destined to meet these crack German panzer divisions in battle, and it would smash them. It was destined to carve out, on Europe's battlefields, one of the most brilliant combat records of any U. S. division in World War II.

These are some of the battle laurels which the Fifth Armored wears:

It lead the encircling movement in France which swung in back of the German Seventh Army and snapped shut the trap on this enemy force at the Falaise Gap;

It was the first division to reach the Seine River;

It was one of the first divisions to enter Belgium;

It was the first division to reach Luxembourg;

It was the first division to fight on German soil;

It was the first division to plunge through the Siegfried Line;

It was the American division, which, after the thrust across the German heartland, lay closest to Berlin; it was halted on the west bank of the Elbe River, 45 miles from the enemy capital, not by the Germans but by orders from SHAEF.

And although it amassed this impressive record of combat accomplishments, the Fifth Armored came through the war with a casualty rate that was among the lowest of all U. S. battle-scarred divisions. This attests to the speed and efficiency with which it executed its assigned missions; the excellence of its staff work and the hardiness of its soldiers. It also attests the genius of its leader, Major General Lunsford E. Oliver, who, two years after the close of hostilities, was to be told by his officers and men that "no division had a more beloved leader."

But it also has been the fate of the Fifth Armored to have its deeds little known. Because it was always in the vanguard, the division's identity was kept well concealed under such anonymous tags as: "Patton's ghost troops," or "First Army armored wedge," or "Ninth Army spearhead." And when much later the layers of censorship were finally rolled back and announcement was made of the division's accomplishments, the headlines were busy with much more immediate events. Therefore, this story is told so that others may know and Fifth Armored veterans may not soon forget.

II

WHAT'S IN A NAME

Ft. Knox

1 October 1941–10 February 1942

JUST AS Wellington traced the successes of British troops to the playing fields of Eton, the Fifth Armored's victories in Europe had their roots in the sands of the Mojave, the mud of Tennessee and the snows of upstate New York. It was a difficult and torturous path which the division had to follow before it reached the field of battle. It spent 34 months and traveled thousands of miles preparing to meet the enemy.

The first four months of the division's life were spent at its birthplace, Ft. Knox. Here, too, it was given its name even before it was formally activated. On 10 September 1941 it was decided to call the Fifth Armored the "Victory Division." It was a name which proved to be exceptionally appropriate, for three years and one day after it was adopted, the division led the victorious Allied ground forces into Germany.

The name was suggested by Pvt. Sidney Huttner, Battery B, 58th Field Artillery Bn. (armd). In an explanatory piece which he submitted with the suggested name, Pvt. Huttner pointed out that the Roman numeral equivalent for the Fifth Armored was V and that this symbol was then being used by the peoples of Europe's Nazi-occupied countries to express their faith in the ultimate victory over the enemy. Pvt. Huttner wrote this piece on 7 September 1941 while en route to Ft. Knox. For his effort he was rewarded with a furlough.

Members of the fledgling division began knuckling down to the grim and monotonous and sometimes interesting business of learning how to fight a war. There were hundreds of individual jobs that had to be learned, everything from cooking to taking apart tank motors. There was the ever-present close order drill with its annoying insistence on complete uniformity of dress. And there were dirty jobs to be done: washing dishes, cleaning latrines, loading trucks, firing stoves, hauling ashes.

On 10 October 1941 the division received its first medium tanks when five N-3's were driven into the 81st motor park.

On 27 October it was assigned its first mission: to guard the gold bullion deposited in vaults at Ft. Knox by the U. S. government. The initial alert platoon given the job came from the 85th Reconnaissance Battalion and was commanded by 1st Lt. John P. Gerald, later, as a Major, killed in action near the German border.

On 11 November the division made its first public appearance when artillery, infantry and engineer units paraded with other Ft. Knox units through the streets of Louisville in an Armistice Day celebration.

When the declaration of war on Germany came 11 December 1941 the training pace was quickened. And plans were rushed to move the division to its new station, Camp Cooke, California.

Originally the Fifth Armored had been activated as a heavy armored division. It consisted of three tank regiments, a brigade headquarters, an artillery regiment, an artillery battalion, an infantry regiment, a reconnaissance battalion and an engineer battalion.

But on 1 January 1942 the division's organization was completely revamped. Of the original three tank regiments, 81st (medium tanks), 34th (light tanks), and 31st (light tanks), it was decided to inactivate the 31st; the other two regiments dropped their light and medium designations and instead each was given one light tank battalion, and two "medium" battalions. No "heavy" tanks were seen throughout the war.

The 46th Armored Infantry Regiment, which originally had two battalions, was assigned another. The division's brigade headquarters gave way to two combat command headquarters.

Other units inactivated were the 21st Ordnance and 19th Quartermaster Battalion. In their place appeared the Maintenance Battalion, Supply Battalion and Train Headquarters and Headquarters Co.

The 65th Field Artillery Regiment was changed to a battalion and the 95th Artillery Battalion was formed. The 58th Artillery

Battalion remained unchanged. The 85th Reconnaissance and 22nd Engineer Battalions also remained unchanged.

After the reshuffling had been completed, the division settled down for another cold month of training. Then in the second week of February orders went out for the Fifth Armored members to pack up their equipment. With their horseshoe rolls on their backs they marched off to the railroad station. But not everyone went west. Just as the Fifth had been formed from cadres supplied by the Third and Fourth Armored Divisions, it left behind a cadre for the Eighth Armored Division.

As the California-bound train pulled away from the red clay wasteland there were few regrets among the Fifth Armored men. Behind them they left some medium and old "Mae West" light tanks, the mud, the tents, the stoves, and the fire shovels.

The Fifth Armored's first Chief of Staff at Ft. Knox was Col. John B. Wogan; he later became a major general and commanded the 13th Armored Division.

Brigade Commander at Ft. Knox was Brig. Gen. John S. Wood, who joined the division on 1 December 1941.

First commanders of the 81st and 34th were Col. Vernon Evans and Col. Robert W. Grow, respectively; both became major generals later in the war.

First commander of the 31st were first Col. Guy W. Chipman and Col. Sereno E. Brett.

First commander of the 46th was Lt. Col. John H. Ringe; Col. Floyd W. Waltz arrived late in January and took the regiment to Camp Cooke.

First commander of the 65th was Lt. Col. J. J. B. Williams; Lt. Col. Harold W. Blakely assumed command on 18 October.

First commander of the 58th was Major John G. Howard; Lt. Col. Samuel V. Krauthoff was first commander of the 95th.

First commanders of the 85th and 22nd were Lt. Col. Frank A. Allen, Jr., and Major Reginald L. Dean, respectively.

III

BETWEEN THE FLOWER BEDS AND THE SEA

Camp Cooke, California

15 February 1942–1 August 1942

CAMP COOKE, CALIFORNIA, is literally a garden spot. It borders the multicolored Lompoc and Santa Maria Valleys, which are the greatest flower seed-growing areas in the United States. But actually the camp is no bed of roses.

Located high above these valleys on a mesa that juts out into the Pacific, the military reservation is swept by high winds and frequently is engulfed in blankets of dripping fog. While its colorful neighboring valleys glow with rows of sweet peas, larkspur, nasturtiums, zinnias and other blooms, the camp's uncleared areas are covered with sage brush. Where this brush has been cut away the surface is either sand or cream-colored diatomaceous earth. There are also rows of tall stately eucalyptus trees, which were planted when the reservation was still a ranch to shield it from some of the winds off the sea.

The camp's military structures are set back about a mile from the reservation's eight-mile coast line. These buildings were all new when the Fifth Armored made its home here in February. The veterans of Ft. Knox's Tent City were happy to find oil-heated barracks, modern kitchens and elaborate motor parks.

Even before it was out of its steel diapers the Victory Division began to feel the war's hot breath. Before the California-bound soldiers had left Ft. Knox they had been issued several .50 caliber machine guns. Anti-aircraft Plan A had been ready to go into effect during the trip if the Jap should strafe the train. Gun crews had been prepared to rush these ground mount fifties out of the cars and start blazing away at the enemy planes. During the five-day trip "old timers" taught the rest of the soldiers how to field strip these machine guns.

On 24 February, just nine days after the division arrived at its new home by the sea, a Japanese submarine surfaced about 10 miles north of Santa Barbara and started lobbing shells into the Elwood oil fields. At Camp Cooke, about 55 miles north of this spot, the 22nd Engineers (which was the "Alert Battalion" that night) sent patrols to the beaches. The remainder of the division stood by for action. But that night there was no further enemy activity. The following night word was received that unidentified planes had been fired on by coastal anti-aircraft batteries at Long Beach and the camp had its first blackout.

During March olive drab was painted over the bright yellow exteriors of all the camp's buildings. And the glass in all the windows facing the sea was painted over.

Many "vacate camp alerts" were issued by the Western Defense Command during the division's early months at Camp Cooke. Frequently they came in the middle of the night. Fifth Armored men had to haul their equipment to the motor parks, load up the tanks and halftracks and head out on a 15 or 20 mile motor march.

While the Japanese fleet was maneuvering in the North Pacific during the last week in May, the Fifth Armored was on special alert status. The division, less Combat Command A, occupied the reservation's coastline and made plans to counterattack any enemy landings. CC A, under the command of General Wood, moved to Alondra Park on the southern edge of Los Angeles. Its mission here was to repulse any enemy paratroop landings near the plane factories and the Airports. When the Battle of Midway started the alert was ended.

Despite these numerous alerts the division continued its basic training according to the original schedule mapped out by the War Department Mobilization Program. In March over 9,000 men had arrived at Camp Cooke to fill out the armored skeleton which had been formed at Ft. Knox. These men had come straight from induction centers, mostly midwest centers, such as Camp Grant and Ft. Sheridan, Ill., and Ft. Snelling, Minn. But there had also been big contingents from other states, such as Ft. Dix, N. J., and Ft. Bliss, Texas. These men were given the regular 13 weeks of basic training and then six weeks of specialized training.

In the individual alerts and exercises that required participation of the entire division, flexibility in the attacking formation was becoming popular. The division commander combined his tactical units in whatever type of striking force he thought could best meet the individual "enemy" situations. He massed his tanks in a simple powerful steamroller force, or employed all the infantry units in the traditional type of attack force, or formed combination tank-infantry battalion teams. This last formation was a forerunner of the even greater tank-infantry integration which the division would achieve by the time it reached actual combat. Then it would have "married" tank-infantry companies that proved so devastating to enemy forces.

While still at Camp Cooke the division also started developing the combat command type of tactical headquarters. CC A was first commanded by Brig. Gen. Wood and later by Brig. Gen. Harold W. Blakely, CC B's first commander was Brig. Gen. Sereno E. Brett. CC A's tactical units included: the 34th Armored Regiment, 71st Armored Field Artillery Battalion, and the 1st Battalion of the 46th Armored Infantry Regiment. CC B's organization consisted of: the 81st Armored Regiment, 47th Armored Field Artillery Battalion, and the 2nd Battalion of the 46th. The remainder of the units formed what was known as the Division Reserve.

By mid-summer the Fifth Armored was beginning to shape up as a fighting force. On 1 August 1942 its strength was 15,000 men.

But America's armies were continuing to expand and the division was again called upon to contribute some of its strength to the formation of still another armored division. In August many of the soldiers who had started with the division at Ft. Knox packed up and departed for Camp Beal, California, as a cadre for the 13th Armored Division.

Orders went out for the rest of the division to pack up, too. During the first week of August it rolled its tanks and halftracks onto railway flat cars and blocked them in place. Then while part of the personnel mounted the trains, the rest climbed into wheel vehicles and started on a 250-mile overland journey. Their destination was a hot spot on God's scorched acres bounded by Needles, Blythe, and Desert Center in California's Mojave Desert.

IV

WIND, SAND AND SUN

The Mojave Desert

August to December 1942

IN THE MOJAVE DESERT the Fifth Armored received nature's Baptism of Fire. Here in this hot dry basin at the height of summer the sun's uninterrupted rays beat down with an intensity that drove the temperature as high as 130 degrees. Men had to swallow several salt tablets each day to keep from losing consciousness. They had to keep their heads covered or quickly become victims of sun stroke.

During the first three weeks in this inferno no heavy work was permitted from ten to two each day. Men lay panting under their shelter halfs hoping the evening would come quickly. And then when darkness with its cooling relief did come, they lay behind their netting wondering about the rattlesnakes, tarantulas and scorpions which holed up during the heat of the day and crawled around at night.

Usually a death-like stillness prevailed on these vast open expanses with only the heat waves rising from the hot sand. But often this stillness was broken by the violence of an electrically-charged wind storm which would rage across the desert floor churning the sand into choking clouds and ripping the shelterhalfs and other canvases from their moorings.

By the end of August the heat had abated slightly and men had become somewhat acclimated to the hot dry atmosphere. Then the actual maneuvers began. And as the huge fleets of tanks, halftracks and trucks moved out over the open wastes they stirred up billows of dust which became a serious problem for both men and machines. The men clapped dust respirators or handkerchiefs over their mouths and nostrils. Over their eyes they wore goggles. In the diesel tanks the dust packed between the clutch plates so that shifting became almost impossible. Oil in air cleaners had to be changed daily, otherwise the dust got into the motors and would scar the piston walls.

While members of the Fifth Armored battled the heat, dust and the "enemy", their thoughts often strayed to another desert. In the North African desert one of the war's crucial campaigns was being fought. There the British 8th Army was starting its long drive to push Rommel's panzer forces back from the gates of Egypt. Victory Division men wondered if they were being trained to fight eventually on this North African desert. Their interest was heightened in this engagement on the other side of the world when five soldiers who had just returned from a nine-week stay in the North African theater joined the Fifth Armored on 20 September.

These tankers had been sent to Egypt from the Ft. Knox Armored Force Replacement Center. Attached to the British forces, they had manned American tanks which were under enemy fire for eight days. They had participated in a three-day engagement with German tanks and had been bombed by enemy planes. These soldiers and the Fifth Armored units which they joined were: Cpl. William E. Grove, 85th; T/5 Benjamin F. Folsom, Hq. CC B; T/5 William E. Malpede, Hq. CC A; Pfc. John Aspesi, 34th; and Pvt. John Sullivan, 81st.

As thick as the dust clouds throughout the maneuvers were, the rumors that the division at any moment would be shipped to that other desert. For some members of the Fifth Armored these rumors proved to be true. In September two artillery battalions, the 58th and 65th, quietly withdrew from the maneuvers and from the division. The 58th arrived at Casablanca 11 November 1942 and fought in North Africa and Sicily. At the time it left the Mojave this battalion was commanded by Lt. Col. Bernard W. McQuade, who later was killed on "D" Day during the invasion of Normandy. After the 65th, under the command of Capt. Edward A. Bailey, left the division it did not go immediately overseas. It remained in the desert for several weeks and arrived in Casablanca 26 January 1943. It, too, fought in North Africa and Sicily.

The withdrawal of these battalions from the Fifth Armored did not leave the division short of artillery units for the remainder of the maneuvers. On 10 Septembers two more artillery battalions arrived from Ft. Sill. They were: the 71st, commanded by Lt. Col. I. B. Washburn, and the 47th, commanded by Lt. Col. Harvey K. Palmer. They had been Artillery school troops and were already familiar with marking base points and firing for effect.

The Fifth Armored's actual tactical maneuvers in the Mojave consisted of eight field problems. Each was from four to six days long, followed by a rest and maintenance period. The enemy, always far superior, was represented sometimes by other troops. On the broad expanses between the jagged ridges General Heard, the cavalryman, had an opportunity to employ all the trickery and deception of an armored division in corps operation. During one problem the 85th was sent off 20 miles to one flank to stir up a large column of dust. This drew the enemy reserves out of position. And then the 81st and 34th concentrated on a narrow front to crash through and "destroy" the enemy.

During the final problem the "red" enemy forces consisted of the battle-ready 3rd Armored Division. And it fell victim to the Fifth Armored's chicanery. A Fifth Armored Company commander called over the "enemy" radio channel to come over to the corral near the highway for gasoline. The "red" tank battalion innocently assembled in the face of the Fifth Armored's massed tanks and anti-tank guns to be "destroyed."

Later in the same problem, however, the Third Armored retaliated for this ruse. An "enemy" liaison group managed to capture a Fifth Armored task force commander by boldly walking up to a headquarters sentry and asking him, "Which way to Colonel Boyer's Command Post?" The "enemy" party was escorted right into the blackout C P tent.

The tactical details of the desert warfare, as portrayed by the long arrows and the pincer operations on the acetate-covered maps never quite filtered down to the average soldier to permit him to visualize the "routed enemy's burning columns and his overrun positions." But the training nevertheless was valuable to all members of the division. By November all crew members were qualified drivers. Tank maintenance crews thoroughly learned their jobs by keeping vehicles rolling through the knee-deep dust and the endless miles of sand. The driving experience enabled the division's motor columns to move like clockwork. And each man had become an experienced individual cook and could live alone in the field.

Over 100 newly-commissioned officers from the Armored Force School and the Infantry School joined the Fifth Armored during the maneuvers. These lieutenants later became the company commanders and unit staff officers when the division made history in Europe.

At the conclusion of the maneuvers the division assembled near the little city of Needles. This community on the Colorado River is the oldest city on the desert. Here the division spent a month waiting for transportation back to Camp Cooke and repairing the damages done to the vehicles during the three-month grind through the sand.

Then, during the final week of November, the division left this scene of its play war, where there had been also a few real casualties.

V

THE MAN FROM NORTH AFRICA

Camp Cooke, California

December, 1942–March, 1943

WHEN THE FIFTH ARMORED came out of the hot crucible of the sun and journeyed back up the California coast, the tanned soldiers viewed Camp Cooke in a new light. They had a new appreciation for its plumbing, mattresses and mess halls. They decided it was not such a bad place after all.

After shaking the sand from their clothes and equipment, they settled down to more rehearsing for battle. They concentrated on combat firing and platoon and company problems. The artillery battalions received new M7's and used the range south of the Santa Ynez River. Tank and infantry battalions fired into the ocean from the sandy hills of Tangair Range, which extended from Port Petrol south to the river. Bushes on the range became enemy machine guns and were blasted with tank shells and hand grenades.

Training was as realistic as possible. Tank battalions buttoned up and fired at each other with .30 caliber ammunition. Infantry dug in and listened to artillery shells whistle overhead and explode 600 yards to the front. The 85th reconnoitered half the state of California. And the 22nd threw bridges across the Santa Ynez River and laid mine fields all over the reservation.

During January and February all platoons of the division were tested for combat efficiency. General Blakely examined the tank platoons while testing of the infantry platoons was conducted by Brig. Gen. Eugene A. Regnier, who had joined the Fifth in December, and had succeeded General Brett as the commander of CC B.

During this post-desert period members of the division were also enjoying their first furloughs. These first trips as soldiers back to the homes they had left as civilians were strange and memorable experiences.

Then one day in early March everyone put on his o.d.'s and field jacket, lined up and marched down to the field house. Here a tall, lean-cheeked, gray-haired soldier was introduced as the Fifth Armored's new commander. He was Major General Lunsford E. Oliver. There was a tan on his face but it had not been acquired in the Mojave sun. He had just returned from North Africa where he had led the First Armored's Combat Command B in the American forces invasion of that continent. General Oliver described the fighting on North African battlefields where American units had, for the first time in this war, encountered the German Wehrmacht. And as the assembled soldiers listened intently to his grim words they realized that the war was far from won, that much difficult and bloody fighting lay ahead, and that the Fifth Armored would play an important role in this tremendous military effort.

Many changes in commanders were made during the 13 months on the west coast. Gen. Wood left the division in June to command the Fourth Armored Division and Gen. Blakely became the new CC A commander. Col. Roy L. Dalferes joined in November to become the Division Artillery Officer. Gen. Regnier arrived in December to succeed Gen. Brett as commander of CC B.

Col. John T. Cole arrived in September to command the 81st Armored Regiment. Among the battalion commanders were: 1st Bn., Lt. Col. Littleton A. Roberts, Maj. William R. Kirchner, Lt. Col. Joel B. Stratton, and Lt. Col. Moderwell K. Salem; 2nd Bn., Maj. Jesse M. Hawkins, Jr., Maj. LeRoy H. Anderson; 3rd Bn., Maj. Robert P. Smith, Jr., Maj. Richard W. Ripple.

The 34th Armored Regiment commanders were: Col. Frank A. Allen, Jr., Lt. Col. Thomas W. Roane, and Col. Emerick Kutschko. Among Battalion commanders were: 1st Bn., Lt. Col. Horace W. Forester, Lt. Col. Halbert H. Neilson, Lt. Col. Charles E. Morrison and Maj. Luther L. Willard; 2nd Bn., Maj. Clyde A. Burcham, Lt. Col. Gustavus W. West, and Lt. Col. Richard H. Jones; 3rd Bn., Lt. Col. Paul C. Febiger, Maj. Joseph J. Baker, Maj. Thomas H. Dowd, and Maj. William A. Hamberg.

During desert maneuvers Col. Harry L. Reeder succeeded Col. Waltz as commander of the 46th Armored Infantry Regiment before Col. Glen H. Anderson arrived to become the permanent commander. Battalion commanders included: 1st Bn., Lt. Col. Howard E. Boyer; 2nd Bn., Lt. Col. Earl S. Gibson; 3rd Bn., Capt. William H. Burton, and Lt. Col. Edgar A. Gans.

The 95th Field Artillery Battalion was commanded by Maj. Malcolm K. Benadum, Maj. LeCount H. Slocum, and Maj. Daniel H. Heyne. In December, Lt. Col. James W. McNeer joined the battalion and remained as the commander throughout the war.

Successive commanders of the 85th Reconnaissance Battalion were: Lt. Col. Thomas G. Dobyns, Maj. Wayne J. Dunn, Lt. Col. Gustavus W. West, and Maj. Kent Fay.

As chief of staff Col. Wogan was succeeded by Col. Cornelius M. Daly. At the end of maneuvers Col. Leo. G. Clarke was assigned the job.

Two members of the war-time division staff started their duties at this early date. Maj. Lonsdale P. MacFarland took over the G-2 position from Lt. Col. Rufus L. Land and Lt. Col. Charles E. Morrison was succeeded as G-4 by Maj. Harrison R. Entrekin, who had served as Asst. G-1 since the activation of the division. Lt. Col. Edward G. Farrand was G-3 and Lt. Col. Weeden B. Nichols became G-1.

THE FIFTH ARMORED'S NEW COMMANDER

Maj. Gen. Lunsford E. Oliver graduated from West Point in 1913 with a commission of Second Lieutenant in the Corps of Engineers.

During World War I he organized and trained several railway engineer battalions and rose to the rank of Lt. Colonel. After the war the most important of the many engineering jobs he undertook was the Mississippi River Flood Control Project.

General Oliver graduated from the Engineer School at Ft. Belvoir in 1916, the Command and General Staff School at Ft. Leavenworth in 1928, and the Army War College in 1938.

In 1940 he was assigned to the Armored Force at Ft. Knox as the Armored Force Engineer. During these early days of armor, General Oliver directed the experimental work which resulted in the development of the steel treadway bridge that later carried American tanks across all the rivers in Western Europe.

Assigned to the First Armored Division in January 1942, he commanded Combat Command B. He was promoted to Brigadier General on 16 February 1942. Going overseas with the division 6 May 1942, General Oliver's command trained in Northern Ireland during the summer and autumn. In September he was called to London to assist in planning the invasion of North Africa.

When the Allies invaded Algeria General Oliver's command landed at Oran. Two weeks later his command moved east into Tunisia and fought its first major engagement at Medjez-el-bab from the 6th to the 10th December 1942.

General Oliver was promoted to Major General on 20 November 1942.

When the remainder of the First Armored Division arrived in Africa General Oliver returned to the United States to command the Fifth Armored Division, bringing, as aides, two veterans of the early fighting in North Africa: Captain Ray Cannon and Lt. Frank Poole, whose experience and reports helped members of the Fifth Armored Division to realize the realities of combat.

Desert 136 degrees.

See the "M" — Medium.

The Colorado.

Our first real Medium

On the go.

Assembly before Maneuvers.

Mud home in Tenn.

Chow time in Tenn.

Four days growth.

Hurry up and wait.

Once a week in Tenn.

"Build a bridge here!" he said.

The Cumberland.

VI

PREVIEW IN TENNESSEE

24 March–1 July 1943

General Heard had forged the Fifth Armored Division into a mighty lance. Now it remained for General Oliver to temper it, bring to it razor-sharpness and to drive it into the heart of the Wehrmacht. But the first task which befell the new division commander was to lead his troops against one of the most unpleasant foes of all ground forces: Mud.

Soon after General Oliver's arrival the Victory Division men turned their vehicles over to the Sixth Armored Division, stuffed their belongings into barracks bags and climbed aboard eastbound trains. Their destination, they were told, was Tennessee, where they would participate in more maneuvers. Many believed, however, that the division was actually headed for an Atlantic Coast port of embarkation.

But the trains went no further east than Tennessee. There the soldiers were taken in trucks from the railhead and hauled to open fields near Manchester and McMinnville. These fields were soft and damp. As soon as the men and vehicles started moving about in them, they turned quickly into sticky quagmires. During the first three weeks in Tennessee it rained frequently, snowed once and was bitter cold every night. This was an abrupt change from the heated barracks and conveniences of Camp Cooke. But the ingenious use of logs, clapboard, straw and sawdust made homes of the shelterhalf in the fields and woods. With the numerous small log cabins that were erected many areas took on the appearance of early American frontier settlements.

Fifth Armored men spent the initial week in the field getting reacquainted with pup tent life and learning how to conquer the mud. They were also put through a vigorous physical conditioning program which consisted chiefly of long hikes. During this period, too, units began receiving their quotas of tanks, halftracks, peeps and trucks. New gasoline-driven tanks with the automatic transmissions were assigned to the tank platoons. It was the first time the crews had seen the V-type engines and enthusiasm for them was high. Mechanics started arriving back from Ft. Knox where they had been attending special schools. They had been taught how to keep these tank engines running and they now spouted such terms as "insoluble long-fiber grease," "concentric and excentric carburetors," and "dead track blocks."

By the time the maneuver exercises or mock battles got under way during the last week in April, chill winds and dampness of the winter's end had disappeared and spring was coming in. The weather grew milder; the forests started turning green; plowed furrows appeared in the fields; and the streams became warm enough to make baths a pleasure. The vehicles still kept mostly to the roads, except, of course, when they pulled into bivouac or detoured around wooden bridges that could not support the heavy tanks. Many of the roads that wound precariously through the hills were very narrow and more than one vehicle toppled down an embankment.

Many of the four-day tactical problems included a crossing of the Cumberland River. The initial jump to the "enemy" bank was always made by infantry in assault boats. After the bridgehead had been secured the 22nd Engineer Battalion would construct a treadway bridge. Then the tank regiments would pour across this bridge, break out of the bridgehead and "destroy the enemy."

After the treadway bridge had been constructed during the first river-crossing maneuver, a telegram was received from Washington forbidding treadway bridges to be used by 30 ton medium tanks. To demonstrate that the bridge was capable of supporting these tanks General Oliver climbed into one and took it across the river. In subsequent river crossings all the division's vehicles used the bridge.

Through the spring days and nights as the tanks and halftracks rumbled over the slippery unreconnoitered roads and through the narrow passes and forests, many Victory Division men believed this experience was a waste of time. They thought such movements would never be made in actual combat because the field manuals stated that tanks should avoid areas where freedom of maneuver would be hampered.

Contrary to this belief, however, the maneuvers in Tennessee were in many ways a preview of the conditions of the Fifth Armored would encounter later in Europe. Many of the long night marches across Tennessee were identical to those made later in France—except that the distant figures slinking in the shadows were 79th Division doughs and not German soldiers. And the mud which the Fifth came to know during its early weeks in Tennessee would be met again along the Siegfried Line and in the Huertgen Forest.

As the muddy roads turned to dust under the hot June sun and the swarms of flies and chiggers descended on the bivouac areas, the Division completed its tactical exercises and rolled its vehicles onto railway flat cars. It was on the move again. This time to northern New York state.

VII

PINE NEEDLES, SNOW AND APPLES

Pine Camp, N. Y.

5 July—10 December 1943

THE GI LOOKED at every camp with a jaundiced eye. He had his own particular terse and derisive comment for each new military post to which he was sent. His descriptive tag for Pine Camp was "a place where there are two seasons—winter and the Fourth of July."

The Fifth Armored GI would add grudgingly, however, that he was happy to arrive at this northern New York state camp in the summer of 1943 and leave behind him Tennessee's humid June heat. Despite the GI's exaggeration, the camp enjoys the normal four seasons, although nature does seem to place its emphasis on the winter months. Even in summer the pine-scented air is usually cool and brisk. The reservation is not far from the St. Lawrence River and some of its firing ranges are on the shores of Lake Ontario, which is about 37 miles from the camp.

Hopes of the Fifth Armored men that they would be able to relax in the pleasant atmosphere of this new camp after the rigors of the maneuvers soon were shattered. Shortly after their arrival it was announced that the division would begin an intensive training program. It was basic training all over again with a few new embellishments. The morning drill and calisthenics period was lengthened and there were long marches and other physical conditioning exercises. All the division's members were later put through the XIII Corps' stringent physical fitness tests, which included running, crawling and carrying tests and a long speed march.

As psychological training, division members also had to go through obstacle courses. In one of these they had to crawl through barbed wire entanglements while explosive charges were set off near them and streams of machine gun bullets were fired a few feet above their bodies. Another obstacle course was designed to quicken men's mental alertness. It included booby traps, trip wires, snipers, partly-concealed enemy equipment and electrified fences.

Greatest emphasis during this tuning-up period, however, was on weapons proficiency. Long hours were spent field stripping and reassembling the different guns and learning to identify their individual parts. Each man wrote a field message each day to satisfy G-2. Units took turns spending several days at Stoney Point on Lake Ontario where they practiced firing on the rifle ranges from dawn until dusk and pulled targets in the pits until their arms and backs ached. In the tank gunnery training, crews tried to hit the target with the first round and were expected to bracket with at least the first two rounds.

Answering a distress call in September from the fruit growers of central New York state who could not obtain sufficient help to harvest their apple crop, the division asked for volunteers from among its members to do the job. About 1,000 men readily put away their rifles and went off for a month to pick apples. Later in their army careers they would once again come to know apple orchards familiarly—in Normandy.

Pine Camp is remembered by most Victory Division men chiefly as the place where the War Department's scalpel cut away some of its bulk. Combat experience and the observations of maneuvers in the U. S. had convinced some of the army's high architects that armored divisions could operate more efficiently and effectively if they were reorganized and reduced in size.

In the streamlining process the Fifth Armored's two tank regiments were broken up into five separate battalions, two of which were transferred out of the division. The infantry regiment was changed to three separate battalions, with no regimental headquarters. Two companies of the engineer battalion were taken out of the division and two troops were added to the 85th, which was redesignated as a Cavalry Reconnaissance Squadron, Mechanized.

Generally, the effect of the reorganization, which took place officially on 20 September, was to reduce the number of units, eliminate the regimental headquarters and divide the division into three fairly set combat teams: Combat Commands, A, B, and R. Each team had a tank battalion, an infantry battalion, an artillery battalion and separate companies of reconnaissance, medical and engineer troops. The reshuffle also strengthened combat command headquarters, giving each of them a headquarters company of its own. And it created a new combat command, CC Reserve.

Appointed to command the new combat commands were: General Regnier, Combat Command A; Colonel Cole, Combat Command B; and Colonel Anderson, Combat Command R. Earlier Lt. Col. Farrand had been made Chief of Staff.

It was not long after their arrival at Pine Camp before the Victory Division men had heard numerous impressive accounts of the low temperatures and deep snows which visited the section during the winter months. And when in October they began receiving issues of cold weather clothing and orders went out to winterize all vehicles, these veterans of the Mojave feared that their destiny's pendulum was now swinging them into the other extreme of nature. Swiftly word swept through the barracks and day rooms that the division would participate in winter maneuvers.

Not too happily did the Fifth Armored members watch the brilliant colors of northern New York's fall fade and the first snows arrive with November. Unit training continued and a few nights were spent sleeping out in the snow trying out the new winter sleeping bags.

But during this activity an undercurrent of new rumors began to stir. It was said that the maneuvers had been called off and that the division was going to move again, perhaps toward a port of embarkation. Supporting these rumors were unusual occurrences such as the visit of Undersecretary of War Robert P. Patterson to witness a combat firing demonstration.

One of the last exercises held at Pine Camp was a demonstration of air power and ground anti-aircraft defense. Participating units were 1st Lt. Richard A. Biederman's A/34th and Capt. Arthur J. Elmore's B/15th.

Then on 25 November came the order for the Fifth Armored to pull up stakes in northern New York State and move to the Indiantown Gap Military Reservation in Pennsylvania. Winterizing vehicles was immediately halted and supply sergeants called in all the new winter clothing.

General Regnier was in charge of the advance party which left on 30 November for the division's new home, while the remainder of the division followed ten days later. The tanks and halftracks were taken by rail. But the wheel vehicles were driven in a cold overland trip; water froze in the canteens of men riding in the backs of the trucks.

The division had missed taking part in full-scale winter maneuvers. Later, however, it would fight actual battles in the snow.

In the reorganization of the Fifth Armored the following major changes were made:

UNIT	REDESIGNATED AS
34th Armored Regiment (Less 1st and 3rd Battalions, Band, Maint., and Rcn. Cos.)	34th Tank Battalion
81st Armored Regiment (Less 3rd Battalion, Band, Maint., Service, and Rcn. Cos.)	81st Tank Battalion
3rd Battalion, 34th Armored Reg.	10th Tank Battalion
46th Armored Infantry Regiment (Less 1st and 2nd Battalions)	46th Armored Infantry Battalion
1st Battalion, 46th Armored Inf.	47th Armored Infantry Battalion
2nd Battalion, 46th Armored Inf.	15th Armored Infantry Battalion
	85th Cav. Rcn. Squadron, Mecz. (Less Trs. D and E)
Rcn. Co., 34th Armored Regiment	Tr. D, 85th Cav. Rcn. Sq., Mecz.
Rcn. Co., 81st Armored Regiment	Tr. E, 85th Cav. Rcn. Sq., Mecz.
Maint. Battalion, 5th Armored Div.	127th Ord. Maint. Battalion

TRANSFERRED FROM THE DIVISION

1st Battalion, 34th Armored Reg.	772nd Tank Battalion
3rd Battalion, 81st Armored Reg.	707th Tank Battalion
Co. E, 22nd Armored Engineer Bn.	989th Treadway Bridge Co.
Co. D, 22nd Armored Engineer Bn.	
Supply Battalion	

General Blakely was transferred from the division on 28 August; he went overseas with the 4th Infantry Division and at the war's end was Major-General and the division commander.

In July Lt. Col. John B. Rosenzweig was made commander of the 47th Armored Field Artillery Battalion and Maj. F. Boynton Butler, Jr. became G-3.

Lt. Col. Richard H. Jones was made commander of the 772nd Tank Battalion with the original light tank unit being augmented with personnel from the Maintenance and Headquarters Companies of the two tank regiments.

Lt. Col. Richard W. Ripple was given command of the 707th Tank Battalion.

The 989th Treadway Bridge Command and Company D, 22nd, were transferred to XIII Corps with no changes in personnel.

Lt. Col. Earl S. Gibson was given command of the 46th and Maj. John S. Wintermute was made commander of the 15th Armored Infantry Battalion.

VIII

WOULD YOU STILL BE MY DARLING

Indiantown Gap, Pa.

10 December 1943–4 February 1944

INDIANTOWN GAP is about 140 miles from the sea but during the war it was considered part of a Port of Embarkation. Here was the start of the long and tedious processing which ended many weeks later at the gangplank. By the time a soldier reached the end of this line, he had, among other things, been inoculated with malaria, typhoid and booster tetanus shots; his slightly worn shoelaces had been replaced with a new pair; his unit had completed the Army Ground Force Battalion tests; and he had said his good-bye.

The assembly-line pre-shipment preparations were carefully sign-posted by voluminous POE instructions. Company commanders and unit staffs dug through these directions, mapped out their programs and then recorded each man's individual progress. The overseas-bound GI had to complete his marksmanship firing, go through the infiltration course, take a furlough, observe the attack of a fortified position, see the required training films, get a new set of dog tags along with other new clothing and equipment, pass through the poisonous gas-filled chambers, fire a bazooka and throw two grenades. It seemed a soldier just couldn't get on a boat until he had thrown two hand grenades; to meet this requirement some men had to be taken out after dark to the ranges where they threw their grenades by the light from truck headlamps. In the evenings after chow troops were assembled in the mess halls so that personnel officers could personally interview each man and verify the entries in his service record.

Even medical officers had become militarized in their thinking. "Soldiers are returning from furloughs with civilian diseases," declared Lt. Col. Joseph O. Boydstone, Division Surgeon, at a meeting of unit commanders. Efforts were redoubled to prevent the spread of these colds and influenza infections, brought back from the "civilian" world.

The tank, artillery and infantry battalions and the 85th completed the Ground Force tests in January. A team from XIII Corps conducted the exercises in the frozen, windswept valley beyond Blue Mountain ridge west of the camp. High scorers in each group were: the 34th Tank, 95th Artillery and the 15th Infantry.

Lights burned long and POE instructions became dog-eared as the furious bee-hive activity continued. Soldiers in supply rooms and motor parks shook their heads and muttered, "Madhouse." But each platoon leader and company commander knew in great detail the status and rate of progress of the men in his own little orbit of training. Gradually the division worked its way toward the gangplank.

To bring the infantry battalions up to strength approximately 250 non-commissioned officers from the inactivated 181st Infantry Regiment were added to the division. These well-trained soldiers from New England were quickly converted into armored infantrymen. The fact that each company had two 1st sergeants was no problem for 1st Sgt. Garvice R. Duckworth. He wrote the words "Tactical" and "Administrative" before the names on the overseas rosters.

During this period Maj. Francis W. Marks* became G-1 to complete the division staff for the duration of the war and Maj. Roland S. Biersach* was assigned command of the 127th Ordnance Maintenance Battalion.

All the division's tanks, halftracks and other vehicles were turned in to the post during the last few days of January. Then on 4 February the Fifth Armored was en route to Camp Kilmer, N. J. This was the last stop before boarding the trans-Atlantic transports. During the four days here activity reached a feverish pitch as the last minute shortages were filled, final rosters prepared, numerous showdown inspections conducted and instructions given on how to abandon ship and load life boats in the event of a torpedoing.

Finally on 9 February the Fifth Armored members hoisted their

-----

* (later Lt. Col.)

packs and horseshoe blanket rolls to their backs and marched down to Camp Kilmer's loading platforms. From here the trains took them to ferry boat slips in Jersey City. As they went from the trains to the ferry boats each man also shouldered his duffle bag in addition to his pack and gun and other equipment. The ferry boats glided down past the skyscraper-crowded tip of Manhattan Island, gleaming in the sunlight, to Staten Island where the vessels which would carry the Fifth Armored to England were docked. Many men gazed for the first time on the Statue of Liberty towering above New York's harbor. Many, too, looked upon it for the last time.

The Victory Division sailed from the Port of New York before dawn on 10 February 1944 in two ships. General Oliver was on the army transport Edmund B. Alexander and General Regnier was in charge of the troops on the British ship Athlone Castle.

At this point in the war the submarine menace had been brought largely under control. Ships were now crossing to Europe in gigantic spread-eagle convoys, hauling the thousands of tons of supplies that were turning the tide of the struggle. The Fifth Armored sailed in one of the largest of these Atlantic convoys. On bright days ships could be seen as far as the horizon in almost every direction. The aircraft carriers, with their decks loaded with strapped-down planes, rolled and dipped in the swells and the watchdog destroyers knifed in and out among the transports ready to go into action at the first sign of a U-boat.

This wartime voyage to Europe was no rest cure. Troops slept on canvas bunks four tiers high that were packed together below decks in stifling atmospheres. Because of the enormous number of men who had to be fed only two meals were served each day. For the first of these meals men began lining up early in the morning. Chow lines with clanking mess kits continued to stream through the mess halls almost all day long and soldiers were still being fed late in the evening.

On the boat deck of the Edmund B. Alexander General Oliver could be seen nervously pacing back and forth. This was his second crossing of the Atlantic in World War II. Behind him lay the battles in North Africa. Ahead was the difficult role his Fifth Armored Division was to play in Europe.

On other parts of the ship, between inspections, exercise and KP, men were playing a new card game called Up-the-Duck-and-Down-the-Cumberland, along with the old stand-bys, Hi-Lo Seven, and Baseball. And many men inappropriately were whistling and humming the popular tune, "If I came Home Tonight, Would You Still Be My Darling. . . ."

IX

OVER THERE

England

24 February 1944–July, 1944

GREAT BRITAIN had been at war almost four and a half years when the Fifth Armored arrived there on 24 February 1944. During those many grim months of conflict this island people had felt the enemy's wrath at first hand. Whole blocks of their cities had been crumbled by the luftwaffe's raiders. They knew well the terrifying screech of the bomb, the violence of the concussion, and the cries of the wounded. The air raid shelter, the blackout, and the nightly drone overhead of enemy planes had become an integral part of their lives. This was a theater of war and the ever-present threat of a death-dealing enemy pervaded the atmosphere and shaped all life there.

Signs of the enemy's handiwork were immediately visible to the Victory Division members as their transports nosed into the mouth of the muddy Mersey River. In the stream were the partly submerged wrecks of bomb-battered vessels.

It was late afternoon when the Edmund B. Alexander and the Athlone Castle tied up at the Mersey Docks in Liverpool. Over the city lay one of the famous English fogs. In a single line with their duffle bags on their shoulders and their packs, guns, gas masks and other gear hanging on them, the Fifth Armored men filed off the ships and down the docks to the waiting trains.

There was no flourish of trumpets or other fanfare to welcome the division after its safe 13-day crossing of the Atlantic. No time was available for such things now. Troops were arriving almost every day from the U. S., crowding on to this island in preparation for the coming assault against the continent. Waiting in the bomb-scarred station, however, were British Red Cross girls who served coffee and doughnuts to the troops before they boarded the small English railway cars.

As the trains pulled away from the docks in the fading light, the soldiers stared out at the rows of British homes with the little air raid shelters in their backyards. Soon the blackout blinds were drawn and the trains rolled along in the darkness. Men dozed and awoke intermittently to hear the engine's high-pitched whistle crying shrilly in the night. Before daylight troops had unloaded from the first trains at the city of Swindon and at two nearby camps, 175 miles to the south of Liverpool.

Most of the division was assigned to Quonset huts and British barracks in the Chisledon and Ogbourne St. George Camps, while the 15th Armored Infantry was billeted in Swindon. The three artillery battalions and the 85th Cavalry Squadron moved directly to Perham Down Camp in the Salisbury area. All these billeting arrangements had been made by an advance party, commanded by Col. Cole, which had crossed earlier in the Queen Mary. Personnel from the Third Armored Division had drawn the equipment for the individual kitchens and had a hot meal waiting for the Fifth Armored members when they arrived that cold morning after the all night trip from Liverpool.

The Fifth Armored's first cold damp six weeks in England were spent in drawing equipment and small unit training. It was also a period for getting acquainted with this foreign country and learning the countless regulation of the ETO (European Theater of Operations). Food was in short supply at the time and efforts were made to conserve it; soldiers were warned to take no more than they could eat and some first sergeants stood by garbage cans to make certain no edible food was discarded. Fuel was also short and fires were permitted in the little stoves that heated the Quonset huts only during the early evening hours. There were visits from old friends in the 58th and 65th artillery battalions, former division units, and from other battle-wise veterans of the North African campaigns.

Almost daily the huge mass formations of Allied planes roared overhead going and coming from their forays on the enemy's continental installations. This was the period when the Luftwaffe was being dealt the crucial blows from which it would never recover. At night German aircraft were often in the skies above the division areas and from the English people Fifth Armored men were learning to identify these enemy planes by their sounds. From the English people, too, division men were being taught how to observe security regulation; lifelong residents of English towns claimed, when asked, not to know the directions to neighboring communities only a few miles away.

On weekends many men visited the cities of Bath, Bristol, Cheltenham, Oxford and London (where they saw inhabitants of the city sleeping nights on the station platforms of the Underground or subway). For their social assault on this new land many men had come prepared with gifts of such scarce and coveted items as nylons, lipstick and gum.

Early in April preparations were being made for the division to start field maneuvers and training in combat firing. But these plans were abruptly halted when an order came down from higher headquarters with the swiftness and disruptiveness of a V-bomb. It instructed the division to "proceed to southern England and operate the camps in the marshalling areas there for amphibious exercises and the invasion of Europe."

"This is a slug in the jaw to our combat training," General Oliver told the men in each battalion as he explained this new assignment. But he added that it was a necessary job and that the Fifth Armored would do it well.

On 10 April the division moved by train and motor convoy to the southwest tip of England where it took possession of the seaside camps and hotels in the Truro, Plymouth and Torquay marshalling areas. These hotels and camps (pyramidal tent communities strung out along the edge of fields and partly concealed from air observation by camouflage nets and called "sausages") served the important leading parts of Falmouth, Plymouth, Dartmouth and Torquay. General Regnier remained at Ogbourne St. George with the rear echelon of division headquarters 127th Ordnance Maintenance Battalion and the 145th Signal Company. Extensive alterations and maintenance were continued on the combat vehicles by the 127th while the 145th conducted a radio operators school.

The marshalling area camps were set up to accommodate the assault troops which would conduct practice invasions on English beaches and finally sail across the channel for the invasion of the continent. The troops' stay in the camps varied from a few hours to three days, depending upon the arrival of their invasion craft and the rate at which these ships were loaded. They came without kitchen and supply troop, knowing that the camp personnel would cook their food and fill out their last minute equipment shortages. When the ships were loaded they moved out into the channel, turned and "attacked" a section of the English coast. The engineers would precede the amphibious tanks, LST's and infantry craft. After a practice assault, the troops would move inland and again assemble in the marshalling camps to await transportation back to their permanent stations.

To perform the cooking and housekeeping duties at the marshalling camps the Fifth Armored was completely revamped for the two-month period. All the infantry battalions plus CC Reserve headquarters were placed under the command of Col. Anderson and assigned the camps in the Torquay area. The tank battalions plus CC B headquarters and the 22nd Engineers under Col. Cole, were assigned the camps in the Truro area. The artillery battalions plus division artillery headquarters operated camps in the area west of Plymouth, under Col. Dalferes. And the camps east of Plymouth were run by Division Trains, the 85th Rcn. Squadron and 75th Medical Battalion under Col. Nelson. The forward echelon of Division Headquarters was located at Tavistock, north of Plymouth.

Many Fifth Armored men called the operation of these camps "K.P. in England" as each company had to run four to six messes or hotels. To do this a call for volunteers was sent out to the tank crews, artillery sections, and infantry squads. The results were surprising. In one battalion 72 men qualified as 1st cooks. Later in combat when men had to prepare their own meals these soldiers with culinary talents became very popular members of their tank crews and infantry squads.

Inspections of the camps in the marshalling areas became so frequent that battalion operations officers wrote training memorandums on "How to Conduct Inspecting Officers Through Kitchens."

Toward the end of May assault troops again started to move into the Fifth Armored's marshalling camps as they had done several time before. At this time of the year with summer fast approaching and British double summer time in effect, the sun did not set until late each evening and out-of-doors it remained light until almost 11 o'clock. So on Sunday, 28 May, it was very near midnight when most men retired that night.

But they had not been in their bunks long before aircraft motors could be heard in the skies over some of the division's areas. Soon the long bluish beams of the anti-aircraft lights were searching the sky. And then while most men were still in their bunks, the planes began to dive and send their bombs shrieking to the earth.

In Torquay a pair of bombs bracketed Col. Anderson's command post at the Livermead Hotel; others hit several homes and a civilian-occupied hotel in the town. Some oil tanks were set on fire in the Truro area. During the raid Staff Sgt. Alfred J. Libby, of the 15th Inf., carried four civilians out of Torquay's Bay Court Hotel after it was hit. For this action he later received the first award for heroism made in the division. The morning after the bombing the German radio announced, characteristically, that Torquay had been left in flames.

The assault troops continued to pour into the camps all during the first week in June. And then toward the end of the week they began boarding the ships. From the vast number of troops that had come to the camps this time, the thoroughness of their preparations and the strict secrecy, many Fifth Armored men suspected that this would be no practice invasion. But they did not know for certain until the morning of 6 June when a heavy rumble rolled across the channel from France, violently shaking the window panes in their frames, and the German radio announced that Allied troops had landed on the beaches of Normandy.

The Fifth Armored's housekeeping duties in the southwest of England were completed. Now came an eleventh-hour period of intense training before the division moved on to the battle field.

On 10 June Col. Anderson moved the three infantry battalions and the 22nd Engineers by train from Torquay to the Barnsly-Wold range near Cirencester and about 20 miles north of the Ogbourne St. George camp. Truck drivers had preceded the train to Ogbourne St. George and were waiting at the station with the vehicles so that the troops could be taken directly to the range.

During the three weeks here the training day was 15 hours long. Every man fired a qualification course with his individual weapon, including assault and transition firing. Machine gun crews fired both ground and vehicular courses. The 22nd Engineers also completed training in the use of flame throwers.

Between 10 and 15 June the remainder of the division assembled at the West Down Camp. Here Col. Cole directed the tactical training of the tank battalions. He worked them from dawn until dark on the ideal rolling terrain.

Gen. Regnier was in charge of the tank firing at Minehead, on the Bristol Channel, during this period. One tank company at a time moved to this range and participated in intensive combat practice firing. Crews fired at moving targets and from moving tanks.

The artillery battalions resumed training on the Imber range at the West Down Camp. In charge of them was a new Division Artillery Commander, Col. Douglas J. Page, who had been executive officer of the 9th Infantry Division Artillery in North Africa. Another North African veteran, Col. Hugh J. Fitzgerald, was assigned to CC B as deputy commander.

Late in June the Reserve Command, under Col. Anderson, was assigned as a fighting combat command by Gen. Oliver and was called Combat Command R.

On the last day in June all the division troops assembled in the Tilshead Camp for the last few weeks of training.

The rehearsals were almost over.

X

A MILITARY WEDDING

DURING THE Fifth Armored's final days in Britain, General Oliver called together his unit commanders. He had one last task he wished to perform before he took his division into battle. He wanted to join his tankers and infantrymen together in combat teams, which he dubbed "married companies." This union, in its ultimate effect on the enemy, would later prove to be as devastating as the joining of fire and brimstone.

General Oliver performed these marital ceremonies very simply. He told his commanders that within each combat command he wanted each individual infantry company to be "married" to a tank company. And within each married tank-infantry company he wanted each infantry platoon "married" to a tank platoon. According to his orders, the tankers and infantrymen in each of these married platoons were to eat and live together during their remaining days in England; this was to enable them to get to know each other well, because in battle they would fight together.

The idea for these wedded companies was conceived by General Oliver while he was in North Africa. There he saw how much the tankers and infantrymen relied upon each other in combat and how effectively they functioned as a striking force when they worked closely together as a confident, well-knit team. He, therefore, believed that this tank-infantry cooperation should be nurtured beforehand and not come about by chance during a battle.

It was this close tank-infantry cooperation which later enabled the Victory Division to move with such swiftness through German defenses during its drive across France. In leading the American armies, each of its armored columns consisted of a line of tanks interspersed with infantry filled halftracks. The married companies formation worked so well for the Fifth Armored in France that it was soon adopted by other armored divisions. And since the war it has become standard tactical teaching in the departments of armored force service schools.

In combat the division's married companies also had two other members on their assault teams: the artillery and fighter-bombers. Among the lead tanks of each advance column was the artillery's forward observer. Whenever the column stumbled into an enemy roadblock the forward observer would radio back to his battalion, whose mobile artillery pieces followed along further back in the column, and in a few moments shells would come crashing down on the enemy's resistance point. In like manner, the air-ground liaison officer would call for air support when it was needed and soon the planes would be bombing and strafing the target.

The division's combat commands, during a combat mission, were each divided into two task forces, one slightly larger than the other. The largest task force consisted of the headquarters company of the tank battalion plus two tank and two infantry companies. The smaller task force consisted of the headquarters company of the infantry battalion plus one tank company and one infantry company.

Throughout most of the Fifth Armored's campaigns the combat commands were made up of the following task forces:

Combat Command A's largest task force consisted of Headquarters, A and B companies of the 34th Tank Battalion, Plus A and B companies of the 46th Infantry Battalion: its smaller task force consisted of Headquarters and C Companies of the 46th Infantry Battalion, plus C Company of the 34th Tank Battalion.

Combat Command B's largest task force consisted of Headquarters, B and C Companies of the 81st Tank Battalion, plus B and C companies of the 15th Infantry Battalion; its smaller task force consisted of Headquarters and A Companies of the 15th Infantry Battalion, plus A Company of the 81st Tank Battalion.

Combat Command R's largest task force consisted of Headquarters, A and C Companies of the 10th Tank Battalion, plus A and C Companies of the 47th Infantry Battalion; its smaller task force consisted of Headquarters and B companies of the 47th Infantry Battalion, plus B Company of the 10th Tank Battalion.

XI

VIVE LA FRANCE

Utah Beach to Le Mans

26 July–8 August

TO THE peering eyes of the men on the decks of the LSTs (Landing Ship, Tank) and the LCIs (Landing Craft, Infantry), France lay like a long thin line on the horizon, slightly greener than the sea. And beyond was the unseen thick green line of the massed German Seventh Army. These men were approaching another continent and also another world—combat. Their passports to this new world were the live rounds of ammunition they carried in their belt pouches and in their tank racks. Behind them were many thousands of difficult hours of drilling, maneuvering and learning how to fight in a modern war. Now they had finished firing at paper targets. Now they faced the Germans, who also carried live ammunition in their leather pouches.

The Fifth Armored had boarded the vessels at battered Southampton on England's south coast and made a smooth crossing of the channel during the night. On 26 July it was nearing Utah Beach, where other GIs and D Day had smashed a bloody entrance into Normandy. In the sea some distance from the land could be seen the superstructures of a wall of submerged ships; they had been sunk there as a breakwater to protect the beach from the waves. At high tide each LST, carrying Sherman tanks, halftracks and other vehicles, rammed its bow onto the beach. Then, after the tide had receded and the big bow doors had been swung open, bulldozers quickly built a ramp up to the exit; and the vehicles rolled out of the ship, onto the shore.

It was dark before all the unloading was completed. And with the night came the enemy planes which were kept out of the beachhead skies during the day by the ubiquitous Allied aircraft. But in the darkness they came to dump their bomb loads; and up from the ground to meet them went long streams of red-blinking tracer bullets and bursting ack-ack shells. Assembled on the beachhead was the war's greatest concentration of anti-aircraft batteries. Some of the Luftwaffe's bombs exploded near an LCI, loaded with Fifth Armored men. Other division members already ashore huddled beneath their vehicles to shield themselves from the ack-ack fragments which came down like hail from the skies.

While the Fifth Armored was disembarking in France on 26 July, endless columns of bomb-heavy allied planes, marking the skies with their long white streaks of vapor trails, mercilessly were blasting near St. Lo a breach in the tight semicircle which enemy forces held around the Normandy beachhead. Through this gap in the German defenses, strewn with dead soldiers and burned-out vehicles, poured First Army tanks and infantry to exploit and widen the breakthrough.

After it landed at Utah Beach the division moved from the shell and bomb-churned seaside area and assembled in forests and fields near St. Sauveur Le Vicomte. Here under pleasant mid-summer French skies Fifth Armored men carefully inspected the scattered equipment and personal belongings (mess gear, clothing, weapons, ammunition, photographs, letters, helmets and food) left behind by the hastily departing Germans. These traces of a retreating army were to become a familiar sight to Fifth Armored men along the road to Germany during the weeks and months to come.

The Fifth Armored was placed on the secret list of General George Patton's Third Army and attached to the XV Corps. To the world it would be known as part of "General Patton's Ghost Troops." From a mobile corps reserve division its status was quickly changed to an armored division to be used for exploitation behind enemy lines. And it was to be the first American armored division to be assigned such a mission.

On the first day of August it moved to a new area just north of the Periers-Lessay road. This was its initial night move behind friendly lines. Along the route was the litter of smashed enemy equipment and the bodies of German soldiers and animals with their sweet sickening smell. The last vehicles pulled into the new area by 10 the following morning. Then an hour later came the division's first order for action against the enemy. It was instructed "to proceed south without stopping, cross the See and Selune

Rivers, assemble south of the Selune, seize the town of Fougeres, and reconnoiter vicinity of St. James, St. Martin, and St. George for further action."

This was a big order for an untried division. But the Fifth Armored for a long time had been preparing for the role it was now about to play on this European battlefield. The tankers and infantrymen rolled up their bedrolls and tied them on their vehicles; they slid shells into the chambers of the big tank guns and also made certain that their machine guns and other smaller caliber weapons were loaded. Then they started the engines of the Sherman tanks and halftracks and rolled onto the roads. They were ready to go.

Preceding the division, the long probing fingers of Lt. Col. Kent Fays 85th Cavalry Sq. pulled out at 1430 hours and began to reconnoiter the bridges and roads along this southward route by which the division was slipping out of the Normandy beachhead and thrusting deep into enemy territory.

In this rush down the Normandy Peninsula toward Avranches, CC A and CC B moved abreast in two columns. But soon they found themselves entangled with troops of the VII Corps, which were moving east into the First Army zone. Serious traffic tie-ups developed which delayed the tails of columns for such long periods that Division Headquarters lost radio contact with the Combat Commands. The congestion became so acute at the St. Denis bottleneck, where the route crossed the Avranches-Brecey road, that General Patton ordered the division to halt its march and pull off the roads.

This order, however, failed to reach CC A and CC B, and they continued rolling south.

Late that afternoon, when the traffic snarl was its worst, General Patton called a meeting of those divisional commanders who could be assembled quickly.

The tension was extremely high. Everyone knew that if enemy bombers discovered this knot of men and vehicles jammed up around St. Denis, a severe blow could be struck against the advance. General Oliver and the other divisional commanders wondered if their heads might not roll because of this tie-up.

General Patton strode into the anxious gathering and opened the meeting.

"Gentlemen," he said, "we are in a hell of a mess, and it's all my fault."

Then he explained that in his haste to send the units south he had given orders directly to the division commanders without informing his staff.

"Now we shall just sit here until my staff can work out schedules and routes," he declared. "Then we shall continue."

That night CC R assembled at Le Mesnil Villeman but CC A and CC B did not halt, never having received the order to do so. Through the moonless night they continued, clanking to the south over the strange roads. Their route was often obstructed by the French civilians who were either fleeing from or returning to their homes; they rode in big blue two-wheeled horse-drawn carts which were stacked high with bedding and other possessions.

The night was also filled with the rushing roar of artillery shells belched out by both the German and American batteries. Enemy bombers, hovering over part of the route, dropped flares and then followed these with bombs. When a segment of a column became separated from its lead elements, tank and halftrack commanders were able to decide in which direction to go at each fork or crossroads only by getting down on their hands and knees in the road and with their flashlights seeing which way the tracks led.

But despite the congestion and confusion and the fact that this was their first night of real combat, CC A and CC B had arrived by dawn at their originally designated areas near St. George and St. Hilaire du Harcouet, south of the Selune River.

Later that day CC R pulled up stakes at Le Mesnil Villeman and reached Marcilly to the south by 8 in the evening. As the combat command's vehicles were leaving the road and going into its assembly area here, 13 Luftwaffe fighter planes dived out of the skies and strafed the columns. The enemy craft were pursued, however, by four P-51s which shot down three of the enemy raiders. About this time, too, the 85th Cavalry Sq. made its first contact with enemy units near the line St. Ellier-Fougeres.

It was during these moves that men of the Fifth Armored first witnessed the jubilation of the liberated French people; they expressed their joy and gratitude by strewing flowers on the tanks and other vehicles, by handing up cider and calvados to the troops and by kissing and hugging the dusty soldiers. Similar roadside demonstrations would be encountered all the way across France and Belgium. The troops also were meeting for the first time the bands of Free French, the underground French fighters, who now appeared with their odd assortments of knives and guns and with their Cross of Lorraine arm bands. They immediately went to work rounding up French collaborators and any "Boches" who were still in the area.

From 3 to 5 August the division was in XV corps reserve south of the Selune River just behind the 79th and 90th Infantry Divisions. Roadblocks were set up to the south by CC A and CC R, and preparations to launch possible counterattacks were made by CC A and CC B. It was expected that the Germans would launch a large scale attack to retake Avranches and thus cut off the U. S. divisions that were south of the town. But the anticipated enemy attack was not made. The Germans continued their night bombings but caused no extensive damage. Meanwhile enemy stragglers moving at night were often picked up.

Plans were made for the capture of the city of Fougeres, which lay further to the south. It was decided that CC A and CC B would attack simultaneously with the 79th Division. But the Germans did not defend the city and the 79th Division occupied it late on 3 August.

The next day the Fifth Armored was directed immediately to furnish 100 trucks to transport doughfoots of the 79th and 90th Infantry Divisions. These trucks were supplied from unit trains and it was necessary temporarily to dump their loads of fuel and lubricants in order for them to complete the mission.

During the halt in the St. James-Ducey-St. Hilaire area, small retreating enemy groups were continually washed up against Fifth Armored roadblocks. Civilians reported that German tanks and artillery were in many nearby areas. Among the more than 100 prisoners taken were men from these enemy divisions: 5th Parachute, 2nd SS Panzer, 266th Infantry, 17th SS Panzer Grenadier, 91st Infantry and service units.

But there was no letup in the pressure being applied to the

Germans now that they were disorganized and on the run. The Fifth Armored's role in this effort was to advance on the right flank of the corps, remaining in readiness to support the attack of the 79th and 90th divisions, and to extend the front to Chateau-Gontier, and possibly as far south as Angers. It was also to be prepared to execute a quick envelopment around any stubborn knot of enemy resistance that might block the advance of the infantry.

The division was scheduled to hit the road again on 6 August. Its 100 fuel trucks had not yet returned from their detail with the two infantry divisions, so the 3912 Q.M. Truck Company was attached to the division; it was ordered immediately to secure gasoline at the Army Truckhead and to join the column at St. James the next morning. But the fuel was not available when the trucks arrived and the quartermaster trucks, therefore, did not return before the time of departure. The Fifth Armored pulled out without refueling and headed south from St. James to Fougeres and then to Vitré.

After CC A and CC B were south of Vitré and advancing on the Mayenne River, the division received orders, about 1430 hours to "push rapidly forward to seize and hold Le Mans."

Plans for a lightning pincers attack were hastily devised. CC A and CC B were ordered to advance in parallel position on the city. CC A would cross the Mayenne River near Chateau-Gontier and, proceeding east through Grez En Boufre, Bouessy, and Chantenay, would block all enemy movement south and east out of Le Mans. CC B, crossing the river at Houssay and plunging through Villier, Meslay, Cheville, Love, Chassile, Coulans and La Milesse, would seal off all enemy movement west and north out of the city. CC R, in reserve, would follow CC A to protect the right flank, while Division Headquarters and the Trains would follow CC B.

The attacking units trundled along swiftly and by midnight of 6 August, the very day the attack order had been received, CC B was across the Mayenne at Houssay and CC A was mopping up in Chateau-Gontier. The Division Command Post was at Houssay on the west bank of the river. In the early hours of the morning of 7 August the quartermaster truck company arrived with the gasoline and the empty tanks of the Shermans and the halftracks were refilled in the darkness.

Before dawn the armored spearheads were again on the roads grinding east to encircle Le Mans. But CC B's Task Force Wintermute, while passing across the front of the 79th and 90th divisions, found the Laval-Le Mans highway being used by the 106th Cavalry (XV Corps); they were preceding the advance of the shuttling 79th division. To avoid this congestion CC B was given a new route south of the Laval-Le Mans highway and CC A was shifted further south. CC A was instructed to swing in a wide arc south of the city and block all roads to the north and northeast; CC B would block those to the east, while CC R would choke off those to the south.

CC A had left Vitré at 0730 hours the morning of 6 August and by 1610 hours its married B Companies, which were leading the single attack column, had pushed through light scattered resistance and had reached the outskirts of Craon. Just before the head of the column reached the bridge in Craon it was blown up by the Germans who continued to defend the opposite bank with small arms fire. By fanning out to the north and south of the second platoon discovered a bridge north of the town and the column was rerouted over this crossing with little delay.

The first heavy resistance was met at Chateau-Gontier. Here the bridge across the Mayenne River had been partially destroyed and it was defended on the far side by antitank guns. These guns disabled one tank of B Co., 34th Tank Bn., and also hit General Regnier's tank.

Dismounting from their halftracks, the infantry crossed the river, and, fighting throughout the night, drove the German soldiers from the town. The enemy force was estimated to be one infantry company supported by antitank guns and mortars. A Co., 22nd Engineer Bn. immediately went to work on the bridge and traffic was moving across it by 7 the next morning.

The CC A column poured through the town and continued its advance until 1510 hours when it was halted by a stubborn force at Poillé-Sur-Vegre. This force was attempting to keep open the Prulon-Le Mans escape route.

Some P-47 fighter bombers arrived over the column just in time to join the fight. Diving on the enemy positions, they dumped their bomb loads and all resistance here was completely neutralized by 1700 hours. While this fight was in progress orders changing the attacks routes on Le Mans were received.

When the head of the column reached Fille it took the road to Spay by mistake. The remainder of the column, with A Companies leading, crossed the Sarthe at Fille and continued on the assigned route. B Companies crossed at Spay and continued on a parallel road until it was possible to get back on the main route. A German bivouac area was caught between these two parallel columns and 30 Wehrmacht vehicles were destroyed. An infantry company and an engineer company were captured. During the scrap Lt. Marvin Orgill, B Co., 34th Tank Bn., changed tanks three times; he abandoned a tank each time it ran out of ammunition.

At daylight 8 August, the column stopped to refuel in the southeastern suburbs of Le Mans. The gasoline trucks pulled up alongside the parked tanks and halftracks and the five gallon cans of fuel were handed up to the crews.

In the village of Yvre the head of the column caught up with some retreating tanks. Lt. Thomas Burke, B Co., 34th Tank Bn., saw two German tanks moving toward the main intersection of the town. Rushing his platoon into the village, he sent his tanks down different streets. The Sherman commanded by Sgt. Shiverski met a German tank head-on and in rapid fire pumped six rounds of armor-piercing shells into it. Lt. Burke then knocked out the other enemy tank as it tried to get away down the street. Outside the town enemy infantry had ironically dug ground defenses in a graveyard. The 46th Bn. infantrymen dismounted from their halftracks and, attacking with artillery and tank support, rooted them out or made their choice appropriate.

As the lead tank crossed the Paris-Le Mans highway about 20 enemy ammunition trucks were leaving a bivouac area in an attempt to escape toward Paris. The gunner of the lead tank, Cpl. Joe Perry, fired as rapidly as his gun could be reloaded and he destroyed every truck in the group. His rhythmic handling of the 30 cal. and 75 mm. floor firing buttons reminded his friends of his pre-war days as a drummer in a Montana band. During the long day of 8 August "Drummer Perry" fired 87 rounds of 75 mm. and 16,000 rounds of 30 cal. ammunition.

CC A's advance continued until 2100 hours. By that time it had closed off the last escape route north of Le Mans.

Meanwhile, CC B had begun rolling south from the fields near Vitré at 1000 hours 6 August. The combat command attacked in two columns, Task Force Wintermute and Task Force Anderson, with the bridge of the Mayenne River at Houssay as their objective. At Crosse-le-Vivien, Task Force Wintermute enveloped the east flank of the resistance via Astille and Origne. Task Force Anderson continued on the main highway through Quelaines to the objective. At Astille the column was halted briefly when it encountered machine gun and bazooka fire from about a dozen Germans who were in a house on the edge of town. The tanks of Lt. Larry Hitchcock's platoon fired point-blank into the house and killed all of the enemy defenders. The absence of civilians on the streets indicated that more enemy soldiers were in the village, so the column by-passed it to the north.

Just before dark the bridge at Houssay was captured by Task Force Anderson which then pushed on to Meslay-du-Maine for the night. Two German cars loaded with demolitions were destroyed near Houssay by Lt. Leonard Keene's leading tank. A roadblock near the crossroads east of Houssay in charge of Lt. Merle Powers captured one of the dreaded 88 mm. guns as it was being towed south from Laval.

As Lt. John G. Jonasch was organizing the roadblock on the Laval road at Meslay, four Mark IV tanks attempted to smash through it. The Shermans commanded by Sgts. Gene Krafka and William Minturn opened fire at almost point-blank range. One Mark IV withstood all the shells hurled at it and continued through Meslay. It was escaping toward Le Mans when Lt. Robert McNab, aiming at the red flame of its exhaust, pumped a shell into its rear and crippled it. An inventory at daylight of the night's handiwork revealed that in the melee the Germans had lost four Mark IVs, two sedans and a motorcycle.

After refueling from the 3912 Q.M. Truck Company during the night, both columns rolled on toward Le Mans. Resistance was light and many confused and disorganized Wehrmacht soldiers were taken. A French commercial bus loaded with German soldiers turned into the married B Column of the 81st Tank Bn. and the 15th Infantry Bn. It was sprayed with rifle and machine gun bullets; then it caught fire and rammed into a 57 mm. antitank gun.

In the village of Maigne the sniping was very persistent, so the armored column spewed out machine gun and rifle fire in every direction to make the Germans keep their heads down. The tracer bullets, however, set fire to the harvested wheat shocks that had been stored in and near the barns and soon much of the town was in flames. Twenty Germans, attempting to flee on bicycles, were killed.

CC B reached Spay at dark and found units of CC A crossing the bridge over the Sarthe River. The next day, 8 August, the advance continued and the armored column made a wide swing through the checkerboard pattern of streets around the southeast side of Le Mans. By 1800 hours CC B had blocked all roads to the east, and patrols of Task Force Anderson had entered the city.

During this advance, spearheaded by CC A and CC B, Col. Anderson's CC R was in reserve and followed the general route of CC A. It protected the right flank of the division in this sudden drive on Le Mans. In the evening of 7 August a married platoon from Task Force Hamberg's A Companies, supported by the 10th Tank Bn's. Assault Gun Platoon, engaged a force of Germans who were aided by tanks at Chemire-sur-Sarthe. The enemy withdrew after a Mark V was destroyed. They left a warehouse full of supplies.

Snipers remained in many of the captured towns and continued to harass CC R's columns as they pushed on toward their objectives. Late in the afternoon of 8 August CC R moved into the area near St. Gervais and blocked all roads leading south from Le Mans.

The division trains, hauling records and supplies, were commanded by Lt. Col. Glenn G. Dickenson. They followed right on the heels of the Combat Commands in this armored rush into enemy-held territory. Lt. Michael Moran was the first Train casualty; he was killed 6 August near Crosse-Le-Vivien while he was with a billeting party.

Thus, by the night of 8 August the Fifth Armored's tanks and halftracks lay in a tight ring around a city of 75,000 people, which would soon surrender. In the seven furious days and nights this untried division had pushed 180 miles into the interior of France, it had crossed two rivers; and now it faced threats of counter-attacks on both flanks—from forces on the north, on the one hand, which might attempt to squeeze close the breakthrough route and, on the other, from the troops in the Brittany Peninsula which might attack from the south. In this intense rapid-paced armored warfare men of the Victory Division had over night become seasoned soldiers.

XII

THE SICKLE

Le Mans to Argentan

9 August—14 August

Now the momentum was high. The French campaign had reached its crucial point. The Wehrmacht's defenses in Western France were crumbling and Allied commanders were determined that the enemy should be given no time to catch his breath, no opportunity to reorganize and to build up a secondary defense line. Pressure was to be applied relentlessly at all points. While fighter-bombers continued to harass the Germans from the air,* the armored spearheads plunged into the weak spots and systematically sliced up the enemy's several defense positions. Then the infantry divisions pressed forward on a wide front and quickly mopped up the cut-off and disorganized German soldiers, most of whom surrendered without a fight.

Applying this pressure to the fleeing Germans, however, was no easy task. It was as exhausting for the pursuers as it was for the quarry. Fifth Armored soldiers got little sleep during the drive south from their first assembly area in Normandy. During practically all the days and many of the nights they were on the road. When they pulled off into a field to bivouac or set up a roadblock they had to dig in to be ready to fight in place.

Men prepared meals individually. Little cans of pork and beans or hash or vegetable stew or the better selection in the 10 in 1 rations were heated on the one-burner Coleman gasoline stoves. They could also be heated on the motor of a vehicle or at the end of the exhaust pipe. When time was short a K ration was broken open and eaten cold. Sometimes fresh eggs and potatoes were obtained from the French civilians by trading candy, soap and gum. And in the apple orchards, which were frequently used as

*Every German account of this period of the war tells of the dread in which Germans of all ranks held the hated "Jabo".

bivouac areas, swarms of yellow jackets had to be shooed away from the food. The steel helmets with their liners removed were used as wash basins. Men slept in their clothes; they stretched out on their bedding rolls, spread on the ground, with their small arms always within reach.

On 7 August the Germans finally launched the counterattack to close the breakthrough route at Avranches; the Fifth Armored had expected and had been ready for this attack when it had bivouacked in the St. Hilaire-St. James area from 3 to 5 August. Into this effort against the First Army front in the vicinity of Mortain, the enemy threw the 1st SS, 2nd SS, 2nd and 116th Panzer Divisions. The attack continued for three days and finally was abandoned on 10 August.

Having completed the encirclement of Le Mans before dark on 8 August, the next morning the Fifth Armored was alerted for movement to the North. Immediately the 85th Cavalry Sq. hit the road. Its mission was to determine the status of the bridges over the Orne River, 20 miles to the north, and to find out what enemy troops were in that area.

At 1740 hours the detailed order for the attack reached the division from XV Corps Headquarters. It instructed the Fifth Armored to seize crossings over the Orne River for the passage of its own troops and also for those of the 2nd French Armored Division. After they had passed this water barrier, both divisions were to proceed north, abreast of each other, the French on the left and the Fifth Armored on the right, to the Carrouge-Sees line. The 90th Infantry Division would follow the French Armor, while the 79th Infantry Division would follow the Fifth. The French 2nd Armored was assembled near Vitré.

It now became clear what the Allied Armies in France were attempting to do. Like a huge sickle, the U. S. Third Army had cut down and around the German Seventh Army and was now attempting to slice up behind this enemy force. At the point of this sickle was the Fifth Armored Division.

The division's combat commands advanced on their objectives the same evening on which the attack order was received. CC A and CC R rolled forward in parallel positions, with CC R on the right; CC B was in reserve and followed CC R.

Having pulled out of the Le Mans area at 8 that night, CC A three hours later was fighting to hold five bridges over the Orne on a six and a half mile front in the vicinity of Ballon. Two-thirds of the combat command was committed in this night action. For the first time it was encountering concentrated enemy artillery fire. German antitank guns to the north of the river knocked out two M7s of the 47th Armored Field Artillery Bn. and two light tanks and a halftrack of CC A Headquarters. With the support of the 47th batteries and the mortar platoons the bridgeheads were held during the summer night and by daylight the enemy fire had slackened.

That night CC R also seized five river crossings south of Marolles. Two of the bridges were taken by Task Force Hamberg, which pushed well beyond the river to dig in for the night. The Married A Companies, of the 10th Tank Bn. and the 47th Infantry Bn. bivouacked at Peray while the married C Companies stopped south of Marolles.

Throughout the night these companies could hear, just north of their positions, the rumbling of enemy vehicles. It was assumed that these German troops were withdrawing further north. But at dawn on 10 August unexpected hell broke loose in the assembly area of the married C Companies as enemy tank and artillery shells began to thunder down. Instead of withdrawing during the night, the German tanks had jockeyed to a new position on high ground which overlooked the C Companies area. During the first few moments of this sudden morning shelling the commander of the infantry company, Capt. John M. Crafts, was killed; command of the company was then assumed by Lt. Leo Marcikowski. The commander of the C Company tanks, Capt. Francis J. Baum, returned the fire with all the weapons at his disposal. Since the river at their backs restricted maneuver, they fought in place until the A Companies rushed in from the northeast to relieve the pressure.

When the furious fight was over, it was discovered that two enemy Mark IV tanks had been destroyed. Losses of the married C Companies included: four tanks, three halftracks, and 27 casualties.

CC B had left the Le Mans area about midnight 9 August and

had assembled at daylight near Bonnétable, just east of CC R's area. As the 15th Infantry Battalion's commander, Lt. Col. Wintermute, and its S-3, Major Hurley, attempted to drive back to CC B's Headquarters, their peep was struck by a projectile from an enemy self-propelled gun and they were both wounded. The German gunners placed the officers on the enemy vehicle and took them into Bonnétable to a house the Germans were using as a medical aid station. As the rumble of CC B's tanks grew louder the Germans withdrew from Bonnétable and the officers were recaptured. Major Toney Giorlando assumed command of the 15th Infantry Bn. and Capt. Donald Crafts became the Battalion S-3.

The commander of the 81st Tank Battalion, Lt. Col. Anderson, also encountered enemy fire when he attempted to get back to CC B's Headquarters. His peep was ripped by machine gun fire. He and his driver then walked back across the field to the battalion area to get a tank platoon for an escort.

At 8 that morning Division Headquarters issued orders that the advance to the Garrouge-Sees line be resumed. CC A turned over its job of guarding the Orne crossing to the 2nd French Armored Division, which also continued to advance on CC A's left.

In this area north of the Orne, into which the Fifth Armored was plunging, about 50 enemy tanks were active. Enemy soldiers here were members of the 9th Panzer, 709th Infantry and 130th Panzer Lehr Divisions. As the Victory Division clanked northward it encountered German antitank guns at all the main road junctions. By nightfall CC A had run up against strong tank forces at Marolles and CC R was trading blows with enemy forces on the outskirts of Mamers.

But the Wehrmacht soldiers now began to realize that these huge pincers were slowly squeezing shut and were threatening to trap the entire German Seventh Army. So the enemy's counterattack to retake Avranches was given up on 10 August and the Germans decided to withdraw their forces as quickly as possible from France. Every effort, they knew, must be made to keep the lips of these pincers open until the retreating Seventh Army could be evacuated through this gap. The Fifth Armored, therefore, began to pound against extremely bitter and determined resistance.

It found almost all dominant terrain in this northward path being utilized as defense positions.

Therefore, the division's advance on 11 August was much slower than it had been the previous day. Combat Commands A and R were instructed to by-pass the cities of Marolles and Mamers and to continue in the direction of Sees. On the flanks the 85th Cavalry Sq. remained ready to repulse any sneak attacks. Enemy 105 mm. and 150 mm. artillery guns shelled the division's forward elements.

When CC A came upon the approaches to St. Rémy, French civilians reported that the German armor in the town consisted of 23 tanks and one 88 mm. gun. Task Force Burton deployed to develop the situation and received tank fire at ranges greater than 2,000 yards. The 47th and 400th Artillery Battalions went into action hurriedly and pounded the enemy defenses. They were joined by the tank destroyers of A Co., 628th Bn. Then, after the fighter-bombers gave the town a working over, infantrymen of C Company, 46th Infantry Bn., entered. They found that one Mark V had been destroyed and that the other tanks had withdrawn to the northwest.

Higher headquarters informed the division that the large Foret de Perseigné contained two enemy divisions and elaborate supply installations. General Oliver decided that the lack of roads and the defenses of the trees in this woods made it a tank trap. He, therefore, directed CC A to by-pass it to the right.

Formidable enemy resistance loomed in front of CC R's Task Force Boyer when it reached the outskirts of Essay. Here the Column's lead tank was hit by a projectile which passed between the driver and assistant driver without injuring either of them.

Capt. Pool, B Co., 10th Tank Bn., observed five Tiger tanks in the town. This enemy armor was subjected to fire from the 81 mm. mortars and from the guns of the 95th Artillery Bn. Then air support was called for and the fighter-bombers, peeling off and roaring down on the town, bombed and strafed the enemy positions. Columns of black smoke which spiralled up into the sky indicated several hits. Dismounting from their halftracks, the foot troops of C Co., 47th Infantry Bn., closed in and cleared out the buildings as the armored column moved through the town. The Task Force assembled for the night on the high ground just north of Essay. But its action for the day was not yet finished. In the darkness a Tiger tank came creeping back toward the town and was destroyed.

When the leading elements of the Fifth Armored stopped for the night of 11 August CC R was fighting on the edge of Sees and CC A had crossed the Sarthe River, north of the Foret de Perseigné. At 1945 hours the division received orders to "continue on to Argentan, and cut all communications to the north." As the Fifth Armored men slept uneasily that night, the darkness in almost every direction was dotted with the red glow of fires that marked the trail of the day's battles.

At dawn of 12 August both CC A and CC R were on the road pushing forward to take Sees.

CC A with Task Force Burton in the lead, had veered to the right to assist CC R in the attack on the city. Under the pressure of both Combat Commands, Sees fell at 1000 hours. An entire battalion of enemy troops was captured on the road. A column of the 2nd French Armored Division followed CC A's Task Force into the town and the resulting traffic congestion caused several hours delay in refueling the combat command's tanks and half-tracks. Col. Farrand went to the headquarters of the 2nd French Armored Division and asked that their troops be moved out of the city so that CC A could get through Sees and push on toward Argentan.

After CC A got through Sees it was jabbed by the point of a 116th Panzer Division column which was coming from the south-west into the city. The presence of this German division, as well as elements of the 1st and 2nd SS Panzer divisions in this area, indicated that the enemy was making a frantic effort to get its armor out of the closing trap; only two days before these enemy divisions had been in the Mortain area taking part in the unsuccessful counterattack toward Avranches.

A self-propelled 75 mm. gun in the column of the 116th Panzer Division fired on the CC A Task Force and broke a track on each of the two leading tanks of C Co., 34th Tank Bn. The remaining C Company tanks then blasted the enemy force and also enlisted the aid of the 47th Artillery Bn. This forced the German armor to flee toward Mortrée. Before it reached the town three of its small caliber antitank guns were destroyed. Pursuing the enemy into Mortrée, Task Force Burton knocked out a Mark VI at a range of 20 yards. A Mark V backed into a building which collapsed on it. Under a covering fire from the tanks, infantry of C Co., 46th Infantry Bn., dismounted and flushed the enemy soldiers from the town.

In this operation two more C Company tanks were disabled by enemy antitank shells. Lt. Richard J. Monihan, C Co., 46th Infantry Bn., climbed up on one of these burning tanks to rescue a wounded tanker. While he was still on top of the tank another shell smashed into it and knocked both him and the tanker to the ground. But Lt. Monihan picked up the wounded man, carried him to safety through machine gun fire; and killed two Germans. Lt. Monihan was the first Fifth Armored soldier to be awarded the Distinguished Service Cross.

Task Force Bartel passed through Task Force Burton in Mortrée, but was halted by a mined roadblock. This obstacle, however, was removed and at 1400 hours the drive on Argentan was resumed. Company A's tanks were spread out on a wide front as the task force advanced over the rolling wheat fields south of the town. By 1900 hours they were on the edge of Argentan south of the Orne River. Two of the attacking tanks had been knocked out by mines and one had been destroyed by antitank fire.

Not wishing to tangle with the enemy so late in the day, CC A withdrew southwest to the high ground overlooking the town. Patrols sent into the town during the night reported that there was intense activity of tanks and infantry. Throughout the night, the 47th and 400th Armored Artillery Battalions turned their big guns on Argentan and blasted the town and its approaches.

Argentan lay only about 15 miles south of Falaise, toward which the Canadian Forces were pressing from the north. The Germans, therefore, were in a panic. They were trying frantically to squeeze their whole seventh Army through this narrow gap and at the same time struggling desperately to prevent the giant pincers from clamping completely shut.

To the right of CC A the armored column of CC R, after leaving Sees that day headed toward the northeast. With Task Force Boyer leading, it proceeded forward against moderate resistance.

By 1600 hours the married B Companies of the 10th Tank Bn. and the 47th Infantry Bn. were in Nonant-le-Pin. Prisoners captured here said that their outfit, the 12th Panzer Division, was located in the vicinity of Gacé, and that the town was well fortified with tanks, antitank guns, and mines.

From Nonant-le-Pin Task Force Hamberg pushed on toward the reportedly well-fortified Gacé, while Task Force Boyer turned northwest in the direction of the main road junction halfway between Gacé and Argentan. At La Corbette the married A Companies of Task Force Hamberg became ensnared in their first mine field. Coming forward quickly from their place in the column, engineers of C Co., 22nd Engineer Bn., hurriedly uprooted these mines. By 2100 hours the column had established a roadblock at the junction of the main roads, five miles south of Gacé. From the town the task force was receiving artillery and antitank fire.

Just after darkness had descended Task Force Boyer pulled into a position south of Exmes and dug in for the night. A column of German vehicles, led by a Tiger tank, stumbled into this roadblock and all the vehicles soon were burning in the night.

During the day CC B had been ordered to remain in reserve in the Sees-Nonant-le-Pin area.

In the darkness the Fifth Armored soldiers could hear the mass movement of the German vehicles grinding along every passable road in the confusion-filled escape corridor. Many of these clanking enemy columns crashed into the Fifth Armored roadblocks and were destroyed or captured. The artillery pieces poured their whining shells into the gap all through the night. Meanwhile, at their command posts, Victory Division staff officers assessed the results of this active day and prepared attacks to be launched the following day. Enemy losses inflicted by the Fifth Armored on 12 August were officially tabulated as: 301 enemy soldiers killed and 362 captured; 70 tanks, 2 armored cars, 7 artillery pieces and 88 miscellaneous enemy vehicles were destroyed.

Wearily Fifth Armored soldiers watched another dawn break on this French battlefield; and as they waited, poised on the edge of this churning hell, they knew another day of hot and bloody fighting lay ahead of them. This 13 of August was also to be a day of indecision. At the offset the division's mission remained the same; it was to "continue to Argentan, cut communications to the north." But later in the day these orders from higher headquarters would be changed and then changed again.

Under the protective cover of a ground haze, CC A's Task Force Bartel started at 7 that morning to move into position southwest of Argentan for the attack. Plans called for Capt. James McDonough's A Co., 46th Infantry Bn. to enter the town with the close support of fire from the A Co., 34th Tank Bn. Task Force Burton was to make a coordinated attack enveloping the east flank.

But when the echelon of 34th Bn. tanks had nearly reached their jump-off positions, the haze suddenly lifted and left them in full view of the enemy gunners. From the edge of the town came an intense shower of antitank shells which pummeled the A Co. vehicles. Seven tanks and the G-3 halftrack were knocked out. And Lt. Col. Bartel was seriously wounded.

After recovering from the shock of this surprising blow, the task force quickly reorganized under Major Glen L. Foote, now in command. It then tried to smash its way into the town from the south but could not penetrate the barrier of massed Panzer tanks on the outskirts of the city. The supporting fire from the artillery and fighter-bombers did not help greatly in whittling down these defenses because the tanks were well concealed in and among the buildings near the railroad marshalling yards.

The combat command's reserve was then sent around the right flank to cut the road to Gacé. But the enemy, using at least 35 Mark V tanks, continued successfully to resist all efforts to push north of Argentan.

At noon the 628th Tank Destroyer Battalion was attached to CC A. As the combat command staff made plans for another attack that afternoon, the reconnaissance platoon of the 34th Tank Bn., kept a watchful eye on the town. It observed the Germans install a hasty mine field on the edge of Argentan. But before another attack got underway orders were received stating that the 2nd French Armored Division would relieve CC A at 2000 hours.

Early that morning CC R's Task Force Boyer had rolled north four miles to the main road junction between Gacé and Argentan. The Task force anchored extensive roadblocks at this important highway intersection and men encountered here, for the first time, the screaming Nebelwerfer fire.

From its position five miles south of Gacé, CC R's Task Force Hamberg had kicked off early in the day in an attack to seize the main crossroads and bridge just south of the town. To reach its attack positions, the task force had to overcome a sizeable German force. This had alerted the enemy troops in the town who now were ready to counterattack. As the married A Companies of the 10th Tank Bn. and 47th Infantry Bn. approached the crossroads they ran into a wave of attacking German infantrymen, supported by heavy artillery concentrations. The enemy soldiers were repeatedly thrown back, but the artillery fire became so heavy that Lt. Col. Hamberg went to Col. Anderson's CC R Headquarters to explain the situation.

The CC R commander had just returned from Division Headquarters with new instructions. He told Lt. Col. Hamberg that CC B's 15th Armored Infantry had been temporarily attached to CC R to assist in blocking the area south and east of Gacé. Co. B was placed in Croiselles and the remainder of the battalion in the vicinity of Exmes. Later in the day the task force withdrew to the road junction at La Catelle where the force had stayed the previous night. Here a defense was prepared against an armored threat from Le Merlerault.

Before the CC B's 15th Infantry Bn. was attached to CC R, CC B had earlier that day been ordered to pass to the right of CC A at Argentan and then out across the German's narrow escape corridor in an attempt to take Falaise. This order was rescinded about noon when General Oliver conferred with General Haislip. The Corps Commander told General Oliver that under no conditions should the Fifth Armored advance beyond the line Argentan-Gacé because a large scale bombing mission was being planned to blast the area to the north of this line.

It was General Patton who had orally issued the orders for an attempt to be made to close the gap when he had visited the headquarters of XV Corps on the afternoon of 12 August. But at the same time, his Third Army Headquarters was receiving instructions from Army Group ordering the ground troops not to attempt to proceed across the escape corridor. A complicating factor was the fact that the international boundary line between the British and American zones extended northwest through the center of Argentan-Gacé.

Describing these conflicting orders the After Action Report of XV Corps for 13 August states:

"The Commanding General, Third U. S. Army, directed the XV Corps to 'push slowly in the direction Falaise and made contact with Allied forces advancing from the north.' As this action was being initiated orders were received rescinding it and directing the Corps to halt on the Orne River. The Fifth Armored Division to be charged with preventing German use of the roads leading east from Argentan without becoming involved in a serious fight for the town, and with cutting roads leading out of Gacé to the east."

During the day the fighter-bombers and artillery continued hammering the targets in the vicinity of Argentan. One severely mauled enemy column, which decided to abandon its attempt to run this gauntlet out of the slowly closing trap, signaled its desire to surrender to the planes by waving white flags. An order was dropped by the airmen to the commander of the column, which directed him to march his troops to Rodeau. This column grew to 17,000 Wehrmacht soldiers and surrendered to the 90th Infantry Division two days later.

Fifth Armored patrols, which had been probing the Germans' defenses in Argentan during the night, were at daylight of 14 August withdrawn from the city. Then at 0630 hours a shattering artillery barrage was put down on the city as the enemy troops and vehicles continued their frenzied rush to get through the city and out of the pocket. They were harassed, too, by the fighter-bombers which began another day of bombing and strafing the terror-ridden corridor. Confusion now became general among the German forces in this area. Enemy columns of from five to fifty vehicles, all trying desperately to find their way out of the encirclement, were reported in all sections of the division zone. Ten enemy tanks were repulsed when they attempted to charge through CC B's positions just north of Sees. And at 10:30 in the morning a column of enemy foot troops and tanks were bombed between the command posts of the Fifth Armored and 79th Infantry Divisions. During the day the German casualties inflicted by the Fifth Armored numbered:—215 killed and 410 taken prisoner.

Then at 10 that evening orders came down from higher headquarters to the division. Its mission at the Falaise Gap was finished. It had set the trap which would enable other units to bag the game. It was now instructed to be ready to drive east, to cross the Eure River and continue on to the Seine, west of Paris.

XIII

IN THE DISTANCE THE EIFFEL TOWER

Argentan to the Seine

15 August–29 August

LIFE EBBED from the German Seventh Army as the iron grip of the Allied Forces began to tighten around the Argantan-Falaise escape corridor. Closing off the final few miles of this gap was a slow sledgehammer operation that would be completed on 20 August. The Fifth Armored was capable of waging such an offensive, as it would ably demonstrate later in the Hurtgen Forest, but this type of fighting was not its specialty. The division was a rapier rather than a saber. It did its best work with quick piercing strokes that cut to the heart of the enemy's defenses.

It was just such a swift paralyzing thrust that the Fifth Armored again was called upon to perform. The Germans who had managed to squeeze out of the Normandy trap were falling back hurriedly to the Eure River, about 80 miles to the east of Argentan. At this water barrier they intended to establish a new defense line with strong points at Dreux and Chartres. If they were successful, to dislodge them would take a major assault, with great losses in men and equipment. The Fifth Armored, therefore, was instructed to race to Dreux and wrest the town and its river crossings from the Germans before they could solidly entrench themselves. It was also ordered to continue beyond Dreux to the Seine and seize crossings over the river between Meulan and Vernon.

Fifth Armored men were still exhausted from the 58-mile dash up from Le Mans and the skirmishes along the Argentan-Gacé Line. But on 15 August the division turned over its positions along the southern edge of the escape corridor to the 90th Infantry Division and by four that afternoon its tanks and half-tracks were on the road grinding east toward the Eure. It was reported that elements of the 1st and 2nd SS Panzer Divisions were in the vicinity of Dreux and that the 17th GAF* Division having just come down from Holland, was moving across the Seine into the Eure area.

As the division sped through the August night, it was led by CC R on the left and CC B on the right. In reserve was CC A following CC R, while the remainder of the division was behind CC B's column.

CC R's route to Dreux passed through Courtomer, St. Martin, Armentieres and Brezolles. It advanced in two parallel columns with Task Force Hamberg, the 95th Artillery Bn. and C Co., 628th Tank Destroyer Bn. (minus one platoon) on the north and Task Force Boyer, Headquarters CC R, the 47th Artillery Bn. and a platoon of C Co., 628th T. D. Bn., on the south.

After stopping about 3 in the morning to refuel at St. Martin, Task Force Boyer was edging up to the western outskirts of Dreux by noon of the following day, 16 August. But then its advance guard was stopped here by fire from four 88s. The powerful enemy shells destroyed one light tank and killed the platoon leader, Lt. James J. O'Connor. Also the German artillery observers, with the advantage of their position on the Dreux Heights, were able to put down accurate fire on the mobile artillery pieces of the 47th Artillery Bn., forcing Lt. Col. Rosenzweig to move his battalion to a new location.

Racing along on the exposed northern flank, Task Force Hamberg ran into enemy resistance near Crulai. The left flank of the 95th Artillery Bn.'s column was attacked by a platoon of Mark IV tanks that were backed up by infantry and mortars. The artillerymen lost one of their M7s, one halftrack and two other vehicles. Then they leveled their big guns at the advancing Germans and, firing over open sights, smashed three of the attacking tanks and forced the others to retire. Because of this engagement Task Force Hamberg did not come within sight of Dreux until four o'clock on the afternoon of the 16th. By this time CC B had already started to attack the city, so CC R was ordered to block any enemy re-inforcements from moving toward

*German Air Force.

the city from the north and to secure crossings over the Eure from Dreux to Tury.

After their all-night rapid movement from Sees, along the poplar lined highway, CC B's two task forces and the 71st Artillery Bn. arrived in the vicinity of Dreux the morning of 16 August. While Task Force Giorlando, which had led CC B's column in its drive east, assembled just north of Fonville, Task Force Anderson went directly to the river and before noon had captured the bridge across the Eure at Villemeux, south of Dreux. The enemy, completely surprised to find American troops this far east, stumbled about in confusion. To take advantage of this disorganization, General Oliver ordered CC B to attack Dreux without delay.

The Mission fell to Task Force Giorlando. The plan called for the offensive to bear down on the town from the wooded approaches to the south; it would straddle the main highway, with the 15th Infantry Bn.'s A Co. on the right and C Co. on the left. Each company would be supported by a light tank platoon from D Co., 81st Tank Bn. (C Company and the two light tank platoons had been added to the task force's married A Companies to aid in this mission). The attacking companies would also be supported by fire from the field pieces of the 71st Artillery Bn. and by the Assault Gun Platoon advancing along the highway.

Defending the town was a battalion of German infantrymen. They were well concealed along the edge of the woods on the south side of the town. They also had two antitank guns in position with the barrels pointed straight down the main highway.

These Wehrmacht soldiers lay quietly and made no move as the line of A and C Company doughs trudged slowly and cautiously toward the town. Then when the attack wave had approached to within a few hundred yards of the trees the forest suddenly erupted in an outpouring of marching gun, rifle and antitank fire. Stunned by this surprise blow, the dazed GI's were thrown back and two halftracks of the Assault Gun Platoon were destroyed.

Lieutenants Polim and Isaacs quickly reorganized their platoons and then with supporting fire from the tanks, artillery, and assault guns, both companies again rushed the woods. This time they rolled over the enemy's defenses. With direct fire Lt. Melvin Abbott's Assault Gun Platoon knocked out the two antitank guns.

As the attack pushed through the woods and continued on toward the town, a German soldier, who was a member of the medical corps, came forward and offered to surrender 500 Germans in the town. Colonel Cole told the man he would be given a half hour to bring the garrison out of Dreux. Then the task force held its fire and waited, but after the half hour ticked away and no Germans emerged from the town, the attack was resumed. When the GI's reached the built-up sections of Dreux they found that the cagey Germans had withdrawn to a cemetery and were shelling the houses with mortars and artillery. But this final opposition was soon overcome and by 5:15 p.m. the town was in the hands of the Task Force. The happy inhabitants of Dreux then came out of their basements and other places of shelter and gave the Fifth Armored troops a loud and joyous welcome.

This quick capture of Dreux and the Eure crossings on 16 August made it unnecessary for the Allies to launch a large-scale airborne operation to take bridgeheads on the east bank of the river between Dreux and Chartres. It had been scheduled to begin on 18 August.

The morning after Dreux fell CC A arrived about 8 at Blainville, which completed the assembly of the entire division in the Dreux area. At Marville, where Division Headquarters were bivouacked, a lone enemy plane was shot down when it attempted to strafe the Command Post. Meanwhile CC R's Task Force Boyer had moved out early that morning was pushing north of Dreux toward the Avre River, which flowed in from the west and joined the Eure. The task force's right flank was protected by the Eure but the high ground across the river gave the enemy excellent observation of the moving column. By 9 A.M. the lead elements were receiving rifle, machine gun and mortar fire near Muzy. Some prisoners picked up by Task Force Boyer said they were members of the 17th GAF Division and that they had just come down from Holland to stop the Allied drive to the Seine.

Task Force Hamberg, which has been moving forward parallel and to the left of Task Force Boyer, reached the Avre and secured river crossings west of Muzy.

About 5 that afternoon Task Force Boyer attempted to enter Muzy and Motel but the column was repulsed by heavy artillery and anti-tank fire. Later it was learned that these two towns were occupied by the Antitank Battalion of the 17th GAF Division. At the end of the days operation CC R was firmly in control of all the territory north of Dreux to the Avre and west from the Eure to the railroad.

The Fifth Armored now became concerned with a very important triangle which was known as the Eure-Seine pocket. The base of this triangle was a line that extended from Dreux at the left and to Paris, about 44 miles almost directly east, at the right end. The Triangle's right sloping side was formed by the Seine River which flowed northwest from Paris, while the left side of the triangle was formed by the Eure River which flowed almost directly north from Dreux and joined the Seine a few miles south of Rouen.

This triangle, particularly its upper half, jutted deep into the wide escape path which the enemy soldiers, who had eluded the Falaise encirclement, were using to fall back toward Germany. The area, therefore, was filled with these Wehrmacht troops who were determined not only to get across the Seine themselves but also to keep its bridges open so that those behind them might also get across.

On the morning of 18 August detailed orders came down from higher headquarters which outlined the course the division was to follow in plunging into the Eure-Seine pocket. It was not instructed to proceed along the base of the triangle directly east to Paris, as every man had hoped and would have preferred. Instead, the division was ordered to bisect the triangle, to push from Dreux across the middle of the pocket and hit the Seine River near Mantes, about 31 miles northwest of Paris. It was to occupy the area west of Mantes-Gaissiccourt, blocking all roads and protecting the XV Corps' left flank.

This mission was accomplished with lightning speed. While CC R remained in Dreux to protect the bridgehead area, CC A and CC B pulled out of the town by noon on the same day the order was received. Ten hours later both combat commands had arrived at the west bank of the Seine south of Bonnieres. In this race across the triangle they overran several groups of enemy infantry and destroyed one 150 mm. howitzer, two half-tracks and numerous trucks.

That night an unusual scrap occurred at one of the road blocks which had been hastily set up. A Mark V tank, rumbling through the darkness, rammed head on into a tank from C Co., 81st Tank Bn. The Sherman's 75 mm. gun immediately belched out a round of armor-pircing ammunition which struck the gun mantle on the Mark V and was deflected down through the hatch, killing the German crew members. At Gilles the same night the 993rd Engineer Treadway Bridge Co. lost two air compressors and five 2½ ton trucks.

Many prisoners were taken by the roadblocks the next day as several scattered and disorganized enemy groups decided to give up the fight. Without losing a single man, Troop B, 85th Cavalry Sq., captured 142 members of the 116th Panzer Division. But enemy tanks were still active in the upper part of the triangle. To prevent the Germans from floating barges loaded with oil and other supplies down the Seine, Capt. Rolf E. Michelson's B. Co., 22nd Engineer Bn., damaged the locks near Port Villez. Also during the day's operations, Fifth Armored men discovered that SS troops were trying to make their escape in ambulances.

On the Breuilpont-Bonnieres highway the division's tanks were met by an overjoyed American pilot; he had been shot down the previous March and since that time had lived in disguise as a French civilian. To the airman's thrill at being liberated was soon added the happy surprise of a reunion with his brother, Lt. Harry G. Eberhardt of the 46th Infantry Bn.

After it was reported late in the afternoon by reconnaissance observers that enemy activity was increasing in the vicinity of Pacy sur Eure, the 47th Artillery Bn. put down on the town a barrage which destroyed some Wehrmacht vehicles. Then early in the evening a force of about 18 or 20 enemy tanks came charging down from the north into CC A and CC B's positions. The attacking armor, however, ran up against a bristling wall of tank, artillery, and aircraft fire, and six of the Panthers were demolished. When a platoon of Mark Vs tried to move into an assembly area with B Co., 81st Tank Bn., one tank was knocked out and the others fled to the northwest.

After turning the Dreux bridgehead area over to the Seventh Armored Division on the same day, CC R had started moving north along the east bank of the Eure to protect the Corp's left flank. Enemy planes soared in over the column and one was shot down by an antiaircraft unit. In the path of the combat command's advance lay Anet, which was about 12 miles northeast of Dreux. Prisoners, captured along the route, said the town was occupied by the German 47th Infantry Regiment. The combat command's long reconnaissance arms, which reached out like antennae from CC R's main body, contacted the enemy troops in Anet by 4 in the afternoon and discovered one Mark IV tank and 12 other vehicles in the town. The patrols found, too, that 13 supply trucks from the U. S. 79th Infantry Division were trapped in the woods west of Anet.

CC R rescued the supply trucks and then moved to high ground which dominated the town and its surrounding area. The Germans, realizing they had been put in an exposed position by this American maneuver, launched an artillery-supported infantry attack to dislodge CC R from the commanding heights. The green-clad Wehrmacht soldiers came across the Eure between Anet and Ivry. But CC R poured down heavy fire on the attackers and thinned their ranks before the assault could gain any momentum. Then in quick retaliation Task Force Boyer charged down on Ivry.

Before darkness settled over the battlefield that summer evening the superstructure of the Eiffel Tower was visible in the distance to the Victory Division troops occupying the high ground near the Seine. As they looked upon this old landmark, which heralded the presence of the famous beautiful city reclining at its base, these tired soldiers wished they would now be ordered to move southeast along the Seine to liberate Paris. They wanted the coveted privilege of driving the enemy from this prize city, the recapture of which would be celebrated around the world. And they knew that Parisians, overjoyed at being relieved of the German oppression, would receive their liberators tumultuously.

But such fruits were not for the Fifth Armored. Another, more difficult, but not so glamorous task was to be its lot. That night the division was ordered to drive northwest along the Seine, away from instead of toward Paris (which would fall five days later on 25 August). Its mission was to clear the remaining Germans from the upper part of the Eure-Seine triangle and to seize all of the Seine crossings which the enemy had been using in the area.

Thus, on 20 August, the day the Argentan-Falaise Gap was finally closed, the Fifth Armored, more than 115 miles (road distance) to the east of Argentan, began a new pincers movement to envelope those Wehrmacht soldiers who had evaded the Normandy trap but had not yet crossed the Seine. It was not an easy operation; for the division was driving a wedge into an extremely sensitive enemy flank and the Germans fought savagely to prevent any narrowing of their escape route. It meant seizing the important crossings at Vernon and Les Andelys on the Seine and Louviers on the Eure; it meant taking from the Germans their pontoon bridges which they cleverly had concealed along the river banks during the day and then stretched across the water at night. In this manner the Germans shuttled 27,000 troops across the river during the last three nights before the bridges were captured. It also meant battling through numerous heavily wooded ravines where the fanatical defenders fought to the last man.

The attack jumped off at 9:30 a.m. with CC A on the left and CC B in a parallel position on the right. Their objective was the high ground at Heudebouville, 25 miles to the north.

CC A's advance guard consisted of the married A Companies of the 34th Tank Bn. and the 46th Infantry Bn. This vanguard tangled with its first resistance at Douains where two of its tanks were knocked out by enemy antitank guns. Assistance was sought from the 47th and 400th Artillery Battalions which smashed the enemy position with their heavy fire and enabled the column to push on two more miles to the edge of La Heuniere. Here the Germans had 12 to 15 tanks ready to trade blows with anything that challenged them. This tough armor was entrenched in excellent defense positions and fire from their guns swept all approaches to the south of the town. For three hours during the afternoon the fighter-bombers, artillery pieces and tank destroyers brought down on the German tanks all of the thunderous and deadly wrath of which they were capable. But only a few of the Panthers yielded any ground.

During the entire day, however, the enemy lost 12 tanks, destroyed by both ground and air action. CC A's losses included three tanks and three tank destroyers. Also, Lt. Col. Hernandez of the 628th Tank Destroyer Bn. was killed while directing fire in front of his own guns.

Early in the evening Capt. James W. Ray, commander of the advance guard, took the married A Companies around the western side of La Heuniere through a defiladed route to the north of the town, where he assembled near St. Vincent des Bois. Thus the night was spent with the enemy sandwiched between the advanced guard and the main body of CC A.

Patrols which had crept up to the edge of La Heuniere in the darkness reported that the Germans had withdrawn from the town. Major Burton was then ordered to send a platoon of infantry from his task force at daylight through the town to make contact with the advance guard on its north side. But as this force drew near to the village, it was fired upon by from 200 to 300 enemy soldiers who were discovered to be occupying the buildings and well dug-in position in an adjacent field. During the first few minutes of this early morning encounter Major Burton was wounded.

Lt. Col. Case, executive officer of CC A, immediately was assigned to replace the wounded commander and ordered to continue the attack. Instructions also went to the advance guard to wheel around and descend on the town from the north. With this combined assault pressing in upon La Heuniere like a vise from both the north and the south, its defenders were soon killed or routed. Those who fled ran to the east across the front of the machine gun and assault gun platoons of Headquarters Co., 46th Infantry Bn.

After snuffing out this last resistance at La Heuniere, the task force continued on through a nearby wooded area and by late afternoon it was on the outskirts of Mercey. Here Lt. Col. Case called for his supporting artillery batteries to soften up the target before his infantry attacked. But unfortunately he did not wait for the preparatory fire and was wounded as he moved his force against the town. Major Jack Day then assumed command of the task force and before midnight his troops, after winding through a dangerous defile, were within sight of Champenard. During the night Lt. Col. Kenneth Gilson arrived to take over command of the task force.

On CC B's front, the Combat Command had been methodically working its way forward through scattered resistance. Each woods in its path was combed out by the infantrymen who trudged through on foot. Late in the afternoon of 21 August CC B had attacked the Forest of Bizy and had completely cleared it by 8:30 that evening. Then it began advancing on Vernon.

Throughout the day CC R had been in division reserve at an assembly area just south of Cravent. The previous day, 20 August, it had finished mopping up the last enemy hold-outs in the Anet-Ivry area by noon and four hours later had turned over its positions there to the Seventh Armored Division.

At dawn on 22 August Lt. Col. Gilson took his new command into Champenard without opposition. But the flat open ground to the north of the village was within the field of fire of five Mark Vs and one towed 88 which were camouflaged in a woods about 1200 yards to the northeast. As Task Force Gilson tried to leave the village these concealed enemy guns destroyed two of its tanks and three of its halftracks. And CC A Headquarters lost three of its light tanks when its tank platoon tried to move to the right to reconnoiter the route used the previous night.

To clear the wooded fringes around this open area on the north of Champenard Capt. Bland's B Co., 46th Infantry Bn., dismounted from their halftracks and took their bazookas into the woods with them. This pressure applied by the rocket-firing infantrymen forced the enemy tanks to withdraw from the woods. But as they tried to escape to the north they came within view of CC A's tanks which immediately loosed a torrent of shells on them. Four of the Mark Vs were demolished and the fifth was abandoned.

After capturing Vernon, CC B trundled on toward the north.

As Task Force Anderson was grinding forward northwest of Gaillon its married B Companies of the 81st Tank Bn. and 15th Infantry Bn. received machine gun fire from a harvested field. When the married C Companies started past the field, it was discovered that this peaceful-looking pastoral scene was a formidable enemy stronghold; under each wheat shock was a large fox hole in which SS troops lay waiting. As the married C Companies started to spread out in preparation for an attack on this fortified position, enemy antitank shells crashed into two Shermans and two light tanks. This fire came forth from a woods on the far side of the field.

The air and artillery liaison officers radioed for assistance and soon the big shells were whining overhead and the fighter-bombers were diving on the enemy gun positions. At the same time the married C Companies turned their tank, assault and machine guns on these woods. A tracer bullet from one of the weapons ignited a drum of gasoline on one of the Mark V tanks. This blazing marker enabled the Airplane pilots easily to pick out and quickly destroy the other two Panther tanks.

After the enemy's heavy guns on the far side of the field had been eliminated the tank guns shot up the wheat shocks and the unyielding SS troops who were concealed in the fox holes beneath them. Then the infantry moved in and with their grenades and rifles finished off those Germans who still resisted. During the fight not a single SS man offered to surrender. When the Graves Registration personnel gathered up the crop of dead on this wheat field the next day, they counted the bodies of 200 German soldiers.

While Task Force Anderson had been overcoming this enemy strong point, CC B's Task Force Giorlando had continued north along the Seine and by nightfall had reached St. Etienne.

Early in the day CC R had been alerted for the mission of clearing the Forest of Pacy. The attack had begun west of La Heuniere at 4 in the afternoon but it was soon discovered that the enemy had withdrawn from the woods. The combat command had then been given the task of protecting the division's rear from any enemy tanks and artillery pieces heading for the Seine as CC A and CC B advanced northwest in the Eure-Seine pocket.

The following day, 23 August, the division's armored wave continued to tumble forward crushing all the enemy's defenses on which it fell. While B and C Companies of the 46th Infantry Bn. cleared the woods from Champenard to the Gaillon highway, the remainder of CC A swept across the open terrain north of the town. The artillery batteries and fighterbombers were kept busy smashing up two Seine-bound German columns which they caught on the road; one was an armored force heading east toward Gaillon, while the other was a horse-drawn artillery column moving east from Heudebouville. In these attacks from the air the Germans found that they were practically defenseless, even when they attempted to hide. The pilots had learned to spot enemy tank tracks and to follow them until they disappeared in hay stacks, buildings and clumps of trees; these innocently looking objects would then be hit by the airmen with their devastating bombs and rockets.

Ater subduing scattered resistance during the day, CC A's main body reached the line Les Quaizes-Ailly-Gournay by 5 that afternoon. Task Force Bland, a special team consisting of the married B Companies of the 46th Infantry Bn. and 34th Tank Bn. plus one platoon from A Co., 22nd Engineer Bn., passed through Gournay and attacked Fontaine-Bellinger at 6 p.m. Here more fanatical Germans were found to be dug-in under wheat shocks and also in an orchard. These tanks led the assault and blasted the area. Then the infantry, following along in their halftracks, dropped grenades down into the fox holes and killed all the Germans who had managed to escape the fire from the tank guns. Probing further north beyond this strongpoint the task force was hit by 40 mm. antiaircraft and antitank fire from the area east of Heudebouville. Two of its tanks and one halftrack were lost before darkness ended the fight. Throughout the night the artillery pounded the enemy positions in preparation for the attack that was to come the next morning.

CC B's Task Force Giorlando had cleared the woods beyond the main highway southwest of Gaillon during the day. Then at 3:15 in the afternoon it had been placed under the control of CC A for the assault on Heudebouville.

Rain fell on 24 August bringing its ominous warning that the fine warm summer weather with its dry roads and solid ground, which had enabled the Fifth Armored to advance so rapidly, was coming to an end. Now there would be another enemy besides the Germans: mud. But despite the rain the division was determined to make quick work of seizing its final objective in the northern point of the Eure-Seine pocket. To take the town a double envelopment was planned: Task Force Giorlando, on the left, would attack through Gruchet and Ingremare (this left wing punch would also have the support of a force of medium tanks under the command of Major Boxley that would attack from the area north of Ailly); on the right. Task Force Bland would drive in through Gournay and Fontaine-Bellinger; and in the center would be a holding force commanded by Lt. Col. Gilson.

The rain and soft mud seriously hampered the advance. By 1:30 that afternoon Task Force Bland had captured Fontaine-Bellinger and twenty minutes later Gruchet fell to Task Force Giorlando. The road through Heudebouville was cut at 2 p.m. and by 5 that afternoon Ingremare had been taken. Then at 6:30 p.m. Task Force Bland moved into Heudebouville. And the fall of this town ended all enemy resistance in the northern tip of the Eure-Seine triangle.

That night welcome news came down from higher headquarters to the damp and tired men of CC A and CC B. They were ordered to "assemble in vicinity to Mantes-Gassicourt, repair and service vehicles and weapons."

But CC R's tasks in the Eure-Seine pocket were not yet finished. The combat command had been ordered that day to move to an assembly area southeast of Mantes-Gassicourt. It had been intended that CC R would remain here as a mobile reserve, under Corps' control, to back up the 106th Cavalry Group. But while the column was enroute to the Mantes area Corps had sent new orders to Colonel Anderson which instructed him to cross the Mauldre River, attack to the north and clear all the Germans from the pocket south of the Seine, west of Poissy. This change in plans had been radioed to the two task forces and by 10 that night the combat command had assembled west of Beynnes.

As soon as the tide goes out —
we land on Utah.

Normandy via LST.

An unsuccessful strafing mission.

One less Henie Tank.

had to have
outances.

eep rolling.

An even swap.

Coutances wasn't che

Bomb creators were everywhere.

Mademoiselle gives thanks and flowers.

Don't stop — Go on.

Abrnches streets.

These Germans stayed in France.

Hay stacks offered little photection to the Hun.

Thunder-Bolt works 'em over.

The Air Corp beat us to this target.

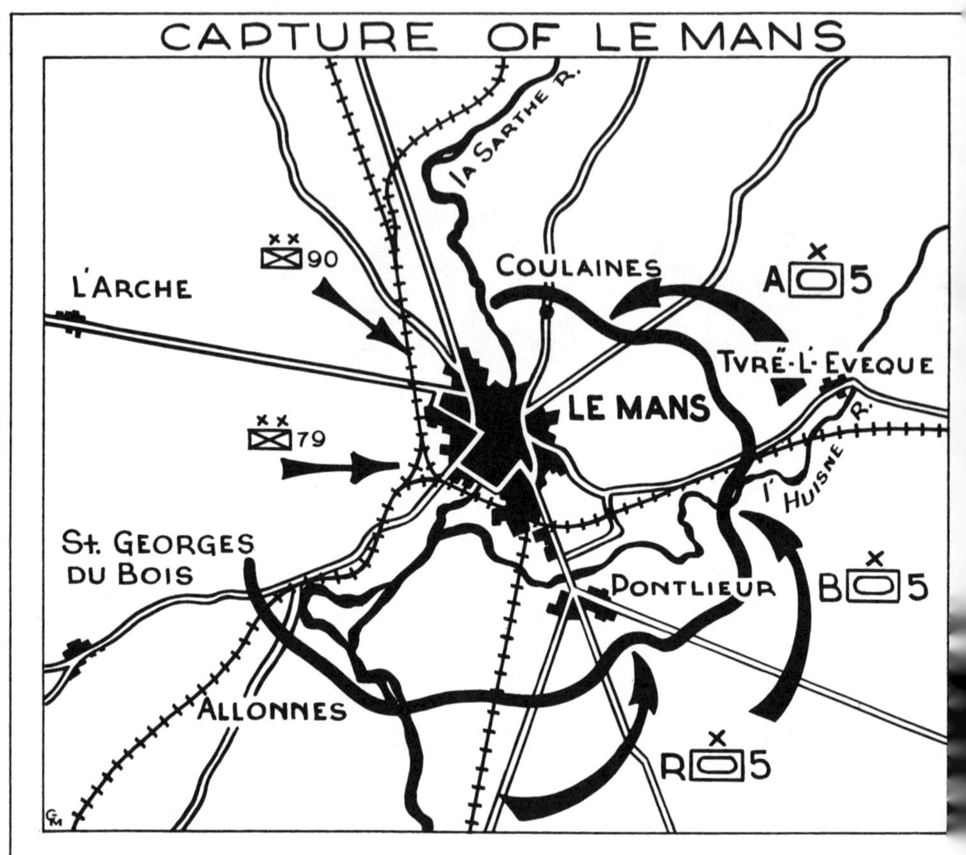

Le Mans — "Won't you stop over, Boys"

Near Le Mans we caught some.

At Sees, France — Gen. Patton, Gen. Oliver, Col. Farrand and Lt. Col. MacFarland.

Prisoners are searched.

We trapped an entire column.

Hitler's Jugend.

Chas. Sotka near Falaise.

Capt. Whitley, Capt. Baum, two DSC's.

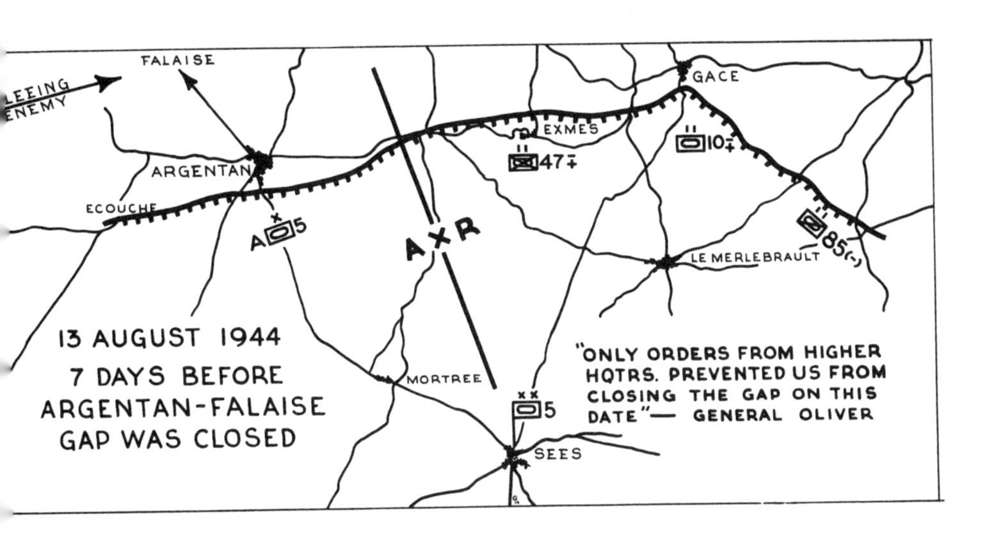

Each town in Falaise Gap had defenders.

One of the Tigers in Argentan — courtesy — 85th Rcn.

The 81st moves into Dreux.

Captain Don Craft questions Free French.

Div. Hq. at Dreux.

The FFI help Capt. Fargon.

— and capture some, too.

The 628th was on the job at Dreux.

The 28th Inf. stayed up with us near the Seine.

St. Germain near Paris was happy.

The town's people greet us.

Cigarette pour papa.

DSO Maj. Foss, Sgt. Schmandt, Sgt. Cook, Sgt. Cohen.

Paris begins living again.

Gen. Oliver passes through Paris.

These Tiger Tanks were hard to kill.

The Compiegne Forrest was in our path.

Bridge over Oise River
Compiegne France.

It was not a restful night that CC R spent in this area. The German artillery observers, perched on the high ground east of the Mauldre from which the countryside west of the river is visible for ten miles, evidently had spotted the arrival of the combat command near Beynnes. For at about midnight German artillery shells with their blood-chilling shrieks began crashing in CC R's assembly area. During the night more than 100 rounds of these 88 mm. armor-piercing shells were hurled at the combat command but no men or vehicles were hit.

After waiting through this anxious night, the combat command lunged forward into the enemy's positions the following day. Task Force Boyer, led by the married B Company of the 10th Tank Bn. and the 47th Infantry Bn., swept through the woods north of Crespières. The tankers and infantrymen ferreted out a Storm battalion, which only recently had been organized in Paris. More than 100 Germans were killed or wounded and the rest surrendered.

All resistance in the area had ceased by 5 that afternoon; the enemy equipment which the combat command captured here included four 88s, four 105 mm. artillery pieces, numerous bicycles and one transport plane.

This completed the division's work of clearing the Eure-Seine pocket and also of annihilating the enemy Combat Team (or Task Force) Wahl-Franke. This had been a provisional unit and had consisted of elements of the 1st and 12th Panzer Divisions, 17th, 2nd and 4th Panzer Grenadier Divisions, 711th Infantry and 7th SS Mountain Divisions. It received new trucks in Paris on 16 August and had been sent to hold Dreux, but the town had been captured before it had reached there. The task force had then been cut up while it fought ferociously to prevent the Fifth Armored from flooding through the Eure-Seine pocket.

On 26 August CC R was instructed to move up to the west bank of the Seine River and outpost the area Les Mureaux-Poisay. Task Force Boyer was strung out from Les Mureaux to Vernonouillet, while Task Force Hamberg occupied the area from Vernonouillet to Poissy. Their job here until 29 August was to harass with mortar and tank fire all enemy movements in the opposite shore. The division's artillery battalions also continued to remain in action, south of the Seine until 29 August. They were given the mission of supporting with artillery fire the 79th and 30th Infantry Divisions which were establishing a bridgehead across the river.

The other two combat commands and the remainder of the division however, moved to the Mantes-Gassicourt area, where they remained until 29 August. It was their first respite from fighting since they had first gone into action on 2 August. Their stay here was devoted to badly-needed maintenance work on their equipment, such as tank and halftrack motors, tank tracks, radios and weapons. While here they also received replacement vehicles for those which had been lost in battle.

During this period, too, men were able to bathe and clean up. For many it was the first time they were able to reserve their clothes since they had left England.

The Fifth Armored's initial, almost-month-long period in combat was of record length. In this long session of continuous fighting from Normandy to the Seine, the division left in its wake a clutter of broken enemy units and destroyed equipment. The division killed 2,811 German soldiers and captured 2,900. It destroyed: 203 tanks, 8 armored cars, 384 motor vehicles, 3 ambulances, 20 self-propelled guns, 87 artillery pieces, and 89 infantry weapons. And it captured: 36 tanks, 8 airplanes and 18 artillery pieces.

In its campaign from Normandy to the Seine the Fifth Armored traveled 405 miles (this figure is the shortest road distance, but many individual maneuvering vehicles piled up more than 600 miles. The drive included: move from St. Sauveur le Vicomte to south of the Selune River, 85 miles; advance to Le Mans, 95 miles; advance north to Argentan, 58 miles; advance to Dreux, 80 miles; advance to the Seine, 35 miles; advance to northwest point of Eure-Seine pocket and back again (26 miles each way), 52 miles.

XIV

ALL IS KAPUT

The Seine to Luxembourg

30 August—10 September

OVERWHELMING OPTIMISM swept through the Allied Forces in Western Europe toward the end of the summer of 1944. And the fountainhead from which these joyous waves expanded was Paris. As the French capital glowed with exaltation in its newly-won freedom and as the remnants of the broken German armies fled through Northern France and Belgium toward their homeland, GIs and generals alike seemed convinced that the war could not last much longer. Except among the Fifth Armored Division Intelligence officers, the air was filled with wild predictions that hostilities would be over in three weeks, two weeks, or even a few days.

But despite their confidence in an early victory the Allies did not relax their crushing pressure on the retreating Wehrmacht. Before they plunged across the Seine to continue the chase, however, some of the U. S. divisions were reassigned to different armies and corps. In this reshuffle the Fifth Armored was transferred from General Patton's Third Army to General Courtney H. Hodge's First Army (26 August). It was also placed in General Leonard T. Gerow's Fifth Corps (29 August). Its team mates in this corps were the 4th and 28th Infantry Divisions. The First Army's other two corps consisted of (VII Corps) 3rd Armored, 1st and 9th Infantry Divisions; (XIX Corps) 2nd Armored, 79th and 30th Infantry Divisions.

As this new advance got under way the First Army's three corps jumped off in staggered formation. The VII Corps' 3rd Armored crossed the Seine east of Paris on 26 August, the XIX Corps' 2nd Armored began crossing in the Mantes-Gassicourt area on 28 August; and the V Corps' Fifth Armored passed over the river in Paris on 30 August.

Although Paris had been liberated from the German yoke for five days when the Fifth Armored finally entered the city, the atmosphere was still charged with a spirit of rejoicing. From windows along the broad avenues hung the long-hidden tri-colored flags, gently stirring in the summer breezes. Happy, colorful crowds, jamming the sidewalks, cheered and waved as the division's tanks and halftracks rumbled by. And whenever the columns halted briefly these exuberant Parisians pressed forward around the vehicles to greet personally the Victory Division men.

It was an exciting, memorable experience for the GIs as they received the plaudits of this grateful city. But their stay amidst these exhilarating surroundings was brief. By noon CC A and CC B were already beyond the city. They were speeding north in order to pass through the 4th and 28th Infantry Divisions. Their mission was to secure crossings over the Oise and Aisne Rivers between Compiegne and Soissons, about 50 miles northeast of Paris.

By late that evening CC B, on the left, was about 25 miles north of the French Capital; both its task forces had met and overcome enemy rear guard troops: Task Force Anderson at Lamorlaye and Task Force Gilson at Senlis. (The 15th Infantry Bn. was now under the command of Lt. Col. Gilson; he had been transferred from the 46th Infantry Bn. when Major Burton had returned from the hospital on 27 August to resume command of that battalion.) The 629th Tank Destroyer Bn. had joined CC A at Claye Souilly during the afternoon and before dark the combat command had reached Nantouillet. Division Headquarters spent the night just south of Ducy after the head of the column had come up against some German infantry troops and antitank guns. Lt. Col. Fay was killed in this action, and command of the 85th Cavalry Sq. had been assumed by Maj. John P. Gerald.

The next morning, 31 August, the division lunged forward in a three-pronged offensive. CC R's column was in the center with CC B on the left and CC A on the right. By about 11 that morning CC B's Task Force Gilson had pushed approximately 12 miles north of Senlis to Verberie, where the enemy had blown the highway bridge. Despite this obstacle, the task force continued its advance and about midafternoon overran and shot up a German horse-drawn column. Further to the left, Task Force Anderson reached Creil at 3 p.m. and found that the important bridge here over the Oise also had been destroyed. Before midnight Task Force Gilson was on the outskirts of Compiegne and was encountering fierce resistance from the Germans in the darkness.

After passing through the doughs of the 4th Infantry Division just before noon, CC A had met opposition from enemy infantry and antitank guns at Morienval three hours later. But a little after 6 that evening the combat command's Task Force Burton had been able to cross the Aisne unopposed at Pommiers; it then assembled for the night five miles north of the river.

In its race to nip at the heels of the fleeing German forces, CC R overran seven enemy artillery pieces south of Bethisy. Next, its two task forces had plunged into the historic Compiegne Forest at Orrouy and Gilcourt. By 8 in the evening they were running into heavy resistance.

As the division continued its rush northward, the trains (supply and administrative vehicles) of each of the combat commands were being protected by the 85th Cavalry Sq. Troops A, B and C were attached to Combat Commands A, B and R respectively.

CC A, now beyond the Fifth Armored's immediate objective – the Compiegne-Soissons line – was attached to the 4th Infantry Division in the early morning hours of 1 September. The new job assigned to its two task forces, which were supported by the 47th and 400th Artillery Battalions was to spearhead this infantry division's advance in the V Corps' eastern sector.

After the 28th Division's 112th Regiment had secured a bridgehead on the north bank of the Oise at Compiegne during the night, B Co., 22nd Engineer Bn., started constructing a 240 foot treadway bridge across the river. It was completed by 6 the following evening and CC B's Task Force Gilson began rolling its tanks and halftracks over the stream. Meanwhile, further down the river at Pont St. Maxence, Task Force Anderson had crossed two hours earlier. During this time, CC R with the assistance of the 28th Division's Combat Team 109 had completed the task of clearing the Compiegne Forest against moderate resistance. But when the combat command had reached Choissy on the river at 2 in the afternoon, it found another destroyed bridge. CC R, therefore, had been ordered to cross over the new treadway bridge at Compiegne.

During the day the division had received new instructions from General Gerow. It was ordered to proceed northward as swiftly as possible to the V Corps' objective, the Belgian border at Condé. CC B, which was now on the north side of the river, was urged, therefore, to continue its advance into the night. Its armored columns rolled on in the darkness, but as Task Force Gilson approached Noyon, about 13 miles north of Compiegne its three lead tanks were knocked out by German antitank guns. Further to the left, a fusillade of 88 mm. shells and bazooka projectiles smashed into three halftracks of the 15th Infantry Bn.'s Co., which was at the head of Task Force Anderson's column. The combat command had run up against the Wehrmacht's 348th Infantry Division, the bulk of which was deployed in this Noyon-Remy area; it had been placed here to stall the Fifth Armored's advance and thus gain time for its own motorized forces to get across the Somme River. CC B was unable to push any further north that night.

But the next day, 2 September, the combat command broke loose and hurtled forward in a spectacular 85-mile dash; it was the deepest drive into enemy territory made thus far in a single day by any outfit on the Western Front. At daylight CC B found that most of the enemy forces which had presented the stonewall resistance the previous night had withdrawn. From its positions south of Noyon it then rolled its halftracks and tanks onto the roads at 6:30 a.m. and pointed them toward the Belgian border.

After grinding through Noyon, it pushed on to Ham, where the bridge over the Somme-Oise Canal had been wrecked with demolitions. Engineers of B Co., 22nd Engineer Bn., were called forward to the site and they quickly threw a 30-foot treadway bridge across the barrier. Crossing the canal and driving beyond Ham, the column then began to pick up speed. It by-passed St. Quentin to the west and, later, Cambrai to the east. Then it shot into Valenciennes and by 10:15 that night was across the Belgian border two miles north of Condé. The first Fifth Armored member to enter Belgium was Lt. Robert A. Lewis, company commander of A Co., 15th Infantry Bn.; he was carried across the border by a jubilant crowd of Belgian citizens.

Fifteen minutes after the division rolled into Belgium an order arrived from the V Corps; it instructed the Fifth Armored to halt its northward drive on the Cambrai-le Cateau line, but the division was already 25 miles beyond this line. When the liaison officer to corps, Lt. Stephen Frankl, drove south to report the division's disposition, he had to travel 120 miles to reach Corps Headquarters.

During its dash north the column was led most of the way by General Oliver, who rode in his peep. Once he spotted an enemy antitank gun which was poised to fire on the column as soon as it started crossing a canal bridge. The division commander moved behind a house at the side of the road and then directed the fire of the column's lead tank, which destroyed the enemy's gun.

At the same time that the Fifth Armored was deftly knifing its way north to Condé, on its left a vast German force was also moving toward Belgium, but more slowly. Consisting of about 50,000 soldiers, it was hastening to get back to Germany. The immediate objective on its escape route was Mons in Belgium. But the arrival of the Fifth Armored at Condé, which lay about 16 miles directly west of Mons, blocked this return path and thus sealed the doom of the German force.

The positions of this huge mass of retreating enemy troops were reported by a Wehrmacht officer, who was picked up by the Fifth Armored along the route to Belgium. Division Headquarters relayed the information to a group of P-47s that were in the neighboring skies. These airmen with their shattering bombs and devastating strafing then spent the entire afternoon ripping into the concentration of men and equipment, especially those jammed up near Beauvais. As the Fifth Armored was quickly called to a new mission and relieved of its blocking positions astride the Germans' retreat path, it did not remain here long enough to gather up any sizeable crop of prisoners from this cut off body. But after the division had departed, the 1st Infantry Division and the 3rd Armored Division captured 45,000 of these German soldiers; many of them were taken near Mons.

It was ironical that this immense German horde should meet its defeat here in the borderland area between France and Belgium; for it was here that von Rundstedt's armored columns, after smashing through the front at Sedan, had broken the backs of the French and British armies in the spring of 1940, and the point from which the British "Old Contemptible" started their historic withdrawal in 1914.

CC A, which had been spearheading the advance of the 4th Infantry Division during the first two days of September, had reached the line le-Cateau-Landrecies. Here, reverting to division control, it assembled in the vicinity of Esnes. Division headquarters was located at Maing, just below Valenciennes, while CC R was a few miles further south.

The Fifth Armored spent 3 September setting up roadblocks and picking up German soldiers who were astonished to find U. S. troops blocking the roads to Germany. About 50 vehicles which came up against these blocks were destroyed. Also during the day, British troops passed to the northwest of the division's positions and closed on the Belgian border.

Counting up the destruction it had wrought on the German Army in its 130-mile Paris-Condé thrust, the division found it had killed 400 enemy soldiers and taken 600 prisoners. It had also destroyed hundreds of vehicles, machine guns and other weapons. North of Valenciennes it had captured 69 two-horse teams and several saddle horses and had been directly responsible for the capture of 45,000 German troops in the Mons area.

On 4 September the V Corps' three divisions began executing a swift and intricate maneuver. They were to pull back from their positions along the Belgian border, swing around to the southeast, and pass behind the troops of the VII Corps in an advance toward Luxembourg. In this 100-mile eastward move the Fifth Armored was led on the left by CC R, which was headed for Charleville-Mezieres north of Sedan, and on the right by CC A, which was driving toward a point south of Sedan. CC B followed along behind CC R; at Brunehamed, however, it would branch off to the south between the other two combat commands and approach Sedan from the west.

Departing at 7:30 that morning from Le Cateau, CC R was off on a record-breaking dash. It shot through Guise, Hirson, Maubert, Fontaine and by 3:40 that afternoon its lead elements were in Charleville on the Meuse River. This was a motor march of 96 miles in eight hours and ten minutes. Because of the extended supply lines, gasoline was extremely scarce and several vehicles with dry fuel tanks had to drop out along the route. After gas had been brought up to them, however, they raced forward to rejoin their units. The fuel shortage also prevented the 95th Artillery Bn. from accompanying CC R on its run to Charleville, but a truck-drawn artillery battalion, the 196th, was able to go along with the combat command.

At Mezieres CC R learned from troops of the 24th Cavalry (also of the V Corps) that the enemy had blown all six of the Meuse River bridges in this area. After reconnoitering for a suitable site at which to erect an emergency crossing the combat command decided to start building the bridge at Warcq. But infantrymen, conducting further reconnaissance on the opposite shore, discovered that there were two canals east of Charleville-Mezieres instead of only one shown on the maps. The bridge over the first canal was still standing but the span over the second was down. Work, therefore, was halted at Warcq and a new site, where the stream could be bridged with only one structure, was sought.

Captain Pasqualino of B Co., 47th Infantry Bn., ordered his company to dismount from their halftracks; then he sent small reconnaissance parties to search along the edges of the river and canals. One of these groups found a dam which, although partially destroyed, could still be used as a crossing for foot troops. Here the entire company made their way over the river and they were followed by members of C Co., 47th Infantry Bn. At nine that evening both these companies charged the high ground east of the second canal which was held by a training garrison of fanatical young Germans. The infantrymen were supported in their assault by direct fire from B Co., 10th Tank Bn., by artillery fire from the 198th Artillery Bn., and by fire from the Assault Gun and Machine Gun platoons of Headquarters Co., 47th Infantry Bn. The enemy defenders had a tremendous advantage. They were entrenched in the rear installations of the Maginot Line. Their positions were high up a 50-foot cliff and were connected by underground concrete tunnels. From their elevated defenses they were able to drop grenades on the attacking infantrymen.

The fighting continued bitterly into the night with the bullets ricocheting off the rocky surfaces. Meanwhile, construction work was begun by C Co., 22nd Engineer Bn. on another treadway bridge south of the cliff. But the Germans had brought up self-propelled 20 mm. antiaircraft guns and poured shells down on the bridge site. A bulldozer was destroyed and the engineers suffered several casualties.

At daylight the next morning, 5 September, the doughs moved against the cliff fortress again and by noon they had rooted out the last of the defenders from the corridors of this Maginot Line installation. Mud and rain hampered the engineers in their construction work but by 5 in the afternoon they had finished their 192-foot treadway bridge. It was the first bridge to be built across the Meuse by Allied forces. One hour later both of CC R's Task Forces were across the Meuse and awaiting further orders from Division Headquarters.

CC A was hard hit by the gasoline shortage. After returning from its mission with the 4th Division, the combat command had filled its vehicles' fuel tanks in preparation for the long drive to the east. But on the extended motor march to the Meuse no gas was immediately available to refuel the tanks and halftracks because the supply trucks had to go all the way back to truckheads south of the Seine River to pick up more gasoline. The lead elements of CC A, therefore, did not arrive at the Meuse until 5:45 in the afternoon of 5 September.

Members of A Co., 46th Infantry Bn., immediately started to ferry across the river at Pont Maugis in a single outboard motor boat that was supplied by A Co., 22nd Engineer Bn. By 9 in the evening the company was holding a small east-bank bridgehead on the flat plain west of Bazeilles and the engineers had begun constructing a treadway bridge. Three hours after midnight, however, enemy infantry launched an attack with machine gun and mortar fire. They forced the bridgehead troops to fall back and the engineers to cease work on the bridge.

During the night a column of supply trucks loaded with 11,000 gallons of gasoline rolled in from the west. This permitted the 47th Artillery Bn. to join the 400th Artillery Bn. and add its support to the bridgehead operation.

Early the next morning members of C Co., 46th Infantry Bn., crossed the river and joined the harassed doughs of A Co. After occupying Balan these two companies then attacked Bazeilles from the north. The enemy soldiers, dug-in southeast of the village, clung tenaciously to their positions. While these infantrymen of A and C Companies fought to enlarge the bridgehead the engineers started work again on their bridge. By 12:20 p.m. they had completed it. And as soon as it was finished a platoon of light tanks rumbled across the structure and went to the aid of the De Federico's mortar platoon, the attack wave pushed beyond two infantry companies. One of the tanks was put out of action by antitank fire.

With the supporting fire from artillery batteries and Lt. Joseph the village. But here the mortar fire from the German positions on the high wooded ground overlooking Bazeilles became so heavy that C Company was forced to fall back to the houses in the village for cover. B Company then passed through C Company in order to outflank the mortar positions from the northeast. Preceded by a crippling barrage from the big artillery guns, B Company filtered into the woods and ferreted out the Germans who were still alive. Among those captured were three officers; one had a map which depicted the enemy's delaying positions between the Meuse and the Luxembourg border, of which G-2 made good use.

After the engagement had been concluded, Task Force Burton came across the bridge and passed through the companies. By midnight it was nearing Douzy.

The job of liberating historic Sedan, a contested city in other wars, fell to CC R's Task Force Boyer. To assist it in this undertaking it was assigned the 15th Infantry Bn. Pushing off early from Mezieres on 6 September, the task force started winding through the narrow, mountainous roads. It had to batter its way through several roadblocks and remove trees which the Germans had felled across the route with explosives. It also encountered in the streets of the villages piles of old wagons and other junk behind which the German soldiers had set up their sputtering machine guns.

At Illy the lead observers spotted a column of 15 enemy vehicles further ahead on the road. This information was relayed to the air support. Then the task force and a group of P-47s attacked the vehicles simultaneously. The slanted streams of tracer bullets from the strafing planes tore into the German column only a few hundred yards from Task Force Boyer's lead tanks. All of the enemy vehicles were demolished and most of their occupants were killed.

Approaching Sedan from the north, the task force decided to circle around and sweep in on the city from the east. When the advance guard reached Givonne, a few miles north of Sedan, it was informed by French civilians that only a few minutes before its arrival a German column headed northeast had passed through the town. The assistance call was again flashed to the fighter-bombers. It was not long before the pilots had located the unfortunate string of vehicles creeping back toward Germany. Swooping down from the skies, they strafed the column from one end to the other and shattered 15 of its 17 vehicles. Later it was learned that this group was the Wehrmacht's 80th Corps Headquarters Column, which had been at Sedan regrouping elements of the German Army.

After the entire task force had gathered on the east side of Sedan, it prepared for the assault on the city. The huge M7 field pieces of the 95th Artillery Bn. started moving into position off the road so they would be able to put down a softening-up barrage on the target. The tank destroyers of C Co., 628th T. D. Bn., going into formation, were ready to blast the enemy armor. The tanks and dismounted infantrymen awaited the order to start closing in on the city.

Then over the radios in the halftracks and peeps came a faint call. It was from CWO Charles Engdahl of Service Co., 15th Infantry Bn. He was trying to contact his company commander, Capt. Clarence Anderson.

"Hello, Sugar Six," he called, his voice coming in weakly. "I have the gasoline supplies. What is your location?" Captain Anderson replied, "I am in Sedan."

"Oh, no, you can't be in Sedan," Captain Anderson said. "We are ready to attack that city now."

But CWO Engdahl *was* in Sedan. Returning from a breakneck run to the gasoline dumps at Ermonville, more than 115 miles to the west, he knew that his battalion was supposed to be in the general vicinity of Sedan and he had taken his column of fuel trucks directly to the city. After radio contact was made with the task force, he reported that the Germans had evacuated the city, except for a few Wehrmacht soldiers who were being rounded up by the Free French forces.

CWO Engdahl soon discovered that a blown bridge prevented him from taking the fuel trucks to the task force's position. But he also found that individuals could make their way across the jack-knifed structure. He then appealed to the Free French for help. One of them sounded a bugle and a group of Free French fighters assembled at the bridge site. Forming a human chain across the collapsed structure, they passed the five-gallon cans of gasoline across the river to the task force on the opposite bank.

Now the checkreins of the extended supply lines began to make themselves felt on the Fifth Armored's advance. With the important Meuse crossings at Sedan and Charleville secure, the division planned to start thrusting its spearheads further to the east. But at noon on 7 September the V Corps ordered the division to halt its advance "due to the limited supply of gasoline." Late that same day the 28th Infantry passed through CC A and CC R and continued toward Luxembourg. To get its fuel the division had to send its trucks on the 200-mile round trip to the First Army supply truckhead, which had now been moved forward to Soissons. And at this gasoline dump the trucks had long waits before they received any fuel and often drew only partial allocations. During its forced two-day wait on the east bank of the Meuse the division furnished 50 trucks to help haul gasoline from Soissons to the First Army's new advanced distribution point at Mezieres.

On 9 September, however, the Fifth Armored got the green

light to resume its offensive. But its operations were to continue on a day-to-day basis, depending on the supply of gasoline. Its advance, led by CC A and CC R, was to cut across the lower corner of Belgium and strike into the Grand Duchy of Luxembourg. CC A, on the right and followed by Division Headquarters and CC B, would drive through Virton and Aubange to Luxembourg City. CC R, on the left, would advance in the direction of Izel, St. Marie, Arlon and Guirsch to Mersch.

As the German soldiers felt this armor pressing closer toward their homeland, their opposition stiffened. They fought with greater fury and filled the paths of the advancing tanks and half-tracks with numerous roadblocks, craters and blown bridges.

Pressing rapidly through Combat Team 110 of the 28th Division, CC A trundled through Aubange, crossed the Luxembourg border and started up the main highway leading to the capital city. At Athus it smashed into an enemy column and destroyed 29 trucks and horse-drawn vehicles, three antitank guns and a large body of bicycle troops. This was accomplished without losing a single man or vehicle. About midafternoon 30 enemy vehicles and two tanks were discovered on the north flank approaching the city of Luxembourg. Pummeled by fire from the artillery pieces and fighter-bombers, all of them were demolished.

When Lt. William Blakely's C Co., 34th Tank Bn., spilled out onto the open terrain west of the city, its lead tank was knocked out by fire from two Mark V tanks, which were on the north. The column pushed forward about 200 yards and destroyed a German tank with a hit in its rear. But then additional enemy tanks in well-protected positions on the south flank opened up and C Co. lost another tank. Lt. Blakely then pulled his tanks back to the cover of a defiladed position and called for air support.

Eight P-47s strafed and bombed the enemy tanks but did not damage them. Then the tank destroyers of A Co., 628th T. D. Bn., fired at them but the shells glanced off the thick front plates of the Panthers without harming them. Finally, a big M7 of the 400th Artillery Bn. was brought forward and with its 155 gun firing direct it smashed one of the German tanks. The others immediately fell back. But at 8 that evening A Co., 628th T. D. Bn., succeeded in outflanking three Mark Vs and destroyed them. At dark the combat command assembled four miles west of Luxembourg City and prepared to enter it the next morning.

Shortly before 10 the following morning, 10 September, CC A's advance guard under the command of Major Foote was grinding toward the highway bridge on the western edge of the city. When they reached the crossing, Capt. Warren Harvey's light tanks found that the Germans were defending the structure with only machine guns. There were also mines lying on the roadway. After Lt. Leonard Hamer of the 22nd Engineer Bn. and Lt. Thomas Grose removed these mines and the machine guns were silenced, the column proceeded into the city.

Behind the leading wave of tanks General Oliver escorted Prince Felix of Luxembourg, who had been in exile for four years, back to his capital. The citizens, doubly pleased to find that their city had been liberated and that their Prince had returned, thronged the streets in a festive mood. But the Fifth Armored did not take time out to join in the celebrating.

While Task Force Burton remained in Luxembourg City as a security guard, the rest of the combat command continued on through the city. During the afternoon the members of B Co., 46th Infantry Bn., dismounted from their halftracks and with the assistance of fire from the 47th Artillery Bn., flushed out a wooded defile east of the city. Then the column pushed on to the Neudorf Airport. But here enemy Panzers and infantry ambushed the advance guard and three tanks of A Co., 34th Tank Bn., were lost. Also in this melee, General Regnier, Major Foote, Lt. Grose, and Lt. Donald H. Coulter with two infantry squads were cut off from the main body of the task force. They took shelter in nearby houses while the artillery and P-47s hammered at the enemy troops and tanks in the area. Then a bazooka team, composed of Lt. Coulter, Sgt. Alfred H. Maffei and Pvt. Arthur H. Gibble, crept through the heavy woods to attack the Panzers. Although the rockets they fired missed their targets, the enemy tankers became frightened and withdrew from these positions. While 120 mm. mortar shells crunched in the landing field area, Lt. Mayo Elliot with a platoon from A Co., 46th Infantry Bn., cleared the buildings around the hangars.

Task Force Burton stayed in the city that night and the remainder of the combat command assembled at the airport.

By its quick entry into Luxembourg City and its environs the Fifth Armored also managed to wrest from enemy hands the undamaged transmitting facilities of Radio Luxembourg. The capture was made by a fast task force commanded by Maj. Jack Day and consisting of a platoon of light tanks from D Co., 34th Tank Bn., and a platoon of infantry from C Co., 46th Infantry Bn. It raced out to Junglinster on the night of 11 September and found the five-towered transmitter undefended. The first soldier to enter the station was T/Sgt. Mitchell Janowicz of C Company.

This station later proved of inestimable value to the Allies in their propaganda broadcasts to the German people. Describing its importance, a Shaef Psychological Warfare representative said, "The greatest single stroke of luck in the whole war was the capture intact of the powerful Radio Luxembourg, second only to Moscow in Europe, and its ready-made audience."

After leaving Florenville, about 15 miles directly east from Sedan, CC R on 9 September had begun passing through the 28th Infantry Division's Combat Team 110. Enemy troops were hastily falling back as this offensive surged toward them. Before darkness settled that night a call was sent back through CC R's liaison officer with Combat Team 110, to the air support. The planes fell upon the retreating Germans and with their guns roaring kept ripping into the columns as long as shooting light lasted. The road, however, was well lighted that night by the glow from the flaming vehicles. When the artillery's reconnaissance plane surveyed the scene of devastation the next morning, it reported the route west from Vance was so cluttered with burned-out vehicles and horse-drawn equipment that engineers would have to clear the highway before it could be used. CC R, therefore, switched its advance path and decided to go by way of Habay la Neuve, Lottert, Metzert, Oberpallen and Useldange. This route passed north of the city of Arlon, near the Luxembourg border, which was reported by French agents to be extensively sowed with mines.

At Habay la Neuve Capt. Arthur Whitley's A Co., 10th Tank Bn., tangled with a German force which tried unsuccessfully to halt CC R's advance. In the exchange of shell fire one of the

Shermans was penetrated by hits on three sides, but fortunately none of the crew was injured and the tank was not destroyed.

By 1:30 that afternoon the combat command was at Mersch, about halfway across Luxembourg. Here C Co., 22nd Engineer Bn., assisted by the Pioneer Platoon of 628th Tank Destroyer Bn., prepared the railway bridge over the Alzette River so that the tanks and halftracks could cross on it. The Germans had wired it for demolition and were covering it with machine guns. Task Force Boyer's tanks, however, quickly shot up the machine gun nests and drove the Germans back before they could blow up the bridge. Then the engineers removed two tons of explosives from under the span's supports. Meanwhile, Task Force Hamberg had found a ford on the river at Moesdorf, three miles north of Mersch, and got across there.

After both its task forces had crossed the Alzette River, the combat command switched the direction of its advance from the east to the north toward Diekirch. Its route ran parallel to the river. As it thrust forward in this direction it jabbed into the flank of an enemy force. Here the fighter-bombers lent their assistance again and they smashed up 70 of the enemy's vehicles. Also during this Dierkirch drive, Task Force Hamberg overran 32 German artillery pieces. When night fell, CC R assembled at Schrondweiler.

CC B, on 10 September, had pushed forward from Petrange between the other two combat commands in the direction of Ermsdorf. When it found that the bridges at Stiensel and Lapstal over the Alzette had been blown, it forded the stream. Its route was over narrow roads and wound through the mountains; also, it was filled with craters and felled trees. But the combat command continued grinding forward and behind it left a trail of destroyed enemy equipment. Time and again the combat command found German rear guards commanded by a German Lt. Appel, who became a well-known figure in CC B headquarters. At the last block, before settling for the night, Lt. Appel was killed while riding a motorcycle toward the attacking elements of CC B. This being done, that night CC B coiled at Blaschette high in the mountains, which were swept by winds from Germany.

XV

CORRIDOR THROUGH THE SIEGFRIED LINE

11 September–22 September

In 41 days of combat the Fifth Armored had come a long way. It was more than 700 miles away from the hedgerows and apple orchards of Normandy. It had fought through three countries. And now it was ready to lead the Allied Armies onto the soil of the nation that had unleached this war on the world.

But to strike this blow against Germany, the Fifth Armored would have to storm the famed Siegfried Line, the crescent of steel and concrete fortifications which supposedly made the Reich impregnable. The division, however, was not deterred by these looming pillboxes. Its confidence was still running high. It was eager to plunge across the border immediately, even though its supply lines were stretched trickle thin, its strength was spread over a wide area, and the bulk of its supporting infantry divisions were miles behind.

On 11 September the division started to fan out along Luxembourg's eastern river boundary. It set up observation posts in this mountainous territory along approximately 33 miles of the German border, extending from Rodershausen on the Our River in the north to Grevenmacher on the Moselle River in the south.

All three combat commands went into the line facing east: CC A was on the south, CC R in the center, and CC B on the north. Leaving the Luxembourg City area, CC A continued east and assembled at Hemstal about 13 miles northeast of Luxembourg City. Its Task Force Burton occupied Biwer (three miles south of Hemstal) after it had turned its positions in the Luxembourg capital over to the 85th Cavalry Sq. (less troops A, B and C). These 85th reconnaissance troops also began patrolling south to the Moselle River on the division's right flank. CC R pushed a few miles further east and assembled at Bruckenhof; its Task Force Boyer occupied Ermsdorf about four and one half miles southwest of the German bordertown on Wallendorf. Moving across CC R's center zone, CC B took over the sector north of Diekirch; its headquarters was set up at Schindler, while Task Force Anderson assembled at Michelau and Task Force Gilson at Hoschied.

While the division was moving its units up to the border on 11 September, an order was sent out to the reconnaissance troops. It instructed them to cross into Germany as soon as possible and find out whether or not Wehrmacht soldiers were manning the pillboxes. In CC B's zone, Capt. Kenneth M. Hayes, commander of Troop B, 85th Cavalry Sq., assigned areas to his reconnaissance platoons to carry out this order. A few members of the 2nd Platoon, a patrol in charge of Sgt. Warner W. Holzinger, were the first Allied soldiers to enter Germany in World War II. It was 4:30 in the afternoon of 11 September when they crossed into the Reich at Stolzembourg.

In addition to Sgt. Holzinger, this patrol consisted of: Cpl. Ralph E. Diven, T/5 Coy T. Locke, Pfc. William McColligan, Pfc. George F. McNeal, Pfc. Jesse Stevens. Also, it was accompanied, appropriately enough, by a member of the French Army, Lt. Lionel A. DeLille, an interpreter.

Describing this historic event, Sgt. Holzinger said, "When we started out on our mission, we took my radio peep with us to keep in touch with the 2nd Platoon and with headquarters. We worked our way down to Stolzembourg. From the citizens we learned there were no enemy soldiers in the vicinity. I have been thankful many times I could speak German.

"The enemy had blown to some degree the small bridge that spanned the Our River. Even at that we were able to cross on it. We could have waded the river, too. On the German side of the river there was a pillbox camouflaged as a barn. It's a good thing it wasn't manned.

"Lt. DeLille and I talked with a German farmer. He told us that the last time he had seen any German troops was the day before. He also told us that if we followed the road up the small mountain behind his farm we would be able to see the first line of pillboxes. So Lt. DeLille, Pfc. McColligan, the German farmer and I went into Germany about 1½ miles where we could get a good view. We studied the pillbox area with our field glasses. None of them was manned. We returned to Stolzembourg where we reported the information to Lt. Loren L. Vipond."

Lt. Vipond then radioed the information to CC B's headquarters, which flashed the news to the world that the Allies had entered Germany. But because the division was still operating

THESE SPACES FOR MESSAGE CENTER ONLY

TIME FILED | MSG CEN NO. | HOW SENT

O (CLASSIFICATION)

MESSAGE (SUBMIT TO MESSAGE CENTER IN DUPLICATE)

No. DATE 11 SEPT 1944

To G-2 5th A.D.

DISMOUNTED PATROLS
CROSSED INTO GERMANY
AT 875530 AT 1815 HRS

OFFICIAL DESIGNATION OF SENDER | 1833 TIME SIGNED

AUTHORIZED TO BE SENT IN CLEAR | SIGNATURE OF OFFICER | SIGNATURE AND GRADE OF WRITER

This is a reproduction of the message announcing the entry of the Fifth Armored Division into Germany. The Fifth Armored is officially recognized by the U. S. Army as being the first of our ground forces to enter the Reich.

under a security blackout it was not publicly announced then that it was Fifth Armored troops which had made this historic frontier crossing.

Additional patrols from CC B and CC R started probing into the Siegfried Line the following day. One of these paid another visit to Stolzembourg. It was made up of Lt. Vipond's reconnaissance platoon plus a platoon of 81st Tank Bn. light tanks commanded by Capt. Harold D. Schiering. Because of the extremely steep terrain behind the town the tank platoon, led by

Lt. Henry Plass, remained in Stalzembourg. Meanwhile Lt. Vipond's platoon, including Sgt. Holzinger, climbed the mountain in order to make a detailed study of the bunker area. Proceeding about a mile further into Germany than the patrol had gone on the previous day sketches were made of the pillbox locations. While the reconnaissance platoon was making this inspection, Capt. Schiering with Sgts. Robert C. Moore and Warren S. Nitschke of D Co., 81st Tank Bn., remained on the high ground just beyond Stolzembourg; here they examined the defenses and interrogated the civilian occupants of a house on the ridge.

After Lt. Vipond's platoon had returned, they started to tell Capt. Schiering's group what they had found. Then as they stood there on the high ground, they saw a column of German soldiers come into view in the distance. The enemy troops had marched down from the north and they continued walking down a second ridge toward the town of Bauler.

"There were about 60 of them," Lt. Vipond said. "They were carrying bundles and machine guns, and they dropped off about six to ten men at each pillbox as they went by."

Capt. Schiering added: "The last pillbox examined by Lt. Vipond's men was occupied by the Germans just a few moments after they had left. The enemy soldiers moved about in a leisurely manner, completely unaware of our presence."

This reconnaissance party, still unobserved by the Germans, returned to Luxembourg and reported that the occupation of the Siegfried Line had begun.

The next day V Corps ordered a show of strength to be made against the enemy's border defenses. At 3 in the afternoon all of the division's big guns, including the artillery pieces, tank and tank destroyer cannons poured out a thunderous barrage of steel that rocked the Siegfried fortifications. From Germany came no response.

Then at 7:25 that evening Corps ordered the division to plunge into Germany and capture the high ground south of Mettendorf, which was about five and one half miles beyond the border. As CC A was still engaged with the enemy along Luxembourg's southern border and as CC B was under Corps' direct control on a two-hour alert call, the mission fell to CC R.

During the remainder of that night CC R's staff drew up its plans for the attack it would launch the following morning. Its preparations had to be careful and thorough because it was embarking on a very precarious operation. With a relatively small force, one combat command plus three attached battalions (1st Bn. of the 25th Division's 112th Regiment, 400th Artillery Bn., and one battery of 987th Artillery Bn.), it would attempt to slice through several miles of territory defended by huge concrete block houses. Its supplies were dangerously low; on 11 and 12 September First Army had to issue 125,000 captured rations. Furthermore, it was invading an area composed of ideal defense terrain; the land was a series of high ridges, deep narrow valleys and forests. This was the plan of attack which CC R's staff worked out: The 47th Infantry Bn.'s three rifle companies would jump off from Luxembourg a little to the north of the German bordertown of Wallendorf; they would wade the Our River (which separated Luxembourg from Germany), scale the steep pillbox-dotted mountainside and seize the first high ridge on the opposite shore. Supporting these infantrymen would be direct fire from the 10th Tank Bn. A few hundred yards south of this operation the 112th Regiment's 1st Bn. would also cross the Our River at Wallendorf; after clearing the houses of the town it would then pass over the southern tip of the same high ridge which the 47th was attacking a little further north; next, it would cross the narrow valley on the other side of the ridge and attack the town of Biesdorf, which was on the next rise about 2,000 yards northeast of Wallendorf. Both battalions would have the support of the big guns of the 95th and 400th Artillery Battalions and also of the 155 mm. "Long Toms" of the 987th Field Artillery Bn. A bridge was to be built at Wallendorf by C Co., 22nd Engineer Bn., while A Co., of the 22nd would go along with the infantry to use flame throwers and pole charges (dynamite charges on the ends of poles) against the concrete block houses. The flanks would be protected by C Co., 628th Tank Destroyer Bn.

At 11 the next morning, 14 September, the first wave of the 47th Infantry Bn., began moving toward the river. They were met, however, by overpowering machine gun fire from the pillboxes on the opposite bank. Prevented from crossing here, they moved further downstream and forded the river at Wallendorf with the tanks of the 10th Tank Bn. As the column pulled up out of the stream and into the town it raked the buildings with all its guns in action. Some of the structures immediately caught fire. Many of the houses, however, were of concrete which deflected the shells. When the German soldiers continued to resist behind these solid protections, the engineers then put their searing flame throwers into use.

After the last resistance in Wallendorf had been snuffed out, the B Co. tanks started up the narrow winding road, directly behind the town, which clung to the precipitous slope like a snake on a rock wall. Lt. Lewis R. Rollin's tank platoon, which led the ascent, sprayed the edges of the road with machine gun fire as they ground up the mountainside. At the top of the rise a German soldier waited with a rocket launcher in his hands; he hoped to knock out the lead tank and thus block the advance of the entire column on the narrow road. His rocket weapon, however, was exploded before he had an opportunity to fire it.

The 47th Infantry Bn's three rifle companies followed the tanks up the steep route. At the summit they spread out over the ridge and with the tanks' help began subduing the individual pillboxes. Prisoners captured in these forward line fortifications said they had moved into them only three days before; the enemy soldiers were members of a home-guard battalion. They also reported that German civilians had been busy for more than a week pumping water out of the concrete block houses. While this battle atop the ridge was in progress, the tanks of A Co., 10th Tank Bn., and the tank destroyers of C Co., 628th T. D. Bn., came across the river to support the attack and C Co., 22nd Engineer Bn., started bridging the stream. The 112th Regiment's 1st Bn., after clearing the houses of Wallendorf, swarmed over the southern end of the ridge and down into the Niedersgegen Valley; they then, according to plan, began probing toward Biesdorf. Toward the end of the day a murky fog began slowly to shroud this battle area.

The Niedersgegen Valley, the lower end of which was separated from Wallendorf by the high narrow ridge, extended northwest along the Gay Creek for about two and one half miles to Niedersgegen. Here it formed a fork; its left arm continued northwest for about another two miles to Obersgegen (also cradled in this section of the valley were the two little villages of Seimerich and Koperich); its right arm fanned out toward the northwest to Kewenig (almost a mile from Niedersgegen) and toward the east to Hommerdingen (about two miles from Niedersgegen).

It was found that the tanks could not descend into the lower part of the Niedersgegen Valley from the section of the ridge directly behind Wallendorf because of the abrupt drop. Reconnaissance, therefore, was conducted that night along the northern half of the ridge to locate a road by which the tanks could get down into and across the valley. It was finally discovered that the only passable route was a road that led through Niedersgegen.

While the CC R force of infantrymen and tankers were atop the fog-engulfed ridge that night, three enemy trucks and a staff car, coming south from Niedersgegen, drove into their assembly area. The Germans, unaware that the fortifications on the ridge had been captured, were hauling food to the pillboxes' former occupants. These vehicles were quickly destroyed.

The wet fog still lay upon the area the following morning. It restricted visibility to 150 yards. But, after CC R's tank and infantry companies reformed into their normal attack task forces, the thrust into the Siegfried Line was resumed. Task Force Boyer took the lead. It traveled north along the road which sloped down into the valley and then turned east to cross the Gay Creek at Niedersgegen. As the column neared this crossing, it observed in the uper right arm of the valley several enemy tanks and other armored vehicles advancing from the east. The valley then resounded with the roar of the booming tank guns as a quick fierce fight flared up between the converging forces. After the Germans lost two Mark IV tanks, a halftrack and an antitank gun, the remaining eight Panzer tanks fell back toward Hommerdingen, about two miles directly east of Niedersgegen. B Co., 10th Tank Bn., had one tank knocked out in the scrap; a shell damaged its track suspension.

As Task Force Boyer started across the Gay Creek, the second tank in the column fell through the bridge. The rest of the task force then forded the stream. It continued up the right arm of the Niedersgegen Valley and passed Hommerdingen. Next, it turned north and spread out on Hill 407 just south of Mettendorf. In this push the column did not encounter serious opposition. It did, however, destroy a large enemy halftrack ammunition carrier and a 76 mm. gun with its prime mover.

Task Force Hamberg also used the ford at Niedersgegen. It followed Task Force Boyer across the creek and then attacked directly east. It cleared Hommerdingen and also Cruchten, which was a little less than a mile southwest of Hommerdingen. By nightfall it had advanced about five and a half miles east of Niedersgegen; it was beyond Nusbaum and Stockem and was holding the high ground south of Bettingen, overlooking the Prum River. It was reinforced that night by the 112th Regiment's 1st Bn. which came north from Biesdorf to join the task force.

Late in the afternoon that same day the 95th Artillery Bn. had moved across the Our River and had climbed the high ridge behind Wallendorf. But as this column of mobile cannons neared Niedersgegen it found that the Germans had filtered down from the north and had recaptured the Gay Creek ford. They were defending it with machine gun and mortar fire.

Thus, as CC R bedded down to spend its second night in Germany, it was completely through the Siegfried Line's belt of scattered pillboxes and was sitting on the division's objectives. And neither of its task forces faced any formidable concentrations of enemy troops. It did not, however, feel completely secure in these new positions. A slight anxiety had been aroused in the combat command by the report that the Germans had regained possession of the Gay Creek ford. This uneasiness was intensified later when it was learned that enemy patrols had worked their way back into Wallendorf about midnight.

CC B was relieved that night from V Corps control, so the next morning, 16 September, it was ordered to lend its support to the assault on the Siegfried Line. Its mission was to widen the base of the bridgehead and clean out the enemy troops that were threatening to cut off CC R from the rear. About four in the afternoon Task Force Anderson and CC B Headquarters crossed into Germany. The tanks and halftracks then moved north through Biesdorf and Cruchten to an area just east of Hommerdingen; here the assault guns of the 81st Tank Bn. went into position and poured fire into the enemy-held woods behind Niedersgegen and Kewenig (which was less than a mile from the Gay Creek ford in the upper right arm of the Niedersgegen Valley).

At six that evening Task Force Gilson passed across the Our River at Wallendorf and then assembled south of Niedersgegen in the narrow valley in order to keep the Gay Creek ford out of enemy hands. To prevent the Germans from infiltrating down from the north and retaking this crossing, the married A Companies of the 81st Tank Bn. and the 15th Infantry Bn. blocked both of the valley's upper arms.

During the afternoon the 112th Regiment's 1st Bn. had jumped off from its positions near Stockem to cross the Prum River at Wettlingen. Reaching the opposite bank and capturing the town, it had pushed further east to the high ground known as Hill 298. In this operation it had been assisted by C Co., 47th Infantry Bn. and C Co., 10th Tank Bn.

Describing the attack, Capt. Leo Marcikowski, commander of the armored infantry company, said: "As we approached Wettlingen an enemy antitank gun opened up from a clump of woods on the western edge of the town. Its shell seemed to whisper 'Hiya Murphy' as it breezed by. Sgt Gordon's crew spotted the gun instantly and his tank wasted only one round in knocking it out."

When the infantrymen began climbing the southwest slopes of Hill 298 their ranks were swept on both flanks by enemy machine gun fire. C Co., 10th Tank Bn., and B Co.'s 2nd Platoon, 628th Tank Destroyer Bn., immediately retaliated; with direct smothering fire they blasted the German gun positions, which were located in stone houses. As daylight faded the infantrymen consolidated their positions on the embattled slopes. But at nine that evening a counterattack of enemy foot troops and tanks rolled down on them from the crest of the hill. The charging Panzers turned on their spotlights in order to direct their tank and machine gun fire against the individual positions of the GIs. This enemy onrush forced the infantry battalion to fall back to the eastern edge of Wettlingen where it prepared to launch another attack the next day.

In the Task Force Boyer area large caliber artillery shells had begun crunching on Hill 407 about mid-afternoon. Then in the early evening machine gun fire was received from the edge of the woods several hundred yards west of the hill. A platoon of tanks and infantrymen from the married B Companies was sent to clear the area. It had to repeat this task twice again before dark.

The Germans were active at other points along the bridgehead's northern flank that night. Enemy patrols and mortar fire harassed Task Force Gilson, which was blocking the two upper branches of the Niedersgegen Valley. Wehrmacht infantrymen threatened CC B's rear by moving into Ammeldingen, a town on the Our River about a mile and a half above Wallendorf. And throughout the night the shrill scream of approaching artillery shells was heard in all sectors of both combat commands.

A crashing hour-long artillery barrage rained down on Task Force Hamberg's D Co., 10th Tank Bn., which was located at Stockem, at daylight the next morning, 17 September. This preparation was followed by an attack of Panther tanks, which descended from Olsdorf north of Bettingen. In the clash two of D Co's light tanks were knocked out by long-range armor-piercing shells. Striking back at the enemy assault, C Co., 10th Tank Bn., moved in from Halsdorf and jabbed into the right flank of the enemy force; it destroyed four Mark IVs and lost one of its own tanks. A second counter-thrust on the same flank was made by A Co., 10th Tank Bn. which was in the draw east of Hill 407. Driving toward Bettingen, it smashed up five more enemy tanks and a 20 mm. self-propelled gun. The remainder of the Panzer force then fell back to Bettingen.

Before the 112th Regiment's 1st Bn. at Wettlingen could carry out its planned attack that morning, it was hit by an unexpected assault of German tanks and infantrymen. Under the weight of this enemy thrust it was forced to abandon its positions in Wettlingen and fall back to the buildings in Stockem. The battalion's withdrawal was covered by the 2nd Platoon of B Co., 628th Tank Destroyer Bn., which exhausted all of its ammunition and lost three of its tank destroyers in this action.

During the morning General Oliver came forward in person to confer with Colonel Cole and Colonel Anderson at their exposed command posts. In view of the fact that supporting infantry divisions were not available to fill in behind the Fifth Armored and protect its rear in the path it was hacking into Germany, he told them to cancel plans for the attack on Bitburg, which was about six miles northeast of Wettlingen. They were instructed to hold their present position, except that all troops could be pulled back out of Wettlingen.

In the woods north and west of Niedersgegen the fighting was hot and bitter that day. Here CC B's Task Force Gilson suffered many casualties from the enemy mortar and artillery fire. When its tank-infantry teams charged a machine gun position on the edge of the woods, the Germans would withdraw deeper into the forest and then reappear later at another point.

CC B Headquarters and Task Force Anderson moved to the reverse slope of Hill 375 just north of Ammeldingen. Only one platoon of the married B Companies of the 81st Tank Bn. and the 15th Infantry Bn., however, accompanied the task force; the others remained behind at Hommerdingen to help protect the artillery batteries there. After completing the move, the married C Companies and the single platoon of the married B Companies started clearing and destroying the pillboxes which were scattered along the high ridge extending from Wallendorf to Gentingen northwest of Ammeldingen.

Although all enemy ground resistance in front of CC R had completely subsided by evening, observers reported that the Germans were building up considerable strength northwest of Niedersgegen. This increased activity here had become evident late in the afternoon when Wehrmacht infantrymen had captured the Our River ford south of Ammeldingen; they had to be driven off by a married tank-infantry platoon. The heavy fog which had hung over the area all day turned to a light rain before nightfall; this made it more difficult for the tanks to operate effectively. Enemy patrols continued to infiltrate through CC B's sector all during the night. They became so annoying that a special force, consisting of a platoon of light tanks from D Co., 81st Tank Bn., and about 20 infantrymen armed with sub-machine guns, were assigned to patrol the road from Ammeldingen to Wallendorf to Niedersgegen; this mission was referred to as the "Milk Run." Also throughout the night the positions of the 95th, 71st and 400th artillery battalions received counter-battery fire.

CC R's fifth day in Germany was relatively quiet. None of its units had to fight off any attacks. Helping to discourage the enemy from initiating any new assaults was a heavy incessant drubbing which the artillery batteries gave the German lines. The combat command's slightly shortened by the withdrawal of the 112th Regiment's 1st Bn. and the 2nd Platoon of B Co., 628th Tank Destroyer Bn., to Hommerdingen. Movements of enemy tanks from the Bettingen area west to the Mettendorf area were reported by the artillery observation planes. Some of these Panzers about nine that evening tried to move down from the north into Mettendorf, but they were driven back by the artillery barrages.

For CC B, however, the day was not so quiet. Task Force Gilson attempted to clear the enemy troops out of the two upper arms of the Niedersgegen Valley. It split up into two groups; one fought its way up the left branch of the valley toward Obersgegen, while the other pushed up the right arm toward Kewenig and Huttingen. The group on the left, driving toward Obersgegen, encountered piles of logs and stones in the road near Seimerich, about a mile beyond Niedersgegen. One tank in this group which tried to return to Niedersgegen struck a mine that had been placed in the road after the column had passed the spot a few hours earlier. In the right arm of the valley the group passed through Kewenig but was counterattacked as it approached Huttingen about two miles northeast of Niedersgegen. The Germans laid down barrages of artillery and mortar fire on the group and Wehrmacht infantrymen blasted it with rockets from the woods on the left flank. Three of its tanks were destroyed. In this close fighting, Staff Sgt. Thomas A. Greene of the 15th Medical Detachment advanced beyond the tanks to give aid to a soldier who had been dazed by the explosion of a rocket. For this extreme devotion to duty he was posthumously awarded the Distinguished Service Cross.

Task Force Anderson continued its job of demolishing the concrete implacements that extended toward Gentingen. It cleared out and blasted with close-range tank fire a total of 35 pillboxes that day. Near Ammeldingen Lt. Victor Anderson's tank exploded a pile of mines. Throughout the day both task force areas were subjected to mortar fire, and enemy activity steadily increased northwest of CC B's zone.

Day dawned on 19 September with a burst of violence for CC R's Task Force Boyer on Hill 407. Shortly after the arrival of daylight on this foggy morning the hill was pounded with the heaviest concentration of artillery fire that the Germans had thus far laid down on this area. The barrages at first landed on the forward slope of the hill; then they were progressively shifted to the top of the elevation and finally down its reverse slop. All elements of the task force were blanketed with the exploding shells, including the supply trains. One shell ripped through CC R's command post tent as Colonel Anderson and Lt. Col. Dickenson were having breakfast.

While the dust from this shattering blow still hung over the hill, enemy tank movement was heard to the northwest. To counter any attack from this direction a platoon from the married B Companies went into position just behind the crest of Hill 426, which was about a mile west of Hill 407.

When the heavy fog began to lift slightly about eight that morning, a force of about 15 enemy tanks and other vehicles were sighted advancing from the northwest toward Task Force Anderson's positions. The married platoon on Hill 426 went into action and at a range of more than 1,000 yards knocked out two of the attacking Panzers by scoring hits on their thin-skinned undersides as they came over a rise in the ground. These two tank losses plus the heavy artillery fire which was thrown at them discouraged the Germans from proceeding any further into the face of this fire. Shifting the direction of their attack, they then exposed their vulnerable flanks to the guns of B Co., 10th Tank Bn., and C Co., 628th Tank Destroyer Bn. These companies poured their direct fire on the Panzers and badly cut up the assault force. The remnants of its armor withdrew as the artillery fire thinned the ranks of its supporting infantry men. When Capt. Frank Pool, B Co., 10th Tank Bn., later inspected the burning tanks, he counted four Mark Vs, six Mark IVs and two halftracks. There were additional vehicles smoldering in the distance.

Other sectors along the edges of the Fifth Armored's corridor through the Siegfried Line also had to withstand enemy attacks that morning. North of Niedersgegen an enemy force of tanks and infantrymen supported by artillery fire descended on Task Force Gilson. Two tanks from A Co., 81st Tank Bn., were destroyed in the fight but the task force succeeded in repulsing the attack and killed 50 Germans in the woods between Niedersgegen and Kewenig. Action flared up on the corridor's right flank when Wehrmacht infantrymen pushed forward into Biesdorf and Panzer tanks appeared menacingly on the edge of the woods to the east. Attempting to counter this move, Battery D, 387th Anti Aircraft Bn., worked the town over with their 50 caliber machine guns. One of their halftracks, however, was knocked out by the Panzer fire from the woods. The enemy effort here was finally crushed when a married platoon from B Co., 81st Tank Bn., and B Co., 15th Infantry Bn., cleared the town at 10:30 that morning.

Shortly before noon it was reported that Wehrmacht infantrymen had infiltrated back into the houses in Wallendorf and were putting machine gun and rifle fire on the Our River treadway bridge there. A CC B force with the assistance of elements of the 387th Anti Aircraft Bn. undertook the job of driving these enemy troops from the town. By three that afternoon Wallendorf was again under Fifth Armored control. In order to help protect the corridor's left flank along the Our River to the northwest a tank destroyer platoon was brought back out of Germany and sent to a point in Luxembourg a little north of Ammeldingen. Increasing pressure from Gentingen was felt by CC B toward the end of the day.

Meanwhile, CC R had been having no easy time of it during the afternoon. Its front had erupted at several points. It had to repell an attack that came from the direction of Olsdorf and Bettingen, another from Wettlingen and Enzen, and finally one from Nusbaum. Also, the drumbeat of bursting artillery shells in both combat command areas continued throughout the day.

The increasing tempo of enemy activity as the Fifth Armored's situation in the Siegfried Line grew steadily worse that day can be seen from a few of the words that Lt. Col. Washburn, commander of the 71st Artillery Bn., set down in his diary. He wrote:

"At 0545 Battalion received 30 rounds of 150 mm. from the southeast . . . 0730 received 18 rounds of 150 mm. from the northwest . . . At noon Battery A moved from right front of Battalion area to right near where they could use direct fire . . . Lt. Harrison wounded while attempting to place fire on self-propelled gun which had knocked out three tanks within 500 yards of Battalion position . . . Battery C firing Charge One at nearly minimum elevation . . . 1030—Battalion conducting fire in four directions simultaneously . . . 1430—Tanks to our front ordered to our rear to clear roads . . . Ammo trucks unable to get through to us . . . Ammo down to less than 800 rounds . . . Notified CC B of situation . . . 1700—Ordered to withdraw to CC B perimeter . . . Battery A ran into trouble at Biesdorf. Capt. Smithers reversed his battery and went out through the Niedersgegen ford. . . ."

Late in the day the 112th Regiment's 2nd Bn. was sent forward to CC R's area to relieve the 1st Bn., which was given the job of defending Wallendorf and the Our River bridge that night. At 6:30 in the evening, however, CC R was ordered to withdraw from Germany and assemble south of Diekirch in Luxembourg. As this move got under way, the division's artillery batteries covered the enemy positions with heavy concentrations of fire to keep the Germans from disrupting the operation. Despite this intense shell fire, Panzer tanks and Wehrmacht infantry emerged from the woods east of Biesdorf and attacked the married B Companies of the 10th Tank Bn. and the 47th Infantry Bn. as they were passing through the town.

The assault was beaten back and the column continued grinding toward Luxembourg. While the 112th Regiment's 2nd Bn. kept the road open from Biesdorf to Wallendorf, the division's artillery batteries displaced west of the Our River an hour after midnight and CC R completed its withdrawal at 4 a.m.

As daylight brightened over the debris-laden hills and valleys that morning, 20 September, the Germans were anxious to find

T. D. means business!

It's kill or be killed.

RR Bridge at Mersch.

Bridge over Mersch — Charlesville.

Rations come up near Sedan.

Enter we must!

The French were thoughtful while we were busy.

Rolling through Luxembourg City.

628th in Luxembourg.

Shells on the way to Ger

rince Felix is welcomed home.

Prince Felix autographs souvenirs in Luxembourg City.

Conquerors of Luxembourg.

A house built over a pill box.

German posters in Luxembourg.

We get our pay even th
we are just outside Gern

On the German border, the Siegfried Line was marked.

WALLENDORF, GERMANY — The junction of the Our and the Sauer Rivers at Wallendorf along the mountainous boundary between Luxembourg and Germany. The town of Biesdorf and the beginning of the Niedersgegen valley can be seen in the background. Many of the destroyed pillboxes are merely white patches on the steep hill behind Wallendorf.

FIRST AMERICAN ON GERMAN SOIL — S/Sgt. Warner W. Holzinger, Troop B 85th Cav. Rcn. Sqdrn. killed in action near Wallendorf.—

Our Tanks burn, too.

Dragon teeth prevent vehicles from crossing.

No rest for our Artillery.

155 mm. Long-Toms supported us at Wallendorf.

: out, Henie, here we come.

allendorf after two days — Later . . . nothing.

Firing on Enemy in Diesdorf.

Stay under cover if you can.

Underground Block Houses must be checked.

Gosh, the Hun is everywhere.

CCR take inventory after Wallendorf.

The Padre came often.

Lt. Col. Boydston
Div. Surgeon.

out whether any Americans were still in Germany. They sent a force of tanks and infantrymen into Niedersgegen from the northeast and quickly discovered that all of the Fifth Armored troops had not departed. They were repulsed by a platoon from the married B Companies of the 81st Tank Bn. and 15th Infantry Bn. Two Shermans, however, were lost in the counterattack.

The Germans then stepped up the intensity of their artillery barrages in the Niedersgegen Valley and on Hill 375. The shell fragments caused so many casualties in the valley south of Niedersgegen that the area was dubbed "Purple Heart Valley" just as Hill 407 had been known to the men of CC R as "Purple Heart Hill." During one of these barrages Lt. Robert A. Lewis, the first Fifth Armored man to enter Belgium, was killed.

The division's artillery batteries were very active that day, too. From their new positions in Luxembourg they pummeled the enemy's positions around Biesdorf and also the Wehrmacht troops facing CC B. A German soldier captured near Hill 375 later in the day reported that 80 members of his company of 100 were killed by the artillery fire in the woods just north of Niedersgegen during the morning.

At one in the afternoon Task Force Gilson began its withdrawal from Germany. Its move was covered by Task Force Anderson on Hill 375 which kept the enemy units north of the valley occupied. After all of Task Force Gilson's vehicles had pulled onto the road, every gun then began spewing out bullets as the column roared out of the valley. From their positions on the high ground around Biesdorf the Germans sprayed the task force with machine gun fire. Along the route were piles of mines which the enemy had been preparing to plant in the road and thus trap the column in the valley. Lt. Col. Gilson was wounded during the withdrawal and as he lay in a ditch alongside the road he motioned to the vehicles to keep moving. Lt. Alexander Fraser, the 71st liaison officer, stopped, however, and after he carried the task force commander to his peep he brought him out of Germany.

That night CC B Headquarters and Task Force Anderson stayed atop Hill 375 while the 1st and 2nd battalions of the 112th Regiment continued to defend the road from Wallendorf to Biesdorf. Enemy pressure, however, began to bear down crushingly on these last remaining projections into the Siegfried Line. Enemy artillery shells rushing through the darkness broke up the Our River treadway bridge at Wallendorf and Wehrmacht infantrymen, who had crept back into the town, started to mine the approaches to the bridge on the German side. On Hill 375, where Task Force Anderson's tanks and infantrymen, as well as soldiers from Hq. Co. CC B had formed into a large circle to defend the elevation, enemy mortars blasted the area throughout the night. Also, enemy patrols were active; they tried to find out whether any of the pillboxes from which they had been driven earlier were still intact.

When daylight came to the hill that morning a platoon of Germans were discovered sleeping near a blown pillbox in the sector defended by the married B Companies of the 81st Tank Bn. and the 15th Infantry Bn. Other enemy infantrymen charged forward against the task force's circular defenses in the heavy fog which clung to the hill in the early morning. The tanks opened up with their cannons and machine guns at short range. And the Fifth Armored infantrymen, remaining in their fox holes between the tanks, cut down the Wehrmacht soldiers as they came out of the mist. When the fog lifted later, 50 Germans lay dead within 40 yards of the married C Companies positions.

During the remainder of the morning enemy troops were on all sides of Hill 375. With the help of supporting artillery fire the task force's tank-infantry teams fended off further enemy thrusts and cleared wooded areas only 400 yards from the top of the Hill. To haul ammunition to the task force the supply echelons of the 81st Tank Bn. and 15th Infantry Bn. found it necessary to use halftracks. The road from Wallendorf to the hill was under enemy machine gun fire all day. A married platoon, however, patrolled this road to prevent the Germans from permanently blocking it and thus cutting off the task force's last escape route out of Germany.

Going to the assistance of the surrounded task force, the 47th Infantry Bn. started to cross the Our River at noon between Wallendorf and Ammeldingen. But as the initial wave of infantrymen waded into the stream they were hit by high velocity shell fire from enemy tanks that had worked their way into Wallendorf.

These Panzers were quickly put out of action, however, by the swift crippling fire from the tank guns of A Co., 10th Tank Bn., which were perched on the high ground in Luxembourg across the river from the town.

After the infantrymen climbed the slopes to the task force, they were distributed along the perimeter of the defenses to reinforce the iron ring around the hill. Throughout the afternoon the incoming mortar and artillery shells continued to bite into the high ground scattering their deadly fragments as they landed. In addition to these unrelenting barrages the Germans late in the afternoon also began using some large caliber artillery shells. Several of these rounds were observed, however, to fall in a wood occupied by Wehrmacht troops. When a column of 15 Panzer tanks, moving west, started to ford the Gay Creek at Niedersgegen in the latter part of the afternoon, they were attacked from the air by the fighter-bombers which destroyed several of them and dispersed the rest.

Just before dark an aid man from the 81st Medical Detachment who was searching for wounded on this littered battle ground, pushed open the door of a camouflaged pillbox. Inside he found a German captain and two lieutenants. The pillbox was about 300 yards from Colonel Cole's command post.

A liaison plane orbited over the Hill at 7:30 that evening. Then through the fading light it dropped a message to the weary troops below. It was an order instructing CC B Headquarters and Task Force Anderson to withdraw from the hill and pull back to Luxembourg that night. There was no cessation of enemy fire as these CC B forces evacuated the hill, wound around the steep slopes to the Wallendorf ford and then crossed the river to Luxembourg. It was out of Germany by four in the morning of 22 September.

While CC B was completing this move, the 47th Infantry Bn., still on Hill 375, made a limited attack to cover the withdrawal operation. The action developed into a night hand grenade battle with the Wehrmacht troops on the north slope of the hill. Twice during the fierce fighting in the darkness Lt. Richard Lewis's platoon of Company B became intermingled with the Germans. At one point in the confusion Lt. Lewis was challenged at such close range by an enemy machine gunner that he could reach out and touch the muzzle of the enemy gun. He answered the challenge with a few quick shots from his carbine.

Then shortly before daylight the infantrymen walked quietly down the slopes of the hill and waded through the water of the Our River to Luxembourg.

Thus ended the Fifth Armored's first venture into Germany. Although the division had been forced to make its first retreat in this Battle of the Wallendorf Corridor, it had nevertheless served its purpose here. First well into Germany, it had drawn a horde of German troops, which prevented them from opposing the Allies' main breaching of the Siegfried Line being made at Aachen (other crossings were also made at Steinbruck, Stolberg, Geilenkirchen, and the effort to cross at Arnhem was made on 17 September). The German units which opposed the division in the action at Wallendorf included: A Panzer Brigade, a GAF Division, a separate infantry regiment, a machine gun battalion, several artillery battalions, a Panzer Lehr Division, and the border troops occupying the pillboxes. The Fifth Armored also severely mauled these enemy units which were thrown against it here. It killed more than 2,000 German soldiers and captured 1,218; of the approximately 100 Panzer tanks which counterattacked it, the division destroyed 45 and the fighter planes knocked out 19 more. But the most important was the fact that it captured and smashed up more than 100 pillboxes in this section of the Siegfried Line (the actual demolition work was done by B and C Companies of the 22nd Engineer Bn.): the removal of these concrete and steel fortifications thus made it much easier for the Allied units to re-enter Germany here when the big push to the Rhine was made months later.

Despite these accomplishments in this battle, the Fifth Armored did not feel happy about withdrawing from Germany after having cut the first corridor through the Siegfried Line. It believed an opportunity was lost here. Its spearhead had extended about seven miles into the Reich; two combat commands lay for two days before Bitburg; it had battered its way completely through the tough belt of pillboxes. It was fully confident then that it could have advanced the remaining 50 miles to the Rhine had it been supported by additional infantry division to broaden the penetration and to keep open its supply lines. But these infantry divisions, involved in petty skirmishing to the north, were not available.

Censorship Is Lifted

Shortly after the Fifth Armored's Wallendorf action the veil of censorship which had covered its identity was removed and the fact that it was fighting on the western Front was announced to the public. Press correspondents were permitted to file stories about its exploits on the continent. Following are two of the newspaper stories that appeared at that time:

New York Times, 1 October 1944

WITH THE FIRST ARMY IN GERMANY, September 30.—General Hodges took security wraps off another of his divisions today and disclosed for publication that the Fifth Armored Division ("Victory" Division) was one of his ace outfits which stormed across France after the American break through near St. Lo. This division entering combat for the first time in the drive across France was in forefront of the spectacular American operation and helped make a lot of tank history.

In the first twenty days of combat the Fifth Armored Division drove 400 miles to the Seine River and was one of the divisions which swept south from Countances and then hooked north from Le Mans to set the Falaise-Argentan trap which gave Von Kluge's Seventh Army such a terrific mauling. Military men will be charting that armored campaign for years to come. The Fifth Armored Division started its operations from assembly area in Normandy's hedge bordered fields in August 1. Tanks plunged through St. Lo gap and reared south to drive deep into enemy held territory. The division proudly boasted that this operation was the first time a full American Armored Division had been used in exploitation mission behind enemy lines.

To accomplish mission the division thrust 150 miles south, then continued 100 miles to Le Mans, then turned and drove 50 miles north to Argentan. Tanks of the Fifth Armored Division were first into both Le Mans and Argentan and were the first armor astride the main highway to Paris. Between Argentan and Gacé the Fifth Armored had one of the toughest battles of the drive. They fought Germans for three days as pincers of trap closing in on the Seventh Army struggling to escape to the east. Then the armor wheeled and pushed on to the Seine. In this drive the division lists, 2,800 Germans killed and 4,300 prisoners of war, with its own casualties extremely light.

Across the Seine, the Victory Division kept wheeling to the east, and fought its way into Luxembourg, and when tanks rolled into the city, the Prince of Luxembourg rode with the Division Commander, Major General Lunsford E. Oliver. Luxembourgers gave the Tank men a rousing welcome along with the Armored Infantry, and quickly recognized the Prince of the Grand Duchy. They stormed his jeep and carried him on their shoulders through the streets.

* * * *________* * * *

Stars and Stripes, 3 October 1944

FIFTH ARMORED MADE THE INITIAL ENTRY IN REICH.

FIRST ARMY HQ., OCT. 2, 1944–The Fifth Armored Division commanded by Maj. Gen. Lunsford E. Oliver, made the initial breakthrough into Germany north of Trier Sept. 11, it was revealed yesterday when the "Victory" Division was taken off the secret list for the first time since it went into action in Normandy on August 1.

The division started from upper Normandy and in 20 days' fighting pushed 400 miles to the Seine River. The "Victory" Division's horseshoe-shaped thrust towards Argentan helped spring the trap on the German Seventh Army in the Falaise pocket. In this operation the outfit advanced 150 miles south, through Fougeres and Vitre, continued 100 miles east to Le Mans, swinging 50 miles north to Argentan.

Men of the Fifth Armored entered Le Mans August 9 and Argentan August 13.

Between Argentan and Gacé, the Fifth Armored engaged the Germans in three days' hard fighting, while Allied units advanced from Caen to Falaise to form the other jaw of the pincers. The Germans, attacked from both north and south and hammered continuously from the air, suffered extremely heavy casualties.

The outfit then drove east 70 miles to the Eure River in a single night and liberated Dreux the following day, August 16. After crossing the Eure, the division remained in contact with the Germans between the Eure and the Seine until the pocked was cleaned out. On August 20, the Fifth Armored reached the Seine at Vernon, 35 miles from Paris.

Other stories about the division which appeared at that time included one in *Yank Magazine*. It was called "The Ghost of Wallendorf" and it described the activities of an alleged woman dressed in white who supposedly aided the Germans in directing their artillery fire by standing on a hill and moving to the right or left.

Another story, which appeared in the *Stars and Stripes,* dealt with an incident in Wallendorf. According to the account, German tanks appeared in Wallendorf each night, while the Fifth Armored was fighting beyond the town, and shot up its supply trucks. These Panzer tanks supposedly made their entry and exit from this cutoff town through a tunnel.

What probably gave rise to this story was the appearance of the four enemy tanks in Wallendorf during the CC B's last day on Hill 375. These tanks were destroyed by A Company of 10th Tank Bn., firing from across the river. Maj. William Daniel, executive officer of the 10th, said later: "There were four enemy tanks in Wallendorf which we knocked out when we were firing in support of CC B. Company A did the job. I saw it."

XVI

WET AUTUMN

23 September—30 November

On the Western Front the hot dry summer had given way to a wet autumn. Skies overhead were gray and overcast and almost every day they spilled out rain onto the battlefields. Under this drenching downpour the ground softened and then, as it was churned up by the trucks and armored vehicles, turned into quagmires of mud. With the mud, too, came an end to the spectacular lightning advances. As the Allies dug in along the border, it was realized that gains from now on would be counted in yards rather than miles. Gone with the warm summer were the high hopes that a German collapse were imminent . . . or, at least, they should have been.

While CC R and CC B had been breeching the Siegfried Line at Wallendorf, CC A had been busy protecting a 26-mile stretch of the Luxembourg border that extended from Wallendorf south to the Third Army boundary at Niederdonven. Patrols were sent out daily by both the combat command's task forces. On 24 September a strong demonstration, supported by artillery and mortar fire, was made against Grevenmacher by the married C Companies of the 34th Tank Bn. and the 46th Infantry Bn. A freight train in the city was destroyed and German barracks east of the border were set on fire.

After this show of strength against the enemy, the division settled down in the Diekirch area; its activities during the remainder of September were restricted to patrolling the border from Rodershausen on the north to Bollendorf, which is four miles south of Wallendorf. Fifth Armored men knew for certain that they were in for a winter campaign when, on 28 September, a convoy of 80 trucks left on the long trip to Normandy to pick up the duffel bags which contained each man's winter clothing. When these bags were stored again at Luxembourg City the overcoats and long underwear had been replaced with many German military souvenirs. During this Diekirch period Lt. Col. Dickenson was transferred from CC R to the 15th Infantry Bn.; he replaced as battalion commander Lt. Col. Gilson, who had been wounded. The 127th Ordnance Maintenance Bn. used this breathing period to put more of the division's equipment back in shape. During August and September this battalion repaired 423 medium tanks of which 275 had their engines replaced or repaired; 87 light tanks; 53 armored cars; 102 halftracks; 174 trucks; and 184 peeps.

On 2 October the 8th Infantry Division released the Fifth Armored of its duties along this stretch of the Luxembourg border. Pulling up stakes the next day, the Fifth Armored then rolled north about 40 miles to the Faymonville-Waimes-Butgenbach area in Belgium. This was about four miles from Malmedy; and the area was to become famous a few months later during the Battle of the Bulge. When the division made its move north, this section had not yet been cleared of German troops; enemy patrols still roamed through the dense forests in the border area. A billeting party in charge of Lt. Robert C. Wenger, 22nd Engineer Bn. Adjutant, was captured by one of these enemy patrols near St. Vith.

After the division moved into this new location, the 85th Cavalry Sq. was placed under the direct control of V Corps. It was assigned, along with the 102nd Cavalry, to patrol the Corps' front. While he was accompanying a patrol on this mission on 17 October, Maj. John P. Gerald, commander of the 85th was killed. That same day another patrol was ambushed; its members reported that the German soldiers were wearing American uniforms and using American rifles.

Meanwhile, CC A had been placed in First Army Reserve and had been ordered on 11 October to move to the vicinity of Heerlen, Holland, in the XIX Corps sector. Here it remained until 26 October. CC B had also been placed in First Army Reserve and on 15 October was sent to the Aachen-Kornelimunster area under VII Corps.

On 23 October, the remainder of the division was assigned a sector of the V Corps front, which included the town of Hofen and Alzen. Leaving their halftracks in the rear, CC R's 47th

Infantry Bn. moved into the 5,000-yard front and set up 27 observation posts. These posts were reinforced by shell fire from the 400th and 95th Artillery Battalions and from A Co., 628th Tank Destroyer Bn. The 10th Tank Bn. also assisted in putting down indirect fire on the enemy's position but its companies were rotated so that only one company participated at a time. In addition to this support, the multiple mount 50 caliber machine guns were used in indirect fire against the long range targets. Extensive mine fields were laid in the area.

On 28 October CC B returned to division control and immediately relieved CC R in the Hofen area. The 15th Infantry Bn. took over the positions which the 47th Infantry Bn. had occupied along the border. During this period the first snow fell on this sector of the front. Fifth Armored men in this area also were becoming accustomed to hearing overhead the roar of the buzz bombs which the Germans were launching. CC B remained in position until 10 November when it was relieved by the 99th Infantry Division. It then moved to the Moderscheid-Schoppen area and after a seven-day stay in the snow there it was sent to the bordertown of Rotgen.

In early November CC A assembled in the vicinity of Neudorf, Belgium. Here it prepared to plunge through the Siegfried Line at Lammersdorf: this operation was to be carried out in conjunction with other V Corps troops which were attempting to capture Vossenack and Schmidt to the north. Plans called for the Combat Command quickly to overrun the towns of Simmerath, Kesternich, and Konzen to the high ground east of the German border. The attack was not to be launched, however, until the troops on the north had succeeded in taking their objectives.

Although Schmidt fell on 3 November, the town was recaptured the next day by a German counterattack. In this section, the 707th Tank Bn., which had been Fifth Armored until September 1943, was partially overrun. The planned attack at Lammersdorf was then postponed from one day to the next and finally was abandoned on 10 November. CC A moved to Walhorn on 17 November and remained there on a six-hour alert until the end of the month.

After it had completed its mission in the Hofen-Kalterherberg area, CC R had been placed in VII Corps Reserve. Then on 19 November it was attached to the 8th Infantry Division to take part in the drive through the Hurtgen Forest. On 29 November the division, minus CC R, was attached to the VII Corps and on the following day CC A was further attached to the 4th Infantry Division.

XVII

THE DAYS BEFORE CHRISTMAS

Hurtgen Forest to The Roer River

24 November–24 December

GENERAL DWIGHT D. EISENHOWER said that veterans who participated in the Battle of the Hurtgen Forest place that struggle at the top of their list of hard fighting. Without hesitation men of the Fifth Armored put that ordeal at the head of their list. The month in the Hurtgen Forest was the darkest period in the division's combat history.

In this dense and somber forest of pine, men battled snow and mud and frigid weather as well as an entrenched and fiercely resolute enemy. Tanks were prevented from maneuvering or deploying by the trees, the mud, the ravines and the extensive mine fields. Advances, therefore, had to be made in bitter yard-by-yard struggles against the well-placed Germans who fought here with savage tenacity. The attackers were subjected to tremendous concentrations of artillery and mortar fire directed from observation posts on high ground, across the Roer River. Foxholes offered little protection since the shells burst in the tree tops and sprayed the ground below with their fragments.

After each long, miserable and sleepless night spent in the icy foxholes, men numb from the cold climbed out at dawn to begin another attack. As they pushed forward through the thickly sown mine fields, the bursting shells and sniper fire, they watched their numbers dwindle. Each gain of a few yards exacted a frightful price in dead and wounded. And to the collecting stations in the rear flowed the heartbreaking procession of the wounded, some walking and the others on litters.

While the Fifth Armored was fighting its way through the Hurtgen Forest and across the approaches to the Roer River, the Germans on 16 December began their last desperate attempt to attain victory on the Western Front. Just a few miles south of the

Fifth Armored's positions the enemy threw three armies, a total of 24 divisions, into a gigantic offensive through the Ardennes Forest.

First of the Fifth Armored's combat commands to be committed in the Hurtgen struggle was CC R; it pushed toward the town of Hurtgen and then took Kleinhau, Brandenberg, and Bergstein. Near the end of November CC A entered the fray a little further to the north and nearer to the Roer River; it attacked through Gey, Horm and Kufferath to the banks of the river. CC B, which came into the fight in early December, also made for the river; it attacked through the towns of Langenbroich, Bergheim and Bilstein.

After it completed its mission in the Hurtgen Forest, the Fifth Armored was pulled back into Belgium to help block the Germans' drive toward Liege during the Battle of the Bulge.

Combat Command R

The night of 24 November, 1944, was cold, black and rainy. At 2100 that night Combat Command R started into the Hurtgen Forest. The mission was to take the German town of Hurtgen. The 95th Armored Field Artillery Bn. had gone into position five days earlier. First company to move was B Co. of the 47th Armored Infantry Bn., part of Task Force Boyer. The infantrymen moved out of Rotgen in their halftracks, leaving their married B Co. of the 10th Tank Bn. behind. Too great a concentration of armor, it was felt, would attract heavy artillery fire. The plan for the attack called for two companies, B Co. of the 47th and of the 10th, to meet on the road between Germeter and Hurtgen and jump off in married formation for the attack.

At 2400 B Co. of the 10th left Rotgen and moved toward its designated area on the road. When the infantry company arrived, the men jumped from their halftracks and sought cover in the basements, for heavy artillery was already falling around them.

Marching in a column of twos, the infantry company moved out at 0530 toward the front lines between Germeter and Hurtgen. Rain and snow slanted through the pine trees, turning the muddy roads into quagmires, making their march a step-by-step struggle. The company was led by an 8th Infantry Division guide, one of the 22 men left of his company, and was to follow a path marked with white engineer tape. The heavy artillery and stormy weather had long since removed this marker and the company walked in the heavily mined forest without a marked passage. The Germans had sown the area heavily with schu and anti-personnel mines and almost immediately explosions and cries for "Medics!" filled the forest. At dawn the Germans began to pour in more and more artillery. Small arms fire increased.

Casualties skyrocketed, and when the tanks arrived at the jump-off point at their scheduled time, 0730, the infantry company was badly battered.

On the road between Germeter and Hurtgen, an 8th Infantry Division light tank had struck a mine, blocking the road. A tank retriever went forward to remove it, but the retriever, too, hit a mine and was disabled. An effort was made to dynamite the light tank off the road, but this caused a large crater which made as formidable an obstacle as the disabled tank.

Despite the cratered road and the heavy casualties already suffered by the infantry company, the attack started at 0730. The tanks lurched toward Hurtgen, with Lt. Jack McAuley leading. McAuley's tank neared the crater and he called back on the radio, "I'm going to try to jump the damned thing." His tank gathered speed, roared up the soupy road, his tracks throwing a brown spray of mud to the rear. At the crater's edge the drive put on one final burst of speed, but the crater was too wide. The tank slammed into the crater's side, rolled to the left and lay half on its side, but it was in perfect defilade. McAuley could fire his 75 only by using his elevating mechanism to traverse and his traversing mechanism to elevate. From this position, the officer and his gunner, Cpl. William S. Hibler, fired round after round into enemy positions. The 95th Artillery and Lt. James M. McFadden's 47th Assault Gun Platoon continued pounding the Germans in Hurtgen. B Co. of the 10th Tank Bn. had already lost three tank commanders to snipers who were firing from the woods on the left.

Engineers were called up to bridge the crater so the column could slip around McAuley's tank and push on to Hurtgen. Capt. Charles Perlman, commander of C Co., 22nd Engineers, came up to assist the engineers, was wounded and was evacuated. Heavy artillery and mortar fire rained on the engineers as they worked. Capt. Frank M. Pool, B Co., 10th Tank Bn., commander, was hit by a German burp gun while standing in his turret directing the bridging operations, but refused to be evacuated. He climbed out of his tank to help the engineers and while on the ground was wounded again, this time by mortar fire. He again refused to be evacuated, but was soon so weak from loss of blood that evacuation was necessary. Lt. Lewis R. Rollins took over the company.

By 1030, working under heavy fire, the engineers had bridged the crater. Lt. McAuley ordered Sgt. William Hurley to move his tank over the span so he could fire on the right flank and protect the column, but Hurley's tank hit a mine, again blocking the road. While carrying out these orders, Sgt. Hurley was wounded by sniper fire and was evacuated.

Then S/Sgt. Lawrence Summerfield, who was later given a battlefield commission, managed to snake his tank around the other two disabled Shermans and almost to the bend in the road which led into Hurtgen. Just as his tank pulled up to the corner, a German antitank gun, which had been zeroed on the corner, fired at him and missed. As the shots zoomed by Summerfield's tank, his gunner, Cpl. Benny R. Majka, knocked out the German gun with one round from his 75. Just then another German gun opened fire on Summerfield's tank, knocking it out.

By now it was 1400. P-47's came over to bomb and strafe enemy positions in Hurtgen.

At this time Capt. Richard Lewis' B Co., 47th Infantry Bn., had only 80 men left out of 225. Mines, snipers and artillery had almost wiped out the company. The Anti-Tank Platoon was brought up to serve as litter bearers and emergency aid men, for although the medics worked fast, they found it impossible to care for all the rapidly mounting casualties.

The Anti-Tank Platoon worked unceasingly, treating and evacuating the wounded men. Sgt. Lyndall Mailes and Pfc. Charles M. Drake made trip after trip over the heavily mined ground to evacuate wounded men.

Pfc. Leonard Tanis, B Co., 47th Infantry Bn., noticed that the snipers and artillery seemed to have a working agreement. The crack of a sniper's rifle was frequently followed by an artillery concentration. Wriggling forward to a position from which he could observe, Tanis used his M-1 to kill a sniper who was also directing artillery.

Attack To Kleinhau

By now Capt. Leo R. Marcikowski's C Co., 47th Infantry Bn., had been brought up and was trying to flank through the woods to the left of the road. The mines and artillery quickly took heavy toll and in 15 minutes 50 C Co. men lay wounded on the ground. Their progress was also slowed by Germans firing American machine guns from positions that were supposed to be in American hands. Both infantry companies were by now almost exhausted, even before they had come into close contact with the enemy. The Germans had booby-trapped every ditch and foxhole, and when the men flopped into a hole to avoid the artillery they were blown up by these mines.

It was impossible to employ the tanks or use the heavy infantry weapons. It was a hopeless job to continue the attack. Late that night Col. Anderson told Lt. Col. Boyer to pull his task force out.

Meanwhile, Task Force Hamberg, the married A and C Cos., had been living in the mud and muck just north of Germeter. They stayed there for the next three days under heavy shelling while the 8th Infantry Division, after paying a terrible price, finally took Hurtgen. On the morning of Nov. 29 Task Force Hamberg moved through the 8th Infantry Division to attack Kleinhau. The married C Cos. led the attack, moving up the road between Hurtgen and Kleinhau.

Lt. Robert Leas' 1st Platoon of C Co. tanks swung to the left off the road to provide flank protection and four tanks were immediately stuck in the deep, thick mud. The 2nd Tank Platoon, under Lt. T. A. Maguire, went straight up the road toward Kleinhau, followed by Lt. George Kleinsteiber's 3rd Platoon. A 2nd Platoon tank section under S/Sgt. Edwin Gordon was detached and also sent to the left flank. While he was in an exposed position under heavy fire, Gordon was called on the radio and told he could pull out if fire became too heavy. He preferred to stick at his job. He was later shot by a sniper and was evacuated.

By 1000 at least one platoon of tanks had bulled its way into Kleinhau. The 95th Artillery Bn. continued to pound the Germans during the attack, with Lt. Howard K. Kettlehut going far forward to observe and direct the fire.

At the time the married C Cos. were fighting their way into Kleinhau, the married A Cos. were following them up the road and through the fields to the left of the road.

Lt. William Drennen's platoon led the A Co. attack. It swung to the left off the road and around C Co.'s tanks mired in the mud. Capt. Arthur N. Whitley, A Co. commander, was up with the leading tank platoon. Artillery rained on and around the tanks, for the Germans had direct observation and plastered the area with all their artillery to stop the attack.

Drennen continued to work to the left toward Kleinhau and Lt. Joseph Cardone's platoon ploughed straight for Kleinhau. Cardone arrived in Kleinhau with three of his five tanks. One was knocked out by direct fire and the other received a direct hit in the turret with a German mortar. By 1430 Capt. Whitley's company was in Kleinhau in support of C Co.

Again the two supporting infantry companies were fighting a losing battle with mines, artillery and snipers, trying to keep pace with the tanks.

Capt. Joe M. Beisenstein's A Co., 47th Infantry Bn., pushed toward Kleinhau, working to the left of the Hurtgen-Kleinhau road. Capt. Beisenstein was twice wounded and twice refused evacuation. He continued to lead his company until he was killed by a German artillery shell during the attack.

By early afternoon both infantry companies had broken through to Kleinhau and helped the tanks outpost the town.

At 1800 that night Capt. Francis J. Baum was mortally wounded by a direct artillery hit in his tank. Capt. Baum had gotten out of his tank to check each of his platoons' positions, and had just climbed back into his turret when the artillery shell landed on his tank. He died a short time later in the battalion aid station.

That night, 29 November, the 8th Infantry Division moved into Kleinhau to relieve the two heavily hit 47th Infantry companies. The tanks stayed in the town until the next afternoon, and then pulled out of Kleinhau into a woods west of the town. Artillery and mortars continued to fall steadily.

During all of this action the 95th Artillery Bn. continued to blast German positions with counter-battery and support fire.

Task Force Hamberg stayed in the woods west of Kleinhau until it received orders on 1 December to take the town of Brandenberg, three miles south of Kleinhau. It was the start of another bitter. cruel fight against mines, artillery and the ever-present German snipers.

At 0700 2 December, Lt. Col. Hamberg's forces jumped off, A Cos. leading, Lt. Kenneth Wagner's 2nd Platoon in front. The platoon swung to the right of the road to avoid mines, but almost immediately Wagner's tank struck a mine and was put out of action. Wagner ordered the crew to abandon the tank, and then walked back to the platoon behind him to tell them about the minefield. Lt. Wagner, T/5 Harry Spletzer, his driver, and Cpl. Marty Aceithauer were crouching behind Lt. Cardone's tank to avoid a sudden artillery barrage when the driver, unaware that anyone was behind the tank, backed up, injuring the three men.

Mines Slow Advance

Stopped by the mines, the tankers and infantrymen waited for the engineers to come up and clear the field. While waiting for the engineers to arrive, the A Co., 47th Infantry Bn., halftracks parked in a field less than 50 yards away from a German antitank gun, but after the German crew had looked over the situation, they decided to give up rather than fight. They came out to surrender to Capt. Daniel Wersma.

That afternoon Capt. Samuel Siegler sent two of his D Co. light tanks to investigate enemy movement to the right of the road. Sgt. Chester F. Gorzynski and Sgt. Frank C. Wach took their tanks over. As Gorzynski approached a house in the area, he fired a tentative machine gun burst and almost immediately a German officer and 20 men came out, all carrying white cloths over their heads. Quickly another group of 20 appeared from the nearby woods, and then, as if on signal, Germans came pouring out of the woods and buildings from all sides. In 30 minutes the two light tanks had taken 175 prisoners.

The 1st Platoon of C Co., 22nd Engineer Bn., arrived and worked throughout the night removing mines from the extensive field. S/Sgt. Paul Bragg and his three squad leaders, Sgt. Charles Nader, Sgt. Leslie Hager and Sgt. William Kestner, found the pattern for the field and they and their men went to work with ropes, pulling out the mines. It was a nervous, touchy job. The men never knew when a mine was booby-trapped and they worked hour after hour in the complete blackness clearing the field. German artillery boomed and pounded in the pine trees around them. By morning more than 400 mines had been removed. The engineers had done all they could to clear the way.

While the engineers were pulling out mines, an A Co. outpost guarded the engineers from infiltrating Germans. S/Sgt. Guido Borella, member of the outpost, had just been relieved from guard and had gone into a dugout when he heard the new guards call for help. Scrambling out of his dugout in the pitch black, he discovered that the Germans had infiltrated the outpost line in strength. A damaged tank which had hit a mine stood nearby. Borella climbed into it to utilize the tank guns. He reached for the .50 caliber machine gun and found that the careful crew had removed the backplate to prevent the Germans from using it. Clambering down into the tank, he tried to fire the .30 caliber machine gun. Again the backplate was missing. Borella had never fired a 75 gun before, but he rammed a shell home in the chamber, pressed the trigger and nothing happened—the percussion mechanism had been removed.

Realizing the outpost was badly outnumbered, Borella and three other men started to the rear for help. Going to the company command post, he found Lt. Donald Hughes and told his story. By now it was almost daylight and Capt. Whitley had come to the infantry command post to say the attack was shoving off. The Anti-Tank Platoon followed closely to rescue the outnumbered outpost. When they arrived, they found five men had been carried away as prisoners and three lay wounded on the ground. Pfc. Richard Baer had escaped capture by feigning death after he had been knocked unconscious by a German grenade.

He lay very still in the mud as the Germans milled around him, taking the prisoners and shooting those who tried to escape.

The attack on Brandenberg had jumped off at 0700 with C Co. of the 10th Tank Bn. leading. Lt. Maguire rode the lead tank. He had gone only a few hundred yards toward Brandenberg when his tank hit a concealed mine. He jerked out his command radio, stopped Sgt. Rex Sterling's tank, second in the column, inserted his radio in it, and pushed on toward Brandenberg.

The Brandenberg assault was carefully planned. All firepower was used and Lt. Col. Hamberg later said it was one of the most perfectly timed attacks he had ever seen. As the C Co. tanks roared into town, shooting as they rolled, A Co. tanks and D Co. light tanks provided supporting fire. C Co., 47th Infantry Bn., closely followed the tanks and drove into the town to mop up. Tanks pulled up to buildings, blasted doors and windows with tank guns. Infantry boiled down into basements, digging out the Germans with hand grenades and small arms. By 1200 the town had been cleared and 75 prisoners had been taken. Casualties had again been high, and the wounded were evaculated in halftracks.

During the attack on Brandenberg, Lt. Kleinsteiber's 3rd Platoon of tanks had roared completely through the town and into the next town of Bergstein before he realized he had gone too far. The Germans were taken completely by surprise and not a shot was fired at him. Kleinsteiber hurriedly withdrew when he realized his mistake.

That night, 3 December, the C Cos. consolidated positions in Brandenberg. The married C Cos. were now commanded by Lt. Maguire and Lt. James Painter.

All day on 4 December the companies stayed in Brandenberg under heavy artillery fire. German planes came in to strafe and drop butterfly bombs. The companies knocked down two of the planes.

The "Rubble Pile"

On the same day, Task Force Boyer, which had been in the Germeter area, was called on to help the 8th Infantry Division clear the "rubble pile," a name applied to the eastern tip of Vossenack. It was nothing more than a jumble of blown-down buildings, but the Germans had established a strong point there and already a battalion of the 8th Division Infantry had worn itself out trying to clear the area.

The married B Cos. 2nd Platoons led the assault. Lt. Oliver Goldman and his infantrymen rode the rear decks of the tanks to avoid the heavy anti-personnel minefields. Tank mines stopped the tanks short of the rubble pile, and the infantry piled off and started toward the strong point. Lt. Goldman sent S/Sgt. Steven O'Connel to flank the rubble pile to the left. The remainder of the platoon, five men and Lt. Goldman, started toward the German positions.

Lt. McAuley brought his tanks into position to work over a German machine gun nest on the right flank. Lt. Goldman was called back to the battalion command post of the 8th Infantry Division. A colonel in command of the operation told him the rubble pile had to be taken by the next morning.

The area leading to the rubble pile was so heavily mined that the duck feet on the tanks pulled mines out of the ground as they moved. The tanks were forced to stop because of the mines. It was decided to attack the first thing in the morning.

The Goldman-McAuley married platoons assaulted the rubble pile at 0930 on the morning of 5 December, captured it and found it contained strong dugouts, a quantity of radio equipment and American guns. The married platoon then attacked the next objective, a strongly fortified German fire trench to the south of the rubble pile. With the tanks firing in support, the infantrymen drove into the dire trenches, reported them clear, and the assault force pulled back into Vossenack, its mission completed. Task Force Boyer continued on to Germeter, then followed Task Force Hamberg, that by now was readying an attack on Bergstein.

Before dawn on 5 December, Lt. Col. Hamberg sent a patrol from the 1st and 2nd Platoons of Lt. George W. Basquez's C Troop, 85th Reconnaissance Sq., almost to the edge of Bergstein to check the road for mines and to locate enemy strong points. The 12-man patrol led by Lt. Max Eastman started at 0300, hugging the ditches, trying to avoid the mines and booby trap wires the Germans had laid. Sgt. Raymond Rupelli and Sgt. David Matha helped Lt. Eastman direct the patrol. Working silently, in complete darkness, sometimes crawling on all fours, the patrol reached the edge of Bergstein and heard enemy troops in the town. They found no mines or barbed wire entanglements on the road, and crawled slowly back to the command post in Brandenberg to make their report.

Col. Anderson's entire command was used for the assault on Bergstein. The order of attack was to be the married C Cos., A Cos., then B Cos.

The attack started with the infantry riding into the town on the rear decks on the tanks. The Germans had been waiting for the attack and laid such a tremendous barrage that the infantrymen were forced to leave the tanks and seek what cover they could find on the ground. Leading his company into Bergstein, Lt. Maguire was killed by a direct artillery hit on his tank. Lt. Painter was wounded and evacuated. Lt. Roy Hanf, the only remaining officer in C Co., 47th Infantry Bn., took charge of the company. The married C Cos. ploughed into Bergstein, firing with every gun they had, then veered to the left edge of town.

The two platoon sergeants of the leading C Co. platoons were killed in the attack and their platoons were disorganized. Without hesitation Pfc. Bernard Gallagher and Cpl. David Lacoutere took over the platoons and continued to lead the attack. The pair were later promoted to staff sergeant and technical sergeant respectively.

The married A Cos. followed in the second assault wave. On the way in, a German 75 mm. anti-tank gun with a round in the chamber, ready to fire, was captured after heavy tank fire drove the crew away. As A Co., 47th Infantry Bn., moved in to clean up the German crew, an enemy officer rose out of his foxhole and raised his gun to fire on the advancing infantryment. Pfc. Lester Aurand shot him squarely in the forehead before he could aim his gun.

Following A Co., the third assault wave of married B Cos. roared into Bergstein with Lt. George E. Flower's platoon leading. As they neared the town, Flower's platoon swung to the right to cover Lt. Collin's platoon as it smashed into town. Sgt. Dominic

Bernaco knocked out a German Mark IV tank which was trying to flee south out of Bergstein.

Lt. Goldman's C Co., 47th Infantry Bn., platoon assaulted the first building in the town and dragged out 25 SS infantrymen found cringing in the basement. Goldman was checking the house for further Germans when an armor-piercing projectile whammed through the wall a few yards from where he was standing and went completely through the building. Then a second and a third projectile zoomed through the wall. All missed him. Sgt. Abe Kurnasky's B Co., 10th Tank Bn., tank pulled up to knock out the German gun, but his tank was knocked out and he was killed.

Into the town with the three married companies roared two platoons of C Co., 628th Tank Destroyer Bn., commanded by Capt. Robert C. Jones, and Lt. Basquez's C Troop, 85th Reconnaissance Sq.

CC R quickly outposted the town and waited for the inevitable counterattack. It came the next morning, and was the strongest the Germans had yet launched. During the night the men in Bergstein could hear the Germans warming up their tank motors outside the town and making other preparations to attack.

Counterattack

At 0530 the enemy laid down a tremendous artillery barrage and the attacking Germans came in almost under their own barrage. At least 500 German infantrymen swarmed into the town to hack away at the tired combat command.

The 628th Tank Destroyer men were ready for the German armor when it appeared. Sgt. Woodrow W. Woods' long 90 mm. gun picked off a Mark VI and a Mark V at 1000 yards; Sgt. Frank R. Balough accounted for two enemy tanks, a Mark V and a Mark IV, at 1200 yards; and Sgt. Charles A. Leo blasted one Mark IV only 175 yards from his tank destroyer.

The main weight of the attack was thrown on the married B Cos. which occupied the two southern prongs of the town. The Germans attacked bitterly, stepping on their own dead and wounded to force the attack. T/5 Martin Johnson fired 15 clips from his smoking tommy gun to drive off the Germans in his section of town. S/Sgt. Jack Peterson fired his .50 caliber machine gun continuously until the attack subsided. By 1030, after more than four hours of constant siege, the attack was broken.

Virtually all of the men of CC R were in a state of shock. Their nerves were shot, their physical energy had long since disappeared. They crouched dazedly in their foxholes and basements, loading their guns and waiting for the Germans to come back. They knew they could never hold another counterattack like the last one. There simply were not enough men left. Every hour cost them more casualties, and the counterattack had taken a heavy toll.

In the afternoon another counterattck came, but by this time the Germans were losing heart. The attack was small and was soon beaten back. More attacks were launched on the town, but the Germans never again seriously threatened. The men learned later why the Germans had attacked the town so furiously. The German High Command had offered the Knight's Cross of the German Iron Cross to any unit that retook Bergstein. But the German High Command never had to pay off.

At 0400 on the morning of 9 December the weary, battered men were relieved in Bergstein and started to leave the town. The command had eight effective tanks left out of the 58 with which they had started. Seventy infantrymen were available for full duty of an original strength of more than 750. It had been a costly fight.

Combat Command A

The 46th Armored Infantry Bn. was attached to Combat Team 22 of the 4th Infantry Division 29 November and assembled in the dark and foreboding Hurtgen Forest, one mile west of Kleinhau. That night Lt. Col. William H. Burton, Jr., visited the commanding office of the 22nd Combat Team. The mission, he was told, was to attack from a line running north and south across Hill 401 and to gain the far edge of the woods beyond Kleinhau. CC A was then to attack to take Strass.

The combat command, attached to the 4th Infantry Division on 30 November, moved to the vicinity of Zweifal. Co. A, 22nd Engineers, joined the engineers of the 4th Infantry to help keep open the necessary supply lines to the rear, and the 47th Armored Field Artillery Bn. went into position west of Kleinhau where bodies of dead Germans still lay in the woods about the artillery positions.

Before dawn on 30 November, Major Jack B. Day contacted the infantry unit on the left. Major Lionel R. Fuller and Major Richard W. McKenna, then a captain, set out to contact the unit reported to be holding the line of departure at Hill 401 and Kleinhau. Artillery and mortar fire was falling in the open ground, but they made their way through the darkness from shell hole to shell hole. The enemy held Hill 401, they discovered, and both friendly and hostile troops were in Kleinhau. Fuller and McKenna found the commanding officer of the American troops in the town and explained the proposed action of the 46th.

Meanwhile Lt. Col. Burton had issued a partial attack order and moved out with a small party to reconnoiter to his line of departure. His radio failed. While he was out of communication with his companies, A and C Cos., 46th Infantry Bn., emerged from the woods, moving up to the line of departure in perfect approach march formation. Immediately heavy and continuous artillery and mortar fire and small arms and machine gun fire from Hill 401 and Kleinhau raked the doughboys. A and C Cos. deployed, but were pinned down by the intense and unexpected fire. A complete change of plans was necessary, Lt. Col. Burton realized. Making his way across the fireswept open ground to the lead elements, Lt. Col. Burton ran and crawled to each commander to issue his revised orders for the assault on Hill 401 and Kleinhau. He then helped lead C Co. up the steep slopes of Hill 401 in a successful but bloody assault. Lt. Col. Burton later received the Distinguished Service Cross for this action.

On 401 they captured a pillbox, 50 prisoners and six machine guns. During the assault artillery and mortar barrages pounded the 46th infantrymen and heavy machine gun fire poured in from commanding positions on top of the hill. When C Co., 46th Infantry Bn., was within 200 yards of the hilltop, a self-propelled gun moved out of the woods 200 yards to the left front and opened fire with such speed and accuracy that C Co. was stopped and the success of the entire operation was jeopardized.

T/Sgt. Floyd M. Spray, who was leading his platoon of Co. C, quickly realized that his men could not long survive if they remained under the heavy artillery and mortar barrages. He seized a rocket launcher and, with almost no cover, made his way along the entire front of his platoon to a position opposite the enemy gun. Within 100 yards of the gun he opened fire with his rocket launcher. He forced the enemy gun to withdraw and permitted Co. C to continue the assault. Sgt. Spray was mortally wounded while returning to his platoon.

Co. A, on the right, advanced abreast of C Co. across 900 yards of open ground to take Kleinhau and clear the town of snipers. B Co., although the reserve company, suffered its share of casualties from the artillery and mortar fire. At 1300, part of the company was pinned down by a concealed machine gun 300 yards to the front. S/Sgt. Robert M. Henley, a squad leader from the 3rd Platoon, climbed a tree under sniper fire, located the gun, then wriggled forward and assaulted the enemy position with his tommy gun. He killed or wounded the entire crew and permitted his platoon to advance again.

After the capture of Hill 401 and Kleinhau, C Co., 46th Infantry Bn., continue to attack east and, at 1600, reached the originally assigned line of departure. B Co., 46th Infantry Bn., passed through A Co. and continued the attack east from Kleinhau. In the open ground beyond the town, B Co. was again stopped by a concealed machine gun, this time 45 yards to the right front. Pfc. Albert H. Harrington attempted to crawl up on the enemy and knock out this gun. In so doing he was killed by an enemy sniper, but his heroic act enabled his company to locate and destroy the enemy position.

A short time later the company was again held up by a machine gun. Lt. Brady O. Kelley crawled up a firebreak for almost 200 yards, assaulted the enemy with only his carbine, and killed the entire crew. At 1700, Pfc. William G. Lee, a scout moving to the right of B Co., charged an enemy wire crew of four and killed or wounded them.

The advance of B and C Cos., 46th Infantry Bn., continued through the heavy forest beyond Kleinhau under heavy and continuous artillery and mortar fire, plus very intense machine gun and sniper fire from the concealed enemy. By 2200, they had penetrated 1200 yards into the woods. Co. A came up and the battalion set up defensive positions for the night. Then they began the difficult task of evacuating the wounded, for all three companies had suffered approximately 30 per cent casualties in the day's fighting.

Artillery fire continued throughout the night as the litter parties made their tedious, dangerous way back through the woods to Kleinhau. From Kleinhau, T/5 Harry Rockman, who had volunteered to drive his ambulance to this forward point, carried the wounded back over the dark, shell-torn road to the hospital.

The medics never quit working in Hurtgen Forest. Stories of their bravery were told and retold long after other details of the fight had been forgotten. High on the doughboys' list of heroes is T/5 John A. Dunleavy, 46th Infantry Bn., medical aid man attached to the 1st Platoon, Co. C. He knew no fear except the fear of leaving a wounded man unattended. Ignoring fire that pinned all others to their foxholes, he went from man to man, treating and evacuating casualties throughout the fight, saving an inestimable number of lives.

Casualties Heavy

The battalion spent the night in foxholes under continuous fire and jumped off at 0900 the next morning. In the thick woods visibility was limited to five yards. Contact was made with the enemy immediately. Casualties were again heavy, but there was no stopping the 46th Infantry Bn.'s attack.

At 1100 the 1st Platoon of Co. C, 46th Infantry Bn., moving as skirmishers through a dense growth of short pines, was halted by an enemy machine gun firing 150 yards to the front. S/Sgt. Peter J. Parrow, acting platoon leader, crawled to within 20 yards of the gun and destroyed the crew with hand grenades. He saw another machine gun firing at his men and set out to destroy it. He had gone half the distance when he was mortally wounded by a third gun. His efforts permitted his men to locate the guns and destroy them with mortar fire.

By noon Co. C had advanced 500 yards when the 1st Platoon was again pinned down by a machine gun. This time S/Sgt. Robert B. Dixon crawled forward and destroyed the enemy crew with a hand grenade. As Dixon was returning to the company the enemy laid down a heavy mortar barrage and he was fatally wounded.

At the same time a hostile 75 mm. self-propelled gun opened fire 150 yards from C Co. and the battalion command post. Capt. Robert T. Bland, then acting S-3 of the battalion and one of the fiercest fighters in the division, immediately went forward under this direct fire to the lead company, organized a group of volunteer bazooka teams and moved against the enemy guns. He led his men to a position which, though fully exposed, permitted effective fire against the target. He directed the fire until a shell burst in the center of the group, killing three and wounding the remainder. Capt. Bland, himself, lost his right leg during the attack.

Casualties had been so heavy that Lt. Col. Burton sent for the antitank platoons to come forward as replacement riflemen. While bringing up the Anti-Tank Platoon of B Co., 46th Infantry Bn., Lt. James H. Foster was forced to cross an open field under heavy artillery fire. Running across the field, he spotted a large foxhole and jumped in to avoid the shellfire. The hole was near an enemy machine gun nest. Five Germans, members of the gun crew, were in the hole, their heads bent down to avoid the artillery fire. Lt. Foster, firing his M-1 rifle like a tommy gun, killed all of them.

At 1200 the 46th Infantry Bn. was ordered to withdraw to the positions of the night before and tie in a defense with the 2nd Bn. of the 22nd Infantry Bn. 800 yards further to the rear and 500 yards to the left. The enemy held commanding ground to the right front from which he was directing heavy, accurate mortar and artillery fire. Lt. Edward J. Egan and his assistant, T/4 Wayne Manion, the only remaining forward observer party from the 47th Artillery Bn., stayed forward with the skeleton force covering the withdrawal. Covered by 47th Artillery Bn. fire, the infantry moved reluctantly back, carrying their wounded over the blood-soaked ground they had won at such cost during the morning. The withdrawal was completed by 1500. An hour later a company of German infantry counterattacked, supported by increased mortar and artillery fire. The attack was broken by 46th Infantry Bn. riflemen and machine gunners.

Supplied During Dark

After dark the 46th Infantry Bn. began to resupply and evacuate its wounded. Artillery and mortar shells continued to fall and during the night the enemy sent out patrols. German burp guns fired wildly in unsuccessful attempts to get the 46th Infantry Bn. outposts to reveal their positions.

An attack was ordered at 1000 on 2 December, this time to be supported by B Co. of the 34th Tank Bn. At dawn, artillery and mortar fire increased and casualties mounted steadily. At 1100 the supporting tanks had not made their appearance. The S-3 requested permission to attack unsupported to seize the high ground to the right front. From that point the enemy was directing deadly fire – the heaviest ever experienced by the battalion. To stay in position meant the death of every man.

But plans had ben changed, and the 46th Infantry Bn. was withdrawn to a new position. Here the enemy fire was so accurate and intense that the 46th moved back into Kleinhau, held by the 8th Infantry Division. The wounded were left behind in sheltered positions. T/5 Sigmund Rachwal and Pfc. Dom C. Ansani of the Medical Detachment remained to care for them. The battalion moved back into the woods west of Kleinhau shortly after dark.

At 2200 Lt. Col. Burton, Capt. John J. McCafferty, Lt. Arthur Paul, T/4 Henry A. Wicka and Pfc. George Brodsky went back to see that all the wounded had been evacuated. Lt. Col. Burton contacted two command posts in Kleinhau and was assured at each that the area had been searched and that there were no men left beyond the outpost line. Still not convinced, he continued through scattered artillery fire to a pillbox 500 yards beyond the outpost line. The party approached the pillbox and, while the other members of the patrol covered the immediate vicinity, Lt. Col. Burton kicked open the door and demanded:

"Who's there?"

Pfc. Ansani answered from within. Inside the pillbox Lt. Col. Burton found Ansani and Rachwal with seven wounded men and

10 members of the 8th Infantry Division. Pfc. Brodsky returned to Kleinhau for litter bearers and T/4 Wicka went to the nearest outpost for water. Lt. Paul, Wicka and Brodsky remained in the pillbox to supervise the evacuation of the wounded while Lt. Col. Burton and Capt. McCafferty returned to Kleinhau to arrange for ambulances. All the wounded were evacuated by 0400 the next morning.

The entire action around Kleinhau was the most severe imaginable. The 46th Infantry Bn. had suffered almost 40 per cent casualties, but came out of the battle a tattered but confident outfit. When all went wrong, the officers and men of the battalion rose to the occasion and displayed the utmost tenacity and coolness. In a critical situation there was always a man or group of men who volunteered to deal with it.

Although the 46th Infantry Bn. had been detached from the Fifth Armored for the battle, it was not alone in its fight. The 47th Artillery Bn. gave its best efforts in support. Gen. Regnier kept close supervision over the action through the sleepless nights and days. CC A's engineers worked like beavers to keep open the hopelessly inadequate supply lines behind Kleinhau.

From 3 to 5 December the 46th Infantry Bn. with B Co. of the 34th Tank Bn. and A Co. of the 22nd Engineer Bn., remained in the woods west of Kleinhau, prepared to resist a possible counterattack. Enemy air was active and the 47th Artillery Bn. shot down five German planes. On 5 December this force was moved into CC A's area near Zweifal and, on 8 December, the entire command moved to Hahn.

Gey-Kufferath

The attack plan called for CC A to thrust east from Gey to take Kufferath and Hills 209 and 211, overlooking Winden and the Roer River. This attack was to be made in conjunction with CC B on the right and was to be launched after the 83rd Infantry Division had taken Gey and Strass.

On 11 December, CC A moved into an assembly area on the eastern edge of the Hurtgen Forest immediately west of Grosshau. But Gey and Strass had not yet been captured, and the attack scheduled for the next day had to be postponed. The 46th Infantry Bn. returned to Hahn.

Capt. Thomas Grose's A Co. of the 22nd Engineer Bn. worked under artillery and small arms fire 11 and 12 December to improve and clear the important Grosshau-Gey road.

Gey was still in enemy hands 13 December and the command remained in position under sporadic artillery fire, waiting for the order to attack. Engineers continued their work on the road, using two crabs. At the command post a peep from D Co. of the 34th Tank Bn. hit another mine. Lt. Lionel B. Scott, Lt. Russell Crockett and their driver were wounded as pieces of the peep were blown 40 feet into the air. A field desk in the peep was blown still higher and fell on a CP tent in which Maj. William G. Reynolds and members of his staff were assembled.

Then orders came for the attack. On the morning of 14 December the 34th Tank Bn. Headquarters with married A and B Cos., commanded by Lt. Col. William L. Cabaniss, moved up the road to Gey. The task force was exposed to enemy observation and fire until the 47th Artillery Bn. laid down a smoke screen east of the road. The tanks and infantry slipped through to Gey.

Capt. Raymond W. Weeks, commanding B Co. of the 34th Tank Bn., went forward with the 2nd Platoon. A crab cleared a path ahead through the minefields to within 100 yards of Horm when it was disabled by a mine. The A Co. engineers cleared out the remaining mines.

The 2nd Platoon of B Co. tanks, under Lt. Marvin W. Orgill, deployed to the north of the road and in front of Horm, while the accompanying infantry remained on the road in their half-tracks. Moving through heavy artillery fire, the 2nd Platoon was almost in the town when hostile infantry, bazooka and anti-tank fire opened up. Lt. Orgill's platoon let loose an intense assault fire and prisoners began to stream out of the town.

Lt. Ernest F. Schmidt moved his 3rd Platoon to engage anti-tank guns on the southwest edge of Horm. His own tank knocked out two 75 mm. self-propelled guns at close range, then hit a mine. Sgt. Joseph E. Nemechek moved his tank to an exposed position toward the south of town and knocked out three troublesome self-propelled guns at a range of 1000 yards.

The entire 3rd Platoon fought a nip and tuck battle with the many enemy anti-tank guns in and around the village. A 150 mm. self-propelled gun sighted in the town was destroyed by Sgt. Felix A. Diersing's tank. Sgt. Wilmer Doty's tank was hit on the right side by a 75 mm. self-propelled gun and exploded, throwing him clear. He returned to his burning tank, pulled out his gunner, Cpl. Charles Fuller, then went back to rescue his driver. Two more rounds smashed into the tank, the driver was killed, and Sgt. Doty was seriously wounded.

Many Prisoners

During the action prisoners continued to stream out of the town. Two squads of infantry from the 83rd Infantry Division approached Capt. Weeks and asked if they could be of assistance. They were put to work handling the prisoners.

The B Cos. of the 34th Tank Bn. and the 46th Infantry Bn. reassembled beyond Horm, leaving the town for the A Cos. to mop up. Tanks fired on the commanding hill to the northeast in order to deny the enemy that observation point, but artillery continued to fall as the B Cos. took on more ammunition.

The B Cos. soon took off again toward Kufferath, the 2nd Platoon leading. The tanks and infantry fought forward under heavy artillery fire to within 400 yards of the objective, Kufferath. Suddenly a battery of hidden anti-tank guns opened up from the right flank. Capt. Weeks' tank was knocked out. He jumped out, ran to another tank, and radioed orders for the 3rd Platoon to move up even with the 2nd Platoon. Lt. Orgill swung his platoon to face the enemy guns and took them under fire. His tank was hit, and he was blown unconscious from the turret. Sgt. Diersing took command and directed the fire until Lt. Orgill regained consciousness and returned to the action. In this fierce duel with anti-tank guns firing from positions near Bergheim, B Co., 34th Tank Bn., lost five tanks. It had only three tanks and one tank-dozer when it was ordered into defiladed positions in front of Kufferath.

T/4 Charles H. Munn, whose tank had been knocked out, was making his way to the rallying point when he found Sgt. Franklin Dow lying seriously wounded beside his destroyed tank. Munn picked up his comrade and carried him, under artillery fire, two miles to the aid station in Gey. Pfc. Jack Sweed helped a badly burned comrade to the aid station. In Horm, Sweed was wounded by an artillery concentration, but found an abandoned peep and evacuated casualties from Horm for several hours before he would accept treatment for himself.

The B Cos. waited in their defiladed positions while Capt. Richard Biedermann moved up with A Co. of the 34th Tank Bn., followed by A Co. of the 46th Infantry Bn. A squadron of P-47's came in and clobbered Kufferath, Bergheim and the woods in between. By nightfall Capt. Biedermann's forces were around Kufferath on three sides.

Soft ground and incoming artillery made the work of resupply and evacuation of wounded extremely difficult. Pvt. Charles E. Gariepy, Pvt. William E. Sayre, Pfc. Benjamin Litwak and Pvt. George T. Puskar had worked all afternoon evacuating the wounded by litter. During the night Sgt. George E. Baker of A Co., 34th Tank Bn., joined them to carry out the wounded on the deck of his tank. Supplies were brought in by light tanks towing trailers.

Early the next morning B Co. of the 46th Infantry Bn. jumped off to take Hills 209 and 211. Two tanks had been put back into operation during the night, and Capt. Weeks was able to support the attack with six tanks. The tanks received anti-tank fire from Bergheim. Tank destroyers, assault guns and mortars blasted the town while the B Co. tanks supported the infantry attack by firing 75 mm. cannister shells against the enemy on top of the hills. Two anti-tank guns in the woods to the right knocked out three tanks, but Sgt. William Kundman, A Co., 34th Tank Bn., pounded them with his 76 mm. tank gun, destroyed one and forced the other to withdraw. Four tanks were lost, Lt. Orgill's among them, but the hills were taken.

Cpl. Patsy Letterie and Pfc. Chester S. Bortowski, having left their knocked out tanks, observed another tank burst into flames and a crew member fall unconscious and wounded on the rear deck. Under artillery fire they moved this man to a place of safety and administered first aid.

Supply Routes Shelled

B Co. of the 46th Infantry Bn. dug in on the objective and began to think about resupply. Between them and the supply point was over a mile of open ground pounded by continuous artillery and mortar concentrations. Casualties had been so heavy that carrying parties could not be formed.

T/5 Virgil E. Westmoreland volunteered to drive his halftrack to the rear assembly area for supplies. Leaving his company at 2000, he drove through the enemy fire and over fields where two tanks had been disabled by mines to the supply point and back. During the night he made a total of six trips. On one trip a tire was punctured by a shell fragment. Westmoreland dismounted, changed the tire, and continued with his job. T/5 David E. Bristol and Pfc. Walter C. King made similarly dangerous trips for the Mortar Platoon.

While the B Cos. were fighting for Hills 209 and 211, A Cos. assaulted and captured the town of Kufferath. During this assault S/Sgt. Andrew Hovdestadt, Co. A, 46th Infantry Bn., volunteered for several of the most hazardous jobs. He led aggressive patrols into Kufferath, cleaning out houses and securing the town. The sergeant was clearing the town when an artillery shell burst near him and he fell mortally wounded. Despite his wound, Sgt. Hovdestadt urged his squad to continue the attack, then crawled to a covered position where he helped other wounded men to safety. He died at the battalion aid station.

In the two operations—the taking of Hills 209 and 211 and the capture of Kufferath—98 prisoners were taken, 175 of the enemy were killed or wounded, and 11 anti-tank guns and six machine guns were destroyed.

For the next five days CC A continued to hold the objectives they had taken. On the night of 17 December Lt. Col. Burton took over the defense of the sector with B and C Cos., of the 46th Infantry Bn., and the tanks were pulled back to form a reserve force.

Enemy artillery continued to pound relentlessly throughout the period. At the command post of the 34th Tank Bn. they kept a record of the number of rounds that fell in the immediate area during one night. The total was 825. This extremely heavy fire tore up the telephone wires and disrupted all communication between companies and battalions. T/Sgt. George W. McClung, 46th Infantry Bn. communications sergeant, worked night and day under sniper and artillery fire to keep the vital lines in. At one place he found 17 breaks in his line which had been chopped up by incoming artillery shells. He quickly repaired the breaks, restoring communications.

The 47th Artillery Bn. fired repeated concentrations against the enemy batteries. Meanwhile, a search was made for enemy paratroopers reported dropped on the morning of 18 December, and a close watch was kept for any signs of a counter-offensive from across the Roer.

On 19 December the 15th Infantry Bn. of CC B was attached to CC A and the next day attacked with one platoon of A Co. of the 34th Tank Bn. to take the high ground east of Bergheim. Eight men were loaded on the deck of each tank and the remainder of the infantry deployed to the flanks and rear. The force moved out at 1000 and cleared a draw leading to the objective. One tank was stopped by bazooka fire, but the attack pushed on, forcing back the defending German infantrymen.

Evacuation Under Fire

On the objective, heavy anti-tank and artillery fire from the flanks smashed two more tanks. Lt. Joseph Mullens dismounted to confer with the infantry commander. He and five infantrymen were wounded by artillery fire. Cpl. Michael C. Korinko dismounted from his tank and rendered first aid. The artillery fire became so intense that the wounded could not be evacuated by litter. T/5 Lester R. Holder, who had already been shot out of two tanks, drove his third tank astride the wounded and took all six in through the bottom escape hatch. His tank was hit six times by armor piercing projectiles which gouged deep holes but bounced off.

That afternoon a platoon of C Co. of the 46th Infantry Bn., the 46th Reconnaissance Platoon, and one tank platoon of C Co., 34th Tank Bn., launched an attack on Schneidhausen. The infantry pushed northeast from Hill 211 at 1500 and the tanks attacked the town from the northwest, supporting the infantry assault by fire. Under heavy fire from the village and from across the Roer, the attackers battled to within 100 yards of the town before they were stopped. Then, as darkness fell, they withdrew to Hill 211 for the night.

The next day B Co. of the 36th Infantry Bn. made another attack toward Schneidhausen. Ahead of the infantrymen lay 800 yards of open, rolling terrain. Eight tanks of C Co., 34th Tank Bn., on the left flank of Hill 211 were supporting the action. Moving forward through heavy artillery, mortar and automatic weapons fire, the company came into position for the final assault on the town. Before they could move out the supporting tank fire had to be lifted. Radios failed to make contact with the tanks.

Pfc. John Bowen, a rifle man of B Co., 46th Infantry Bn., volunteered to cross 600 yards of open ground to the west and contact the tanks. This entire distance was under direct observation by the enemy, and the area was subjected to very heavy artillery and mortar fire. Fully aware of the risk, Pfc. Bowen ran for 100 yards through intense fire. An enemy machine gun opened up on him. Bowen dropped to the ground and simulated death. His action diverted the machine gun. He remained motionless for several minutes, then once more rushed forward. Making six rushes, and under fire the entire time, he succeeded in reaching the tanks. The fire was lifted and the assault platoons of B Co. continued on to take Schneidhausen.

Even before the actual assault on the town, B Co. had lost all its officers with the assaulting platoons. First Sgt. Walter Jones (later commissioned a lieutenant) went forward with a SCR 300 radio strapped on his back and assumed command. This radio proved to be the only means of communication with the battalion command post and the supporting artillery. Sgt. Jones acted as a forward observer and directed artillery fire which smashed an attempted enemy counterattack. He then led patrols through the mine-infested town and eliminated the last remaining enemy.

It seemed impossible that the bridge over the Roer River could still be intact, but Sgt. Jones led a patrol out to see. Two men of the patrol were seriously wounded by anti-personnel mines. Unwilling to expose the other members, he continued alone until he could see that the bridge was intact. He then returned, personally checked each of the company's defensive positions and supervised the search for wounded.

Throughout the afternoon T/5 Angelo Aquitieri, an aid man with B Co., had worked under fire to administer to his wounded comrades. That night he, too, was wounded. He found a safe basement in Schneidhausen and had the wounded brought there. Soon there were 32 at the aid station, and all the water was exhausted. The only source was the Roer River, 150 yards beyond the outpost line.

The open ground to the river was fully exposed to the enemy's guns and a bright moon aided German observation. However, S/Sgt. Arthur L. Bading and S/Sgt. Mathew M. Mszauski gathered canteens and set out for the river. Almost immediately the enemy spotted them and laid down a heavy mortar concentration. As they neared the river a sniper opened fire. Sgt. Bading worked his way forward while Sgt. Mszauski deliberately exposed himself. The sniper fired again and Bading killed him with an accurately thrown hand grenade. The two men reached the river, filled the canteens and returned to the wounded.

Throughout the night T/5 Aquitieri continued to work on the wounded, although he became so weak that he had to be helped from one patient to another. When he was relieved at 0900 the next morning, it was discovered that he had a penetrating wound of the abdomen.

Relief

At 0730 on 22 December the 83rd Infantry Division began relieving B Co., 46th Infantry Bn., in Schneidhausen. Because of the shortage of litters, 14 of the wounded had to be left in the basement where they had spent the night. Sgt. Benjamin O. Morisch, in Kufferath, learned of this and organized an aid party with plasma, instruments, litters and litter bearers. He relieved Aquitieri in Schneidhausen and, by 1145, had given treatment to all of the patients. The litter party then started back for Kufferath. Halfway to the town a heavy mortar barrage fell, killing one man and seriously wounding another. Sgt. Morisch rallied his party and continued on to Kufferath.

The relief of CC A by the 83rd Division continued on 22

December. The following day the command moved back to Hahn, and 24 December it moved to Baelen, near Eupen, Belgium. There it was placed on a six-hour alert status for possible operation against the German "Bulge".

Christmas Day was quiet and clear, with the first sunshine in weeks. The alert status was changed to two hours, but the command was able to celebrate Christmas.

Combat Command B

In early December Col. John T. Cole received orders to move his command into the Hurtgen Forest. Its mission: to clear the Germans from the area extending from Kleinhau to Winden, a town on the Roer River. The area was one of the last and most stubborn pockets west of the Roer. The fight to clear that few square miles of ground was the hardest and bloodiest the men of CC B were ever to tackle.

On 9 and 10 December the tanks and halftracks rumbled up the tortuous, muddy trails of the shell-scarred forest.

The combat command assembled in the woods just west of Kleinhau and started to dig in. Almost immediately they were strafed and bombed by German planes flying at tree-top level. The medics counted 18 casualties.

Light snow covered the ground the morning of 11 December when riflemen of the 15th Infantry Bn. dismounted from their halftracks and prepared to attack. At 0745 they moved out, passed the battered town of Kleinhau and advanced toward the high wooded ground a mile to the northeast.

Supporting each infantry company was a platoon of tanks from each of the line companies of the 81st Tank Bn. On the right flank were riflemen from A and B Troops of the 85th Cavalry Recon. Squadron. F Co. of the 85th was attached to the 4th Cavalry Group, working further south. Artillery support was supplied by the 71st Field Artillery Bn.

The reports that the area up to the line of departure had been cleared of all Germans had been highly inaccurate, for when the doughboys started across the exposed ground, a heavy barrage of artillery and mortar fire was laid down on them. They also received accurate small arms fire from their right flank from three machine guns, two bazooka teams and German riflemen concealed in a thick patch of pine trees. One of the first casualties was the commander of the 15th Infantry Bn.'s A Co., Capt. Donald K. Krafts, who was killed.

The assault wave pushed on, but when forward elements started up the slope of the hill, heavy machine gun fire pinned down the attackers.

Despite flying shell fragments and machine gun bullets, S/Sgt. Louis J. San Martino of the 15th Infantry Bn.'s A Co. continued to crawl forward. When he was certain he had located the exact position of the German machine gun emplacement, he signaled to Pvt. Wade N. Spruill who had set up his mortar in a shell hole.

Pvt. Spruill realized he was in full view of the German forward artillery observer and that when he put his mortar into action he would become the special target for enemy shells. Without hesitating, however, he started lobbing shells into the enemy position. His sixth round was a direct hit, destroying the machine gun nest.

Attack! Attack!

The riflemen trudged forward again and advanced until A Co.'s 2nd Platoon, which was in the forward elements, lost its platoon leader, Lt. Bass Redd, who was killed, and its platoon sergeant, T/Sgt. Richard Rosner, who was wounded. When these key men were hit, the other members of the platoon became hesitant and disorganized. The attack bogged down.

S/Sgt. Frank M. DiTaranto immediately assumed charge of the platoon. Exposing himself to heavy fire, he crawled forward from man to man and organized the scattered remnants into a fighting unit. Charging forward again, they reached the edge of the woods.

The 15th Infantry Bn.'s B Co. commander, Capt. Arthur Elmore, was also wounded in the assault, but Lt. Merle S. Power quickly took over, reorganized the company and resumed the attack. He led the assault by preceding the leading elements of the attack wave and continued to push forward until he was killed by a German machine gun.

By now A Co. alone had suffered 60 casualties. Every line

company commander in the 15th Infantry Bn. had been killed or wounded.

Darkness came early that cold winter night and the riflemen dug into the frozen ground to hold their positions. Through the long night spent in their foxholes they had only their overcoats to keep them warm.

Intense artillery and mortar fire made it impossible for trucks, peeps or other thin-skinned vehicles to haul badly-needed supplies up to the front. The 81st Tank Bn.'s D Co. was called on to do the job with its light tanks. Lt. Benjamin T. Potts had the men in his platoon load rations, water and clothing on the rear decks of their tanks and they started toward the forward positions.

In the darkness they missed the guide who was to show them where to unload the supplies. Going beyond the outposts, they went into territory still held by the enemy. Fired on by small arms and mortars, they turned around and started back up the road.

Going back, they found their route around two knocked-out Shermans was now blocked by a light tank from their platoon which had hit a mine. Climbing out of the turret, Lt. Potts got in front of his tank and started to lead it between the two Shermans when it, too, struck a mine. The explosion killed him and seriously wounded his driver, T/4 Peter J. Thauwald.

Heroes Are Made

During the next two days, riflemen from the 15th Infantry Bn. and 85th Reconnaissance Sq. and tankers from the 81st Tank Bn. continued to clear infiltrating Germans from the woods and to hold the high ground despite extremely heavy artillery and mortar fire. Each day the troops hacked their way forward a few hundred yards against bitter enemy resistance. Every advance of a hundred yards meant another foxhole. Every foxhole meant back-breaking hours of work digging through the foot-thick frozen crust of earth.

Heroism was accepted as nothing less than duty in Hurtgen Forest during those days. When he saw his squad leader fall wounded on a patch of open ground, Sgt. John Tivvis of the 15th Infantry Bn.'s C Co. crawled forward to an exposed position and put fire on enemy snipers so that aid men could get to the wounded soldier. He then helped evacuate the man across several hundred yards of ground under shellfire.

Wounded during the first day's attack and evacuated to the aid station, C Co.'s S/Sgt. William Carter returned to the fight and was wounded again the second day. Both times he was told at the aid station to wait for the ambulance which would evacuate him to a field hospital, but both times he slipped off and returned to his company. When he turned up at the aid station the third time the surgeon knew that Sgt. Carter would not go back to his company again. He had been wounded in the foot and could not walk.

The enemy's intense shelling took a heavy toll again the second day. The 15th Infantry Bn.'s new A Co. commander, Capt. Roderick Smith, had his command only a few hours before he, too, was wounded and evacuated. Command of the company fell to the only remaining officer, Lt. Francis C. Darby.

That night, three days and two nights after they had pushed off, the 15th Infantry Bn. reported the strength of its three line companies at four officers and 170 enlisted men. At full strength they had 18 officers and 735 enlisted men.

Reinforcements Arrive

Just before dusk that night Lt. Miles Light moved his machine gun platoon from the 15th Infantry Bn.'s headquarters forward to support the line companies. As they were digging in on the high ground a German soldier came out of the woods and surrendered. It was too late to take the prisoner back to the rear that night so Lt. Light bedded him down in a large foxhole between himself and another member of the platoon. In the morning when Lt. Light checked the other foxholes in the area to make certain his men were awake, he found three sleeping Germans in one hole and four in another. The fighting was that close in Hurtgen Forest.

The difficult job of supplying the dug-in troops in the line continued to be handled by the light tanks of Capt. Harold M. Schiering's D Co. The tanks rolled forward with loads of rations, water and clothing, and returned with wounded doughboys stretched out on their rear decks. Mines planted by infiltrating Germans were always a serious threat to the tanks. This problem was quickly solved on one run by Lt. Henry V. Plass. Pulling his tank up behind a knocked-out engineers' bridge truck which lay at the side of the road, Lt. Plass converted the truck into a mine sweeper by pushing it ahead of him the rest of the way to Strass, where he delivered his supplies.

On the third day of the battle the 15th Infantry Bn.'s anti-tank platoons left their 57 mm. guns in the rear and went forward as riflemen to reinforce the dwindling rifle platoons. The 2nd Bn. of the 83rd Infantry Division's 330th Regiment had been attached to CC B on 12 December. The next day the 81st Tank Bn.'s C Co., commanded by Capt. William L. Guthrie, was ordered to support the 330th Regiment which was holding the sector around Strass on the left flank.

Two of C Co.'s platoons moved out in the early morning. When the tanks reached Schafberg, on the road to Strass, they were fired on by anti-tank guns. Mines prevented the tanks from deploying. In rapid succession four tanks were hit. Three of them burned and the turret was jammed on the fourth.

Although the tank commanded by S/Sgt. Raymond W. Beltz was hit three times, he continued to shell the enemy position until a fourth German projectile whined across the contested ground and ripped into the barrel of his gun. When the men removed the round they had intended to fire, they found a piece of shrapnel from the German shell sticking in its nose.

The scheduled attack by the 330th Regiment was cancelled and the C Co. tanks were ordered to their assembly area.

Medics! Medics!

CC B was now out of contact with the 330th Regiment and it was vitally necessary that communications be re-established. Lt. Carlo Lombardi of the 81st Tank Bn.'s D Co. was asked to attempt to reach the attached battalion with his radio-equipped tank. Between his tank and the 330th Regiment lay a stretch of open mined ground that was covered by direct fire of the anti-tank guns which had knocked out the C Co. tanks. Lt. Lombardi's driver, T/4 Roy P. Rusteberg, ran the gantlet successfully, and communications were re-established with the isolated unit.

The men continued to fight forward, yard by yard, but every

few yards they advanced cost them heavy casualties. Medical officers and aid men worked unceasingly to treat and evacuate the wounded.

At the 15th Infantry Bn.'s aid station the medical officers, Capt. Leroy Holbert and Capt. George Tempel, and their assistants were red-eyed and exhausted. In their medical dressing tent and on all sides of it they treated casualties from all of the units fighting on this sector. During the first day they had cared for 150 wounded men, 200 the second day and 100 the third.

When the wounded started pouring in during the first day, the little detachment found that it could not treat all of them without assistance. Help was sent from their Service Co. and from B Co. of the 75th Medical Bn.

S/Sgt. Edmund W. Harrigan led four peeps up the shell-torn road the first day and evacuated the wounded who were scattered in the fields on both sides of the road. But when the companies pushed further ahead, only tanks could be used to get the wounded out of the cold, muddy fields where they had fallen and bring them back through the concentrations of artillery and mortar fire.

Up with the rifle platoons the 12 medical aid men, only two of whom finally came out of the battle without being casualties themselves, worked day and night bandaging up the wounded and starting them on their difficult trip to the aid station.

After making three attempts to crawl out into an open field to evacuate a casualty and each time being driven back by sniper fire, Sgt. Leon Kraskin, an aid man, stood up and walked to the wounded man. The sniper fired again and the bullet grazed the back of his head, driving a piece of the helmet into his scalp. But Sgt. Kraskin disregarded his own wound and after applying compresses to the infantryman's wounds, dragged him across a hundred yards of ground to safety.

Working right along with the medics were the chaplains of the Combat Command. One G. I. expressed the surprise and lift it gave him in this way: "I looked up from my foxhole and there was ol' Chaplain Palmer. 'You'd better get down in here,' I said to him. 'You do the shooting and leave the praying to me,' he told me, and I'm damned if he didn't crouch right there in the open and say one. It made me feel a hell of a lot better!"

Pfc. L. T. Gotchy, another aid man, worked continuously without rest for two days and nights and finally, against his wishes, had to be evacuated himself. Not only did he care for the wounded, rescuing men from open ground considered untenable by infantrymen, but he also helped them dig foxholes and led tank convoys to and from the rear with loads of rations and water.

Despite the tremendous casualties, lack of sleep and rest and exposure to the bitter cold, the men continued to push forward. It was slow, agonizing fighting. By now the command had worked themselves forward almost to the edge of the woods. Ahead of them lay 1200 yards of open ground, covered by a dozen German guns.

Open Ground is Hell On the Infantry

During all this time, Lt. Col. Glenn G. Dickenson, 15th Infantry Bn. commander; Maj. Charles I. Webb, battalion S-3, and Maj. Emerson Hurley, then assistant S-3, had stayed in the forward positions, encouraging and helping the men. The sight of their battalion officers checking the furthermost outposts and undergoing the same dangers and hardships they were enduring gave the riflemen a morale boost that nothing else could have done at the time.

On the morning of 14 December, CC B attacked across the open ground. B and C Cos. of the 15th Infantry Bn. led, with A Co. in close support. Their objective was a quarry which was in another woods directly across the exposed ground. They planned to assault the quarry and push on quickly to the high ground northwest of Bilstein. A and B Troops of the 85th Reconnaissance Sq. were on the right flank. Each company of the 15th Infantry Bn. was supported by one platoon of tanks from each of the 81st medium tank companies. Ahead of the riflemen, artillery and mortar barrages were laid down by the 71st Artillery batteries and 81st Tank Bn. Mortar Platoon.

As the infantrymen moved down out of the woods to the open ground in the draw, the Germans turned every available mortar and artillery piece on the area. Pfc. Harry Grubert of the Infantry Bn.'s A Co. saw his squad leader killed by a mortar shell. Without hesitation he assumed command of the shaken and disorganized squad.

The forward observer for the 71st Artillery Bn., Lt. William S. Martin, was directing the fire of his batteries on enemy positions when an enemy shell crashed through the underbrush and dug into the ground beside him; it was a dud.

Sgt. Robert Rufiange saw ten members of his platoon fall seriously wounded when his 15th Infantry Bn.'s C Co. reached the draw. He administered first aid to them until all available bandages were exhausted and then under fire he went back and located two aid men. With their help he was able to evacuate the casualties.

Extensive mining and the boggy condition of the ground frustrated all attempts to use the tanks. Three Shermans were disabled by mines and the 81st Tank Bn.'s A Co. commander, Capt. Robert M. McNab, was wounded.

An infantryman who had been hurt when one of the tanks backed up lay 150 yards from the edge of the woods, completely exposed. When he called for help, Lt. Light and Sgt. Clarence H. McNeely crawled out, treated the man and pulled him back to the shelter of the woods.

Artillery, mortars and machine guns blasted and pounded the open ground over which the men were trying to attack. To advance was impossible. Nothing could live in that open field more than a few seconds. The men slowly pulled back from the exposed ground into the woods, carrying their wounded with them.

Speed and Surprise Do the Trick

That afternoon Thunderbolts and Lightnings were called in from the Tactical Aid Command to strafe and bomb enemy positions above the quarry. Sixteen 500-pound bombs were dropped. The bombs landed only a few hundred yards from CC B's forward positions. Blast from the explosions blew in the 75 mm. gun muzzle cover on a tank commanded by Sgt. Salvatore Candito.

The afternoon of 14 December, Col. Cole and Lt. Col. Le Roy H. Anderson, 81st Tank Bn. commander, came to Lt. Col. Dickenson's command post in the forward lines to confer and plan another attack.

The open ground had to be crossed. Col. Cole decided the only possible way to cross it was to mount the remaining infantry on the rear decks of the tanks and depend on the tank's speed to get them across. The attack was set for 0830 the following morning.

Next morning the tanks pulled up to the edge of the woods in a rough V formation, infantry mounted on the rear decks. The tanks roared across the open exposed ground. Churning faster and faster, they reached the halfway mark in the clearing and rolled toward the far edge. They had caught the Germans by surprise. Few shots were fired at them. As the tanks approached the quarry area, they opened up with their tank and machine guns, riddling the forest in front of them. Infantrymen jumped from the tanks and ran toward their first objective with its six antitank guns. They found the guns abandoned or destroyed. The bombing, heavy artillery and crushing tank fire had forced the Germans to retreat. The tankers and infantry moved on quickly toward their next objective, the high ground beyond the quarry.

There's Always Another Objective

Meanwhile the attached 330th Infantry Regiment, supported by the first and third platoons of the 81st Tank Bn.'s B Co., had pushed forward toward their objective, the town of Bergheim. They reached the town at noon.

At first it was intended to advance on the third objective, the high ground southeast of Bergheim, the same day. But little daylight remained of the short December day in which to organize and execute the plan. Riflemen did not jump off, therefore, until just before dawn the next morning. Because the two infantry battalions, the 15th and the 2nd Bn. of the 330th Regiment had suffered such heavy casualties, the attack was carried out by A and B troops of the 85th Reconnaissance Sq.

At 0900 Capt. Weldon M. Wilson, whose 81st Tank Bn.'s B Co. tanks were supporting the 85th, reported that all Germans had been cleared from the objective. He was then ordered to return with his tanks to the assembly area.

Late that afternoon a handful of men, all that was left of the 15th Infantry Bn.'s C Co., supported by the 2nd Platoon of tanks from the 81st Tank Bn.'s A Co., jumped off to attack the little town of Bilstein on the right flank.

As the tanks rolled toward the objective, S/Sgt. James P. Davis, who had become leader of the platoon after its lieutenant was wounded, noticed that only three of his five tanks were grinding across the open ground toward the town. He was unsuccessful in his attempts to make contact with the missing tanks by radio.

Later, when T/4 Herman Hawkins and Pfc. Arthur Medaros crossed the same mined field under fire, Sgt. Davis learned from them that their tanks had been disabled by mines.

Despite the heavy shelling, the riflemen cleared the town just before dark, flushing 17 prisoners out of the basements with grenades.

"In one of the basements we surprised a band of Krauts preparing a hot meal. They had fresh steaks from a cow they had just slaughtered," said Lt. Robert H. Hoffman, commander of the 15th Infantry Bn.'s C Co. "After we sent the prisoners back to the PW cage, we made certain the dinner wasn't wasted. It was our first hot meal in seven days."

After taking its objectives, the 15th Infantry Bn. dug in, and each morning repelled an enemy counterattack. On 19 December the battalion was attached to CC A and the next morning attack orders came down to them again. Their mission was to overrun the remaining enemy positions on the high ground west of Winden.

No Rest for the Engineers

"When we heard that order, we thought the jig was really up," said T/Sgt. William H. Guinn of C Co., 15th Infantry Bn., who had during the action on this front gone from squad leader to platoon sergeant, to platoon leader and finally to leader of the combined remnants of two platoons. "There were only 32 of us left in our company and we thought this attack would certainly finish off the rest of us."

On 20 December at 0915 they jumped off. B and C Cos. and the Machine Gun Platoon led the attack and A Co. was in reserve. By 1100 they had taken their objective, killing the Germans who put up a fight and driving the rest into Winden.

This same morning the 330th Regiment advanced southeast against Untermaubach, but because of the terrain conditions, a cliff on one side of the town, and extensive mining of the approach route, it was impossible to bring up tanks to support the infantry. They were unable to get beyond the outskirts of the town. B and C Troops of the 4th Cavalry Group, however, were successful in taking Bogheim.

After the infantry, without tank support, made another unsuccessful attempt to storm Untermaubach on 21 December, Capt. Rolf E. Mickelson, commander of B Co. of the 22nd Engineer Bn., received orders that his outfit would have to clear the road to the town that night at all costs.

Seven attempts had been made during the day and each one had failed because of the heavy concentrations of mortar and artillery fire that the Germans laid down on the road. That night the enemy guns continued to pound the road with interdictory fire, but Sgt. John J. Morgan and his crack mine-sweeping squad went to work with detectors and probes, determined to open an attack route for the tanks.

Earlier, Sgt. Lee Serratt and his crew had cleared the road from Bergheim to Bilstein so that bogged-down tanks could be evacuated. They had completed their mission in spite of the bursting shells of searing white phosphorous which the enemy had thrown in on them.

There had been no rest for the B Co. engineers during the entire action on this front. In one two-day period they had removed 450 mines, which included wooden box and S type mines and booby-trapped Teller mines. While mine-sweeping teams were busy digging mines out of the supply and attack routes, the rest of the company, working in day and night shifts, cleared the wreckage and debris from the roads. In six days they hauled 45 truck-loads of rubble out of Hurtgen and Kleinhau to repair roads into Obermaubach.

Sgt. Morgan and his men succeeded in lifting all of the mines from the Untermaubach road that night and early the next morning the tanks from the 2nd Platoon of the 81st Tank Bn.'s B Co.

The trees of Hurtgen looked pretty.

There were hidden block houses near Zweifall,

This is the tank we blew off the road.

The snow hit us as we hit Hurtgen.

Looks pretty but it ain't.

These Artille
work night

We covered our Fox Holes against Artillery.

But we couldn't keep them dry.

Cook your own — It's good.

A German tank and crew near Kelinhau.

Gotta write home.

Washing freezes.

Div. Hqs. in the snow.

Sgt. Cimo and Lt. Shanan check a map.

Pfc. Joe Sorobowski and Pvt. Roy E. Jones of 47th Inf.

Pvt. Herman J. Coburn open Xmas package.

A Teller mine — 12 lbs. TNT.

Fire Direction Center.

CCR switchboard in Hurtgen T/S Edgar Hamilton, Leo Millernine.

CCB Hq. near Kleinhau.

Fresh meat helped.

Xmas presents arrive in Hurtgen.

Snow then mud.

T/4 Doyle C. Nethery, T/4 Wayne D. Hood, Hurtgen.

Sgt. Larry Moore keeps it clean.

Maj. Phillipsborn at CCB Hqs. Hurtgen.

TD and Mine Destroyer in Hurtgen.

Lt. Willitz CCB near Kleinhau.

Capt. Lester, Lt. Bonam CCA Vicinity Grosshau.

A. mortar crew fire and dig in.

A TD near Grosshau.

nine exploder on a
didn't last long
h.

This one came into Bergstein and was captured.

Recovering a Tank.

The Dams we wanted
command in Hurtg
flooded the Roer Val
anyway.

liver, Gen. Bradley, Lt. Col.
rland, Gen Eisenhower, Col.
Lt. Col. Entrekin, Lt. Col.
onfer near Zweifall, Ger.

The C. G., the Chief, G-1, G-2, G-3.

The weather is fine.

Do the phones work now?

Near Gey a Bomb crater.

Gey—Let's get the
clear.

The medics had a job.

(Map) Brandenburg and Bergstein are representative of the edge of the Hurtgen Forest near the Roer River. The high ground on the north side of the Roer permitted observation for the enemy artillery and mortar fires even after the Germans had been forced across the stream. The area of the Roer River dams can be seen in the distance.

Cpl. Joe Swigerti.

Truck Engines arrive in Eupen.

Louis Filas—Roger 4 22 Eng. Rcn.

Cpl. Wile B. Foreste, 10th Tank.

T/5 Harry F. Gresham — 127th Ord.

34th Tank — Sgt. Montgomery, Sgt. Tac Sgt. Maffei, Sgt. Raymond, Pvt. Ledbetter, Seldon, Pfc. Persinger, Lt. Rogers, hear ele returns on radio.

T/5 Paul E. Schul, 127th Ord. changes tank engine.

T/5 George Behm 127th Ord. inside tank turret.

ancis Horvath repairs motor.

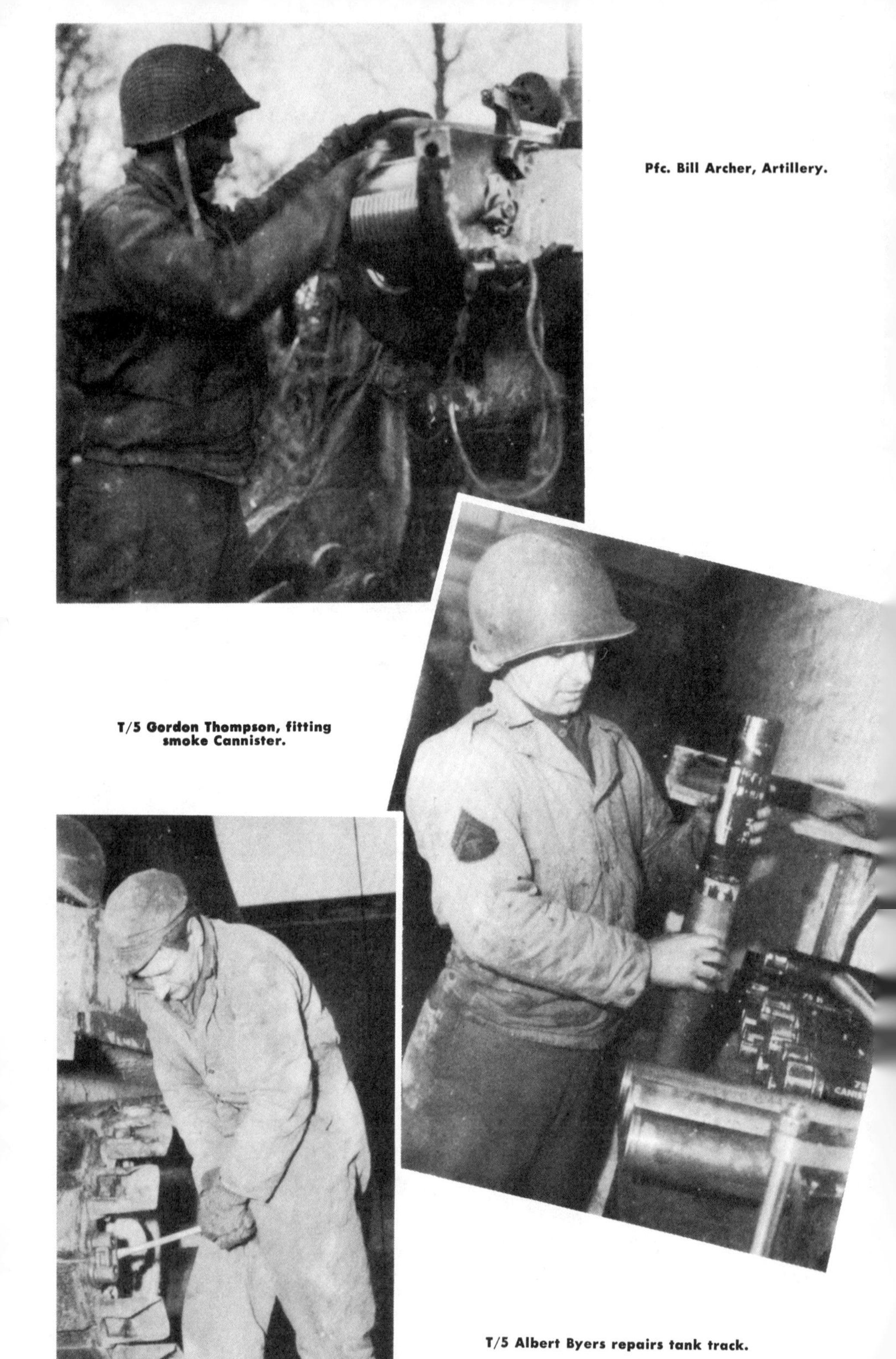

Pfc. Bill Archer, Artillery.

T/5 Gordon Thompson, fitting smoke Cannister.

T/5 Albert Byers repairs tank track.

Tanks tear down telephone wires.

T/5 Lewis Taylor prepares for air attack.

Siegfried line obstacles at Rotgen.

Rotgen, Ger.

At Monschau we hold out during Bulge.

Prisoners in Pepinster.

During the Bulge, we fought b side anyone we could find.

Overhead RR bridge near Malmedy.

erman Mark V al-red to resemble a American tank.

German self-propelled 75 mm. Note the 5th AD markings.

PW's at Eeichersctt by CAA.

1st Sgt. Ernest J. Roberts gets Battle Field Commission by Gen. Oliver and Lt. Col. Anderson, 81st Tank Bn.

Snow near Heudorf. Belgium.

We painted our Tanks white.

rolled into the town, blasting paths for the infantry. Rumbling up to each house in town, the tanks fired a high explosive shell into the front door and literally blew the defenders out into the hands of the infantry.

North of the town, on the road from Winden, a heroic stand was being made by A Troop of the 85th Reconnaissance Sq. By putting themselves into a pocket from which there was no withdrawal, they blocked every attempt by the Germans to reinforce the Untermaubach garrison from the north and made the successful assault on the town possible. For this action they received the "Presidential Citation."

Untermaubach fell at 1600 on 22 December. Two hundred prisoners were marched back to PW cages.

Out of the Line for Christmas

That night, after 12 days of the most bitter fighting, news came to the companies that they would be relieved immediately. Under cover of darkness they were to move out of the front lines and start toward a rest area in the rear.

"When the Germans heard the movement behind our lines, they decided to take advantage of the confusion and launch a local counterattack in our sector," said Lt. Warren A. Hedlin, commander of the 15th Infantry Bn.'s B Co.

In the darkness T/Sgt. Anton J. Kembic could hear the enemy soldiers coming up the hill, clicking the bolts of their guns. Crawling silently forward, he watched the Germans set up a machine gun which was to be the backbone of their attack. Retiring to his foxhole again, he waited for them to fire first so that he could be certain of the gun's position. Then he opened up, knocked out the gun and broke up the counterattack.

CC B was relieved on the night of 22 December, but two days later, on the morning of Christmas Eve, a few infantrymen from the 15th Infantry Bn. were still in the line. On the high ground overlooking Winden, eight men from C Co. huddled in foxholes, wondering how much longer they would be able to hold out.

For four days they had been there, suffering from the cold and sweating out the enemy shells and small arms fire that was thrown at them. During this time their only food had been a loaf of German bread which they had found in one of the foxholes. To quench their thirst they had licked icicles which had frozen on the edge of a piece of canvas.

At headquarters they were listed as "missing in action." No one knew they were there because the officer who had posted them had been evacuated as a casualty.

When in the early light of the morning they saw doughboys and frostcovered tanks emerge from the forest behind them, Cpl. Richard Stephen remarked, "Well, it's another attack."

Grabbing their rifles, they prepared to join the assault. But when the attackers reached their positions, they saw that these men were strangers. It was then that they learned their company had been relieved two days before. Picking up one member of their squad whose feet had been frozen, they headed home to their company for Christmas.

Alerted for Ardennes

The division was pulled back on 24 December to an assembly area in Belgium and was placed in 21st Army Group reserve. CC B bivouacked about four miles northeast of Verviers. On Christmas Eve all units were placed on a two-hour alert. They were ordered to be prepared to move south, if necessary, against the northern edge of von Rundstedt's salient on the Western Front.

Although snow suits were issued and vehicles painted white, the call to go into action against the German "bulge" did not come. Two days after Christmas the 71st Artillery Bn.'s Lt. Alexander D. Fraser and his driver, Sgt. Harold D. Freeman, were killed during a German air attack on Verviers, Belgium. Also killed in this bombing was CC B's Signal Officer, Lt. George M. Willets.

There was more enemy air activity on 31 December when a 500-pounder was dropped in the 71st Artillery Bn.'s area, but it caused no casualties. Then, on New Year's Day, seven ME 109's attacked the CC B area. Five were shot down.

XVIII

SNOW BATTLE

Belgium and Eicherschied

1 January–31 January

Most of January was relatively quiet for the Fifth Armored. As it sat amidst the snow-covered hills of Belgium, the fighting strength which had been drained from the division during the Battle of Hurtgen Forest was slowly infused again. New tanks and halftracks arrived to replace equipment that had been lost in the fighting. And reinforcements were assigned to the division to fill in the casualty-depleted ranks of the companies. Then near the end of the month, after the division had been transferred to the Ninth Army, one of its combat commands was again called upon to go into battle.

Combat Command A was attached to the 78th Infantry Division on 28 January and was given the mission of taking the town of Eicherschied in the Kesternich-Konzen area of the Siegfried Line. The 47th and 71st Armored Field Artillery Bns. moved into firing positions to support the attack.

The married A and B Cos. of the 34th Tank Bn. and the 46th Infantry Bn. plus the 34th Tank Bn. Headquarters Co., comprising a task force under Lt. Col. William L. Cabaniss, moved to the vicinity of Lammersdorf the night of 29 January. Task Force Burton stayed at Neudorf. The night was bitterly cold and deep, drifting snow covered the ground.

The attack on Eicherschied was set for the next morning.

At 0530 on 30 January, after a five-minute artillery preparation, the 78th Infantry Division jumped off, making two diverging attacks. One force pushed toward Huppenbroich; the other toward Imgenbroich. A Co., 22nd Engineer Bn., began work immediately behind the infantry to clear the enemy minefields for CC A's attack on the right flank of the infantry. The married A Cos. were to jump off at 0730, but clearing the minefields was hampered by the deep snow and the attack hour was delayed.

Lt. Leonard Hammer of A Co., 22nd Engineer Bn., directed the work in front of the tanks. Three flails were knocked out by mines and a fourth by direct fire while clearing the minefield.

At 1000 the A Cos. were ordered to attack through whatever mines remained.

Snow Makes Going Tough

Capt. Richard E. Biederman reconnoitered a route for his tanks around an ungapped minefield. A Co., 34th Tank Bn., rumbled down the main road, followed by A Co., 46th Infantry Bn. halftracks, then veered to the left into open country when they found the road blocked. The tanks, moving cross-country, ploughed through the heavy snow, but the halftracks stalled. A Co. infantrymen bailed out of their halftracks and began walking through the deep snow. The tanks churned toward Eicherschied, 3000 yards away, with three platoons in broad wedge formation, firing as they moved. They ploughed over desolate, snow-covered landscape with hedgerows marked by lines of deep, drifted snow. An anti-tank gun opened fire from the east, but a stiff breeze whipped up a cloud of fine snow which helped screen the tanks and its fire was inaccurate. Occasional rounds of German artillery dropped among the struggling infantrymen.

The tanks wallowed on through the snow, drifted in places into 14-foot high banks. They moved in a devious route through the hedgerows after several tanks bellied on large concealed stumps and had to be pulled off.

A Co. infantrymen struggled to keep up with the lumbering tanks, but it was impossible to keep pace. The infantrymen couldn't walk more than 60 to 70 yards without flopping in the snow for rest. Control of the infantrymen was difficult. The extreme cold froze up most of the infantry radios. Machine guns froze, too, and they had to depend on rifles, grenades and bazookas. Two companies of the 311th Infantry Regiment were following A Co., 46th Infantry Bn., and the companies became mixed as the snow capes everyone wore hid all rank and division insignia. Lt. Col. Cabaniss, reconnoitering on foot, was wounded and command of the assault force fell to the commander of the attached 1st Bn., 311th Infantry Regiment.

At 1130 Capt. Raymond Weeks, commander of B Co., 34th Tank Bn., and Capt. John W. Hewitt, commander of B Co., 46th Infantry Bn., came up with one platoon of the married B Cos., tanks towing the halftracks, and formed on the right of Capt. Biederman. Capt. Billy Devault's A Co., 46th Infantry Bn., could be sighted slowly moving up through the flying snow.

By 1230, A Co., 34th Tank Bn., had deployed behind the last defilade before Eicherschied. The infantry still struggled in the snow, far behind, so Capt. Biederman called for a Corps "time on target" concentration on the town. Twenty-one battalions of artillery hit Eicherschied at the same time. The town exploded in one violent mass.

The attack on the town started and the deployed forces moved over the crestline with all guns firing. Debris was still falling from the artillery concentration. Three 88's, camouflaged with white sheets, threatened the advancing tanks, one to the right and two to the left, and all with good fields of fire.

One enemy gun fired three rounds close to Sgt. William Kundman's tank. Kundman swung his turret quickly, his 75 mm. gun roared and pieces of the enemy gun flew into the air. Lt. Otho E. Thomas discovered a second gun and split the barrel with one round. Lt. Gerald F. Axner knocked out the third gun and T/5 Clayton Wainwright jumped from his tank, threw a white phosphorous grenade into the gun position, flushing the gun crew from their foxholes.

"Married Companies" Assault Town

The tanks rolled up to the edge of the town and stood outside, pumping shells into the houses and buildings until the infantry came up. At 1600 the assault was begun by the married A and B Cos. and the 311th Infantry Regiment in close support. A Cos. took the east half of the town, and the B Cos. the west half. Tanks pulled up to buildings, fired round after round of high explosive ino the doors and windows, then doughboys ran into the basements and dug out the terrified Germans. The tank-infantry teams, working with practised precision, cleaned out house after house, block after block. They were old hands at this business and they worked fast and sure at cleaning out the town.

By 1800 the town was clear and outposts were set up. A Co. engineers worked throughout the afternoon to clear the main road into Eicherschied of snow and mines. During the night a 311th Infantry Regiment patrol went to the Roer River and contacted the 8th Infantry Division.

The town finally yielded 230 prisoners, including three women, two in German army uniforms. The prisoners wore makeshift white camouflage suits with diapers, doilies, sheets and tablecloths predominating. They looked dirty, tired and beaten.

Lt. Mayo Elliott, A Co., 46th Infantry Bn., platoon leader, and his men captured a German medical aid station while mopping up the town. The German medics were armed with pistols. "The pistols are for the hopelessly wounded," a German medical officer explained apologetically. "We put the muzzle against the patient's heart, pull the trigger, and he is out of his misery."

At 0800 on 31 December the married A and B Cos. moved out to take the high ground beyond Eicherschied, and gained it with little resistance. That afternoon the 311th Infantry Regiment began to relieve CC A. The relief was completed at 2300 and the entire combat command moved to its former billets in Neudorf.

Men in CC A agreed that taking Eicherschied had been a good operation. Casualties had been extremely low, important ground had been taken and key enemy guns had been destroyed.

In this operation CC A captured or destroyed four anti-tank guns, one 150 mm. howitzer and three 120 mm. mortars. The 47th Artillery Bn. fired 2000 rounds in support and claimed the destruction of five additional anti-tank guns.

On 28 January the Fifth Armored moved to Hergenrath and then, on 5 February, to Herleen, in Holland.

XIX

THROUGH THE CABBAGE FIELDS

Roer to the Rhine

24 February—10 March

IN THE ROER to Rhine campaign the division began to fight the kind of war for which it was designed. Speed and firepower, the division's two important weapons, could be utilized, and enemy defenses crumbled. The division had picked up speed and had started to roll when it was stopped by the Rhine River.

Action from the Roer to the Rhine was characterized by ferocious fighting in the initial stages as the Germans tried to hold their strong prepared defenses east of the Roer. They fought bitterly for every yard of ground. Later, the enemy defenses broken, the division's tanks and halftracks rolled down the highways and cross-country, fighting a running battle all the way to the Rhine.

CC B was the first combat command committed, and struck the toughest defenses. Bad weather, fortified lines and soggy terrain hampered their movement, but the CC B armored columns battered their way through Erkelenz and Rheindahlen and cleared the area to Munchen-Gladbach.

CC A passed through CC B to attack through Viersen, Anrath and to the outskirts of Krefeld.

CC R, the last command into the fight, struck to the Rhine reaching the river at Orsoy after fighting through Huls, Mors and Repelen.

The division artillery fired its biggest mission helping the infantry divisions storm across the Roer River to begin the campaign. They fired more than 10,000 rounds in less than three hours in supporting the assault.

Combat Command B

Combat Command B was chosen to drive the first armored lance into enemy forces which faced the Ninth Army across the

Roer River. On 24 February it moved to Baesweiler, Germany. Then, at 0100 the following morning, it began to move across the river to the bridgehead which the 102nd Infantry Division had secured on the east bank. Task Force Dickenson, consisting of the married A Cos. of the 81st Tank and 15th Infantry Bns. and one platoon of A Troop, 85th Reconnaissance Sq., led the way.

Fires were still crackling and blazing in the battered town of Linnich as the tanks and halftracks rumbled between the charred walls, which leaned precariously over the streets, toward the treadway bridge that spanned the river. The bridge site was concealed under clouds of chemical smoke, but enemy artillery shells were still falling in the area. Enemy planes tried continuously to break through the ack-ack screens to get at the bridge. T/4 Raymond J. Gouck, of the 15th Infantry Bn.'s Service Co., ran out into a street to rescue a soldier who had been hit in the chest by a piece of falling flak.

After CC B assembled south of Hottorf, Gen. Oliver came to Col. Cole's command post and outlined the final details of the command's mission. It was to help the 102nd Infantry Division take Erkelenz by skirting around the town and cutting all communications with Rheindahlen. Also, CC B was to capture the five towns of Wockerath, Terheeg, Mennekrath, Kaulhausen and Venrath in order to secure the XIII Corps' east flank. H-hour was 12 noon, D-day was 26 February.

Col. Cole assigned the job of seizing these first objectives to Task Force Anderson, which consisted of the married B and C Cos. of the 81st Tank Bn. and 15th Infantry Bn. To accomplish his mission as quickly as possible, Col. Anderson divided his two married companies into four groups. In support he would have elements of B Co. of the 628th Tank Destroyer Bn. and the 71st Artillery Bn. He also decided that he would have to overrun the towns of Wey and Hof Roitz, two intermediate objectives, in order to secure the right flank of CC B's zone of action.

"All Objectives Taken"

At noon, under gray, rain-laden skies, the tanks and halftracks spilled out on the Rhineland plains and started rolling toward their objectives.

A Time magazine correspondent who watched the attack from the air wrote:

"From the air in a Piper Cub the tank drive was a thing of the sheerest military beauty: First came a long row of throbbing tanks moving like heavy dark beetles over the green cabbage fields of Germany in a wide swath – many, many tanks in a single row abreast. Then, a suitable distance behind, came another great echelon of tanks even broader, out of which groups would wheel from their brown mud tracks in the green fields to encircle and smash fire at some stubborn strong point. Behind this came miles of trucks, full of troops, maneuvering perfectly to mop up bypassed tough spots. Then came the field artillery to pound hard knots into submission. From the flanks sped clouds of tank destroyers, cutting across the landscape in wild swoops that hit the enemy and cut off communications with bewildering speed."

Artillery and small arms fire was thrown at the waves of tanks, but the heaviest fire was received from Holzweiler, where elements of the 11th Panzer Division were entrenched with anti-tank guns. Direct-fire enemy anti-tank guns knocked out six tanks.

Maintenance men of the 81st Tank Bn.'s B Co. pulled into a field near Wey and, after dodging anti-tank shells and machine gun tracers that whined over their heads, managed to evacuate two disabled tanks. Later they learned that the area was mined.

Six hours and 45 minutes after the assault began, all objectives had been taken. Twenty-five Germans had been killed, 16 captured, and six anti-tank guns and three mortars had been destroyed.

That night, after Task Force Anderson consolidated its positions around Mennekrath, Task Force Dickenson moved forward to the Erkelenz-Terheeg road. The entire combat command prepared to attack in the morning.

Fire Fight

The objective was the town of Rheindahlen, key to the defenses protecting the strategic city of Munchen-Gladbach. Task Force Anderson was to storm the town in a frontal assault while Task Force Dickenson was to knife around to the left flank and cut the railroad on the western edge of the town. Col. Cole instructed his task force commanders to move as fast as possible toward the main objective without stopping to clean out completely the intermediate towns.

The attack kicked off at 0700 and the tanks and halftracks started rumbling across a soft field on which a knocked-down British plane was scattered in a thousand pieces. Task Force Anderson was led by the married B Cos. of the 81st Tank Bn. and the 15th Infantry Bn., which advanced in two assault waves.

First opposition was encountered after they crossed the railroad northeast of Erkelenz and started moving north on the broad plain between Rath and Herrath. Although the towns on the flanks were pounded with artillery fire as the tanks by-passed them, anti-tank shells came whining out of Rath on the left flank, smashed into one of the tanks and set it ablaze. Swinging their 75's to the left, the tanks immediately poured direct counter-fire into enemy gun positions and they appeared to be silenced.

The handful of infantrymen who had been riding on the deck of the demolished tank found themselves the target for German mortar shells after the initial assault waves had pushed on and left them alone on the plain. Backing up into the by-passed town of Herrath on the right flank, they fought their way into one corner of the town, which was still in enemy hands.

"We fired at one of the houses and three Krauts came out with their hands raised," said Pfc. Abraham Lieberman. "I can speak a little German, and one of the Krauts showed us where they had three heavy mortars."

After following a communication line down a street, through a barnyard and kitchen and into a basement, Lt. Vincent Castner walked in and captured four German enlisted men and a captain, the latter an artillery observer.

A German Tank Captured

A little later Lt. Harold L. Spiro, B Co., 15th Infantry Bn., maintenance officer, and a crew of men were working on three halftracks that had bogged down in the soft ground about 200 yards north of Herrath when they noticed what appeared to be a company of enemy infantrymen followed by four self-propelled guns, heading toward the town. Climbing into the halftracks, they turned their machine guns on the enemy column and the Germans scattered and retreated. Before they withdrew, however, the German self-propelled guns opened up and destroyed two of the halftracks.

When Lt. Spiro and his men pulled back into Herrath, an enemy Mark IV tank rumbled out from behind one of the buildings and started down the street. It stopped as the tank commander spotted the Americans. The crew jumped out of the tank, made futile attempts to hide, then decided to surrender.

T/Sgt. Anton J. Kembic and a squad of men, after capturing several prisoners, set up defense positions to hold one corner of Herrath until a battalion from the 102nd Infantry Division arrived to finish cleaning out the town.

When the married C Cos. drew abreast of Rath, more anti-tank shells began to swish across the plain. The supporting batteries of the 71st Artillery Bn. laid down a barrage on the town, and while the smoke from the bursts was still spiraling above the rooftops, a platoon of the 15th Infantry Bn.'s C Co. was sent to reconnoiter the enemy gun positions.

The platoon returned, with the report that no enemy guns could be found in the town. As the C Cos. pushed north behind the B Cos. assault waves, however, observers spotted a column of vehicles 1000 yards away, heading toward Rheindahlen on a parallel route. Through binoculars they recognized the first vehicle as an American light tank. The early morning mist which clung to the plain prevented them from identifying the rest of the vehicles. Because he did not know the exact position of Task Force Dickenson, Col. Anderson ordered the tankers to hold their fire. The two forces continued to advance in parallel paths for more than a mile.

A German Column is Destroyed

But when the lead elements of the married C Cos. reached the northern edge of a woods northeast of the town of Buchholz, they encountered a cross-fire directed at them from the woods and from the column on the parallel route. The vehicles in this column, which had deployed off the road, could now be identified as four German 75 mm. self-propelled guns mounted on Mark IV chassis and a single American light tank, repainted with German insignia. The fire from the woods came from two anti-tank guns which had allowed the initial assault wave to pass unmolested.

The enemy fire knocked out two of the 81st Tank Bn.'s C Co. tanks. The rest of the big Shermans opened up in a thunderous barrage which sent streams of shells pouring both to the east and to the west. All of the enemy guns were quickly silenced, including the captured American light tank.

"If you were to tell me that a column of tanks was fired on by two German anti-tank guns from a distance of only 200 yards and four self-propelled guns from 400 yards, and only two tanks were hit, I'd call you a damned liar. But that's what actually happened," said Capt. William L. Guthrie, commander of C Co., 81st Tank Bn.

Meanwhile, the married B Cos., having rolled forward past Buchholz to Hilderath and finally west to Shriefers, overran six German 170 mm. artillery pieces between Sittard and Schriefers. The lightning speed of their advance had caught these guns unmanned, the crews still sleeping in nearby houses.

But when they reached the approaches to Rheindahlen they ran up against a well of intense fire from anti-tank and flak guns entrenched in the town. Their position became extremely critical when anti-tank guns started blasting them from both their flanks.

Extremely fast, accurate tank fire smashed the enemy on the flanks, and at the same time the married B Cos. moved into defensive positions behind the buildings in Schriefers.

After watching the bursts of artillery shells creep closer toward his halftrack, T/5 Bluford Evans of the 15th Infantry Bn.'s B Co. bailed out of the driver's seat and hit the dirt just as another shell smashed into the empty halftrack and set it ablaze. Cpl. Evans had lost another halftrack under similar circumstances during the drive across France.

When Pfc. John T. Tavoularis jumped to the ground from the tank on which he was riding, he became entangled in German barbed wire. The tank's commander, Lt. Leonard L. Keene, Jr., not knowing that the infantryman was trapped in the rear of his tank, ordered it backed up to avoid the anti-tank fire. Other doughboys looked away as they saw Pfc. Tavoularis fall and the huge Sherman roll back over him. But the earth was soft and the tank, straddling him, pressed him into the pliable ground without injuring him.

"The enemy shells scorched the outsides of four of our tanks and nicked four more, but only two tanks were really knocked out," said Capt. Weldon M. Wilson, commander of B Co., 81st Tank Bn. "If we had moved more slowly in that attack, most of our force would have been completely wiped out. It was speed that saved us."

Rheindahlen A Tough Nut

On the left flank, Task Force Dickenson was pushing forward, but not without difficulty. After crossing the Erkelenz-Rheindahlen road, the tankers and infantrymen found an anti-tank ditch, stretching all the way south to Erkelenz, blocking their route. Col. Dickenson pulled his force back and sent it around to the east of Rath and headed north along the axis of the highway.

Except for sporadic fire from Rath, they did not meet determined opposition until the tanks and halftracks of the married A Cos. came within sight of Rheindahlen. Here, after overrunning three German 75 mm. artillery pieces at Ihipshoven, they became the target for enemy anti-tank guns. Time fire burst overhead.

"We could hear the direct fire shells going over us and we thought they were scraping the top of the halftrack," said T/4 William Henke, radio operator in the 15th Infantry Bn. headquarters. "After the shells went over us, we could see them hit the ground, bounce and then explode."

Toughest knot in the enemy's Rheindahlen defense system was a thickskinned Mark VI tank.

"Three of the Tiger tank's shells ripped into our tank," said Lt. Robert P. Lant, platoon leader in the 81st Tank Bn.'s A Co. "The first two smashed our front sprockets and the third tore off our .50 caliber turret gun. But our 75 mm. gun was still okay, so we slammed about 12 shells back at the German tank."

Climbing out of his disabled Sherman, Lt. Lant boarded another tank whose commander had been wounded. He continued to lead his platoon in its swift advance. As the other tanks moved on, the Mark VI became the special baby of the platoon sergeant, S/Sgt. Jack O. Galpin, and his crew.

"We fired eight rounds to the direct front," said Sgt. Galpin. The Kraut tank was maneuvering around, backing up and coming forward to fire, but I know we hit it at least twice."

While Sgt. Galpin and his crew were firing to their right flank, an enemy anti-tank gun opened up from the left flank and knocked out their tank.

"More of our tanks were moving up behind us, and when ours was hit, the other really poured it into that Tiger tank," said the platoon sergeant.

The Mark VI was finally knocked out by a round from the tank commanded by Lt. Shirley J. Duran. More than 36 rounds had been fired at the enemy tank before it was destroyed.

An enemy infantry attack, two platoons strong, started to move south out of the town toward the married B Cos. Tanks and halftracks leveled their guns into the advancing Germans, swept the ranks with fire, and broke up the assault. The remnants fell back into the town.

Crews of several emplaced 88's came forward and surrendered to Task Force Dickenson, but two anti-tank guns to the north of the town opened up and knocked out four more tanks.

The Air Corps Away From Home

One of these tanks disabled by the high velocity guns was the forward observation post for a section of the 81st Tank Bn. 105 mm. assault guns. It was hit three times. One of the shells, passing through both gas containers, set the tank on fire.

Scrambling out of the assistant driver's seat came Thunderbolt Pilot T. E. Todd, Air Corps liaison officer.

"I instinctively felt for my parachute when I started to bail out," said Lt. Todd, veteran of 51 Thunderbolt missions.

After clearing the tank, he was about to take off across country when he was knocked to the ground by the tank gunner, Pvt. John L. Sullivan, who leaped from the blazing turret and landed on Todd.

With the rest of the crew, he then scrambled into a shell hole as the advancing doughs, mistaking the tankers for Germans, started spraying them with small arms fire. The firing ceased when two crew men crawled toward the infantrymen and identified themselves.

The pilot then decided to tag along behind a column of prisoners moving toward the rear, but incoming shells scattered the group and he found himself again heading for a hole. In on top of him came the tank driver, Pvt. Clarence Bilbrey.

After assisting a wounded doughboy to the medics, he finally reached the command post. Here he assessed his losses, which included his bedroll, binoculars and a wallet containing 200 dollars.

"I also lost my flying boots," he said. "I left them in one of the holes. They're not so good for flying low."

Most of the halftracks of both task forces had become mired down during the cross-country push toward Rheindahlen. Nine halftracks had been completely demolished. And the tankers found that they had left only a limited supply of ammunition.

For the rest of the morning the task forces remained on the southern approaches to the town, but that afternoon Task Force Dickenson, after locating a route around the maze of anti-tank ditches, moved up the western side of the town and cut the railroad. Then, when waves of advancing doughs from the 102nd Infantry division took over the positions to the south of the town, Task Force Anderson moved to the high ground on the southeast corner of Rheindahlen. At CC B headquarters, air panels were laid out and Col. Cole asked the air liaison officer to call Tactical Air Command for air support.

When the skies cleared that afternoon, the P-47's came roaring over, orbiting on the signal panels that pointed to their objective. As they passed over the town, orange puffs of enemy fire rose to meet them. Over the air liaison radio came the message, "Light flak over target."

Column Cover

The artillery liaison officer, Capt. Richard A. Rowlands, radioed from his peep to the 71st batteries for a counter-flak barrage and red and white smoke shells to mark the target. The artillery fire was laid, corrected and laid again. Then the Thunderbolts made a wide sweep toward the target and, peeling off singly, dived and dumped their loads. The town rocked from the tremendous explosions.

Tactical Air Command sent five flights of P-47's to support the CC B assault. Three flights reduced the enemy fire from the woods to the northeast of the town. Two flights attacked enemy vehicles moving east from Viersen and also destroyed an ammunition dump, numerous vehicles and gun positions in the town.

While the noise of bombing and strafing was still rumbling across the plains, tankers of both task forces opened up and laid down a barrage of direct fire on the town. Behind this preparation the infantry pressed in and, flushing out several hundred prisoners, cleared the town without firing a shot.

This two-day battle which smashed a path through the Germans' Roer River defenses and started the rush to the Rhine cost CC B nine halftracks and one peep completely destroyed, and 20 tanks disabled by enemy shells. Task Force Anderson lost eight men killed and 39 wounded, while Task Force Dickenson suffered two men killed and 16 wounded.

Enemy losses were estimated at 150 killed, 150 wounded and 147 taken prisoner. Material captured and destroyed included four 75 mm. anti-tank self-propelled guns, three dual purpose 88's, 12 anti-tank guns of various calibers, three 75 mm. artillery pieces, three 105 mm. howitzers, six 170 mm. artillery pieces, six 120 mm. mortars, two Mark IV tanks, one Mark V tank and one captured American light tank.

Enemy divisions that participated in the defense of Rheindahlen included elements of the 338th Infantry Division and the 130th Panzer Lehr Division.

Only a Mop Up is Left

On 28 February, the day after Rheindahlen fell, CC B consolidated its positions around the town while the 102nd Infantry Division pushed north toward Hardt, to the west of Munchen-Gladbach. CC A passed through CC B to go into action around Hardt and start driving toward Viersen.

On 1 March Col. Cole organized a task force led by Capt. Harold M. Schiering which consisted of D Co. (light tank company) of the 81st Tank Bn., B Troop of the 85th Reconnaissance Sq. and one platoon from the 628th Tank Destroyers. Their mission was to block all roads from Wickrath north through Rheydt to Munchen-Gladbach and to make contact with the 29th Infantry Division which was attacking the strategic city on the right flank.

Capt. Loran L. Vipond's B Troop cleared the woods south of Rheydt that morning and linked up in the city with elements of the 29th Division. That night the D Co. light tanks rolled up the west side of Munchen-Gladbach and occupied the towns of Venn and Poth.

Sent out to police and post "Off Limits" signs in captured Gunhoven, Sgt. Vincent T. Catapano and his CC B Military Police detachment confused the name with Genhulsen, which had not yet been cleared, and drove into the wrong town.

"We thought something was wrong when the people started leaning out of windows waving white towels and sheets," said Sgt. Catapano. "We started asking questions and found we were the first GI's to enter the town."

All three task forces remained south and west of Munchen-Gladbach for the next two days, consolidating their positions and flushing bypassed Germans from their areas. Enemy planes bombed and strafed CC B's scattered position on 3 March, causing some casualties. That night the command moved past Munchen-Gladbach and north to the outskirts of Kempen, where it bivouacked.

On 11 and 12 March the different CC B units occupied the areas in and around the towns of Oedt and Vorst. Here they garrisoned the communities and set up military government machinery. The 71st Artillery batteries took over firing positions on the Rhine River. With a headquarters established at Meere Busch, their mission was to support the 11th Cavalry Group which was outposting the west bank of the river.

All units prepared and waited for the order which would send them on their last campaign on the Westen Front.

Combat Command A

Crossing the Roer River on 26 February, CC A moved up behind CC B as reserve. The combat command had a dual job. It was in immediate reserve and also was to protect the corps' right flank. At noon 28 February the command was relieved from this mission and given the task of attacking northeast from Hardt to pass between Viersen and Munchen-Gladbach, cutting communications south and southeast of Viersen. Early next morning this mission was changed to send the command all the way to the Rhine.

During the night Major Fuller, 46th Infantry Bn. executive officer, led a patrol to the anti-tank ditch north of Hardt. The ditch was undefended, but the road over it was partially damaged. Lt. Frank Czuhajewski, 46th Infantry Bn., led a platoon of dismounted infantry over the ditch and toward the town of Rasseln. There they set up outposts to protect the crossing.

At 0710 CC A jumped off to the east from Rasseln, the married C Cos. of the 34th Tank Bn. and the 46th Infantry Bn. leading. By 0815 the C Cos. were stopped by soft ground and the B Cos. passed through and attacked north up the main road. Tank and machine guns on the lead tanks fired continuously, probing the woods, houses and ditches for Germans. This reconnaissance fire broke the spirit of any Germans who might have wanted to fight and the command moved rapidly through Bockert, Ober Beberich, Unter and Hamm with little opposition. Whenever the column halted briefly, infantrymen piled out of their halftracks and rooted out the German soldiers hiding in basements. Few prisoners were taken, for the speedy advance allowed few halts.

T/5 R. C. Webb, 46th Infantry Bn., searched one house and found seven German officers preparing to sit down to a hot meal. Webb's squad hustled the officers off as PW's, dashed back to the house and enjoyed the hot food before the column pulled out.

"Bring Up the Engineers!"

Despite the German's disinclination to fight the tank column, any vehicle that wandered up a side road away from the main body was greeted enthusiastically by machine gun and bazooka fire.

Lead elements hit a snag when they found the road underpass under the Viersen—Munchen-Gladbach railroad badly damaged and impassable. By 1430 a new route was found and the column rolled on through the village of Robend.

In a few minutes the column was roaring down the main road from Viersen to Anrath. The bridge over the Niers Canal could be seen far ahead, still intact. Lt. Marvin Orgill, B Co., 34th Tank Bn., raced toward it with his point platoon. Shooting as it rolled, the column thundered faster and faster toward the bridge. Orgill was pounding his medium tank 20 miles an hour and was only 100 yards away from the bridge when the explosion came. The Germans had blown the bridge in his face.

"Bring up the engineers," yelled Orgill over the radio, and before the officer could climb from his tank, Capt. Thomas Grose, commander of A Co., 22nd Engineer Bn., skidded up in a peep. He and Lt. Col. Burton quickly examined the bridge, found that one lane had been destroyed and the other was too weak to carry tanks. Already B Co. infantrymen, lugging machine guns and mortars, were scrambling across the blown bridge and fanning out on the other side to set up a hasty bridgehead.

Enemy soldiers milled around in confusion in the distance. Many disappeared into a large barn 1000 yards away from the bridge. T/Sgt. Claude Newton zeroed his mortars on the barn. His third round blew up both the barn and the congregating Germans.

"Move off the road and let the bridge trucks pass," came the call on the radio, and the heavy bridging equipment lumbered by the column, headed for the canal bank.

As the heavy engineer trucks rolled up, Sgt. Mike Woitow began to inspect the damaged span. Since the bridge was only partially demolished, he reasoned that only a portion of the demolition charge had exploded. Deep inside a concrete culvert Sgt. Woitow found a 100-pound live charge. He wriggled his way through the narrow opening and into the culvert. Lying flat in the narrow, cramped space, his arms stretched out ahead of him, Sgt. Woitow began the delicate job of disarming the charge. The men watched breathlessly from the bank until, at last, they saw Woitow inch his way out of the culvert and exhibit the detached fuse.

The engineers went to work, laboring furiously to speed the repair of the bridge. One hour and five minutes later, the span strengthened with 48 feet of treadway bridge, the engineers waved on the tanks and halftracks. The married C Cos. spurted across, pushing toward Anrath four miles away.

Road Blocks Pay Off

Tank machine guns chattered, tank guns boomed as the command cut a swath to Anrath. At 2000 the C Co. tanks and infantry poured into the town, fanned out to cover the town like a blanket. Again speed had paid off. The enemy was completely surprised and three gun crews were captured in their billets before they could man their guns. In many houses lights burned brightly, radios played and hot bread baked in the ovens.

Strong roadblocks were set up immediately on roads leading into Anrath. At one outpost Sgt. Dale Jeanneret snuggled his tank up against a building, pointed his long 76 mm. gun down a straight stretch of road and waited for Germans. Almost immediately a German army truck rumbled down the road toward him. Five hundred yards away the truck slowed down, started to creep toward the town. Jeanneret couldn't see the truck in the darkness, but he heard it coming closer and closer. Now it was 400 yards away, now 300, 200, 100 – and Jeanneret picked up the truck's dim outline in his sight. Fifty yards away the German suddenly saw the tank, turned his truck to flee. Jeanneret took his time, carefully placed his sight reticle on the truck's cab, squeezed his 76 trigger. The gun roared, blast flames from the 76 lighted up the buildings, and the truck exploded as the round struck. Jeanneret played his machine gun around the burning truck to pick up survivors, then relaxed in his seat as he watched the German truck burn.

Roadblocks were an old story to Jeanneret, for he had received the Distinguished Service Cross for knocking out three German tanks by himself on another roadblock back in France.

The companies in town kept busy until 0400, manning roadblocks and cleaning out German soldiers hiding in basements. Lt.

Champ Montgomery, on outpost with his B Co., 46th Infantry Bn., platoon, saw four Germans with bazookas, riding bicycles up the road into town. He nailed all four with his M-1 before they could dismount. A German dispatch rider came into Anrath on a motorcycle, meekly gave up a valuable map showing dispositions of the 15th Panzer Grenadier Division and the 2nd Parachute Division, the German forces defending Krefeld.

Throughout the night the Germans continued to pour into the town, not knowing it was in American hands. All were killed or captured by the roadblocks. The enemy had been building up his forces from Krefeld to Anrath, but CC A's quick capture of Anrath disrupted German plans for defenses along the Niers Canal.

On to the Rhine

Early next morning, 2 April, Task Force Burton jumped off with the married C Cos. leading, headed straight for the Rhine. Just outside Anrath the leading platoon caught heavy anti-tank fire and artillery from the woods northeast of the town. Three halftracks and one peep were quickly lost and the column halted briefly. Capt. Claude E. Cason lost his halftrack and peep and had to rely on hand signals for communication.

P-47's wheeling overhead were brought in to strafe and bomb the woods and CC A artillery pounded the area as soon as the planes cleared. The 3rd Platoons of the C Cos. took over the lead and continued the attack.

The P-47's and artillery effectively neutralized fire from the troublesome woods, but sporadic fire was received along the column until the area was cleaned by the 120th Infantry Division at noon. A later reconnaissance showed twelve 20 mm. guns and six 122 mm. howitzers emplaced in the woods.

Married C Cos. continued leading, working over all possible enemy positions with machine gun and tank fire. Capt. William Blakely's command tank of C Co., 34th Tank Bn., was hit four times with high explosive during the drive, but kept rolling. At 1130 there came a change of orders and the married C Cos. pulled off the road at the crossroads just west of the great Krefeld Steel Works. CC A's axis of advance was changed from north of Krefeld to south of the city.

In the afternoon, C Co. pulled back on the road and continued the attack, moving south and east to avoid the steel works. The column slammed through Votzhofe and Hoxhofe. Just beyond Hoxhofe, Lt. Robert Brown, who was riding at the point, and Capt. Blakely both spotted a long tank column advancing toward them on a road to their right. Capt. Blakely immediately deployed his company to attack the column, then waited. As the column came nearer, it proved to be a combat command of the 2nd Armored Division which had been driving up from the south. Both armored divisions were ahead of schedule and the meeting came unexpectedly.

Late in the afternoon Task Force Burton moved into Fischeln to relieve the 2nd Armored Division. Capt. Blakely's luck ran out for the day and his Sherman was knocked out by a German tank which was firing at a range of 2000 yards from the suburbs of Krefeld.

In Fischeln, more than 8000 German civilians and soldiers had packed themselves into a modern air raid shelter to escape the battle. The shelter was hopelessly overcrowded, but they had entered the shelter voluntarily, so the combat command posted a guard and saw that they remained there. All during the night CC A manned strong roadblocks on roads leading into Krefeld.

End of the Fight

Next day Capt. Thomas Ryan, Sgt. Steven Mainczyk and Lt. Edouard Tresca from the division's CIC detachment and T/5 Lester Kraft from CC A started out to post "Off Limits" signs on the huge Krefeld Steel Works. They found they were the first Americans to enter the mill. Although they were fired on as they entered the plant, they rounded up 14 German prisoners and liberated 1500 hysterically happy slave workers. The steel mill, one of the largest in Germany, employed 4000 persons at peak production, making turret and heavy castings for Tiger tanks.

CC A remained south of Krefeld on the morning of 3 March, prepared to assist the 102nd Division. During the afternoon and evening the combat command moved to St. Hubert, where they searched the town and rounded up weapons and prisoners. Task

Force Jones occupied the towns of Tonisberg, Vluyn and Schaephuysen and also conducted searches.

The married A Cos. were sent on a hurry-up reinforcement mission to CC R, now fighting on the Rhine River at Orsoy. CC R, however, had smashed most of the resistance and needed little help to polish off the fast-crumbling German defenses west of the Rhine. The A Cos. returned to CC A on 8 March.

Combat Command R

CC R entered the fight east of the Roer River on 3 March, when it was ordered to cut communications north of the Moers-Rheinberg area in a drive to the Rhine River.

The combat command was assembled at Rheindahlen. It had crossed the Roer on 26 and 27 February, taking up positions near Hottorf to protect the XIII Corps' right flank behind CC B. On 1 March the command had moved up to Rheindahlen to prepare for the mission.

The married B Cos. of the 10th Tank and 47th Infantry Bns., led by Lt. Col. Boyer, were to cross the Niers Canal at Oedt, move through Kempen and Huls and northeast to the Rhine. The married companies moved out at 1250 on 3 March, with C Co., 22nd Engineer Bn., two platoons of the 628th Tank Destroyers, and a platoon of D Co., 10th Tank Bn., light tanks.

A platoon of C Troop, 85th Reconnaissance Sq., moved out ahead to look for bridges over the Niers Canal when the span on the main road between Greath and Kempen was found impassable. One damaged bridge was found.

T/4 Charles Winslow and his bulldozer of C Co., 22nd Engineer Bn., doubled the column, roared past the tanks and halftracks to the canal. When forward elements reached the bridge, Winslow had it ready for use. The column lumbered across the bridge at 1330, passed through the 84th Infantry Division at Huls and plunged forward, driving 17 miles in a half hour before the column ran into road craters. Dug-in infantry opened fire as the tanks and halftracks rolled to a stop. Lt. Ernest Sauer's Sherman picked off a self-propelled gun that threatened the halted column.

Once again Winslow raced his bulldozer up to the head of the column, with the light tanks of D Co., 10th Tank Bn., clearing the way. While the "little Dog" tanks covered him, his 'dozer churned back and forth, pushing earth into the craters. The road repaired, the tanks and halftracks roared on.

Infantry Assault Hill

At 1600, Task Force Boyer met its first stiff resistance where the road entered a deep cut. Atop a 100-foot hill overlooking the cut, dug-in enemy had prepared to stem the armored advance. While the Shermans blasted at the German 37 mm. guns, machine gun nests and infantry positions, the B Co. infantrymen poured out of their halftracks and assaulted the hill, covered by the tankers' fire. The infantrymen took 50 prisoners and killed the rest of the enemy force, crushing the resistance.

Engines roared as the armored column moved out again. Half an hour later the tanks and halftracks blasted through Tonisburg. Northeast of the town the enemy had blown craters in the road along the edge of a wooded area. The armored column turned right on a secondary road, attempted to attack toward the woods across a field in platoon line. Three tanks bogged down, but were recovered. As the tanks moved through the area, S/Sgt. Robert Graham, later commissioned a lieutenant, spotted a German vehicle in the woods and nailed it with his tank gun.

Out on the main road again, Lt. Col. Boyer's task force lunged forward so fast that it began overtaking fleeing German columns. Outside of Moers the B Cos. were stopped by tank ditches and anti-tank fire. Lt. Cullin's tank was destroyed. Sgt. Graham took command of the leading tank platoon and continued the fight.

Resistance became so strong that a halt was called for the night, and CC R stopped at Neukircherfeld and set up defensive positions. Houses and basements, full of enemy troops, were mopped up until late that night. Twenty-six prisoners were taken in the 95th Artillery battery positions alone. The enemy was active throughout the night, and the troops received small arms, mortar and artillery fire.

That night Col. Anderson sent C Troop of the 85th Reconnaissance Sq. out on a troop mission to probe enemy positions. They met resistance on every route, and determined that the

Near Linnich a Teller Mine.

enkirchen.

for operations across the Roer River.

Across the Roer we get more prisoners.

Linnich was al unpassable.

Sgt. Louis J. Chlin, 47th AIB beside German Mark IV.

Capt. Peterson, 47th AIB.

Conald P. McNeil, T/5 Harold Ashby, Pfc. Jacob F. Hooven fried egg sandwich.

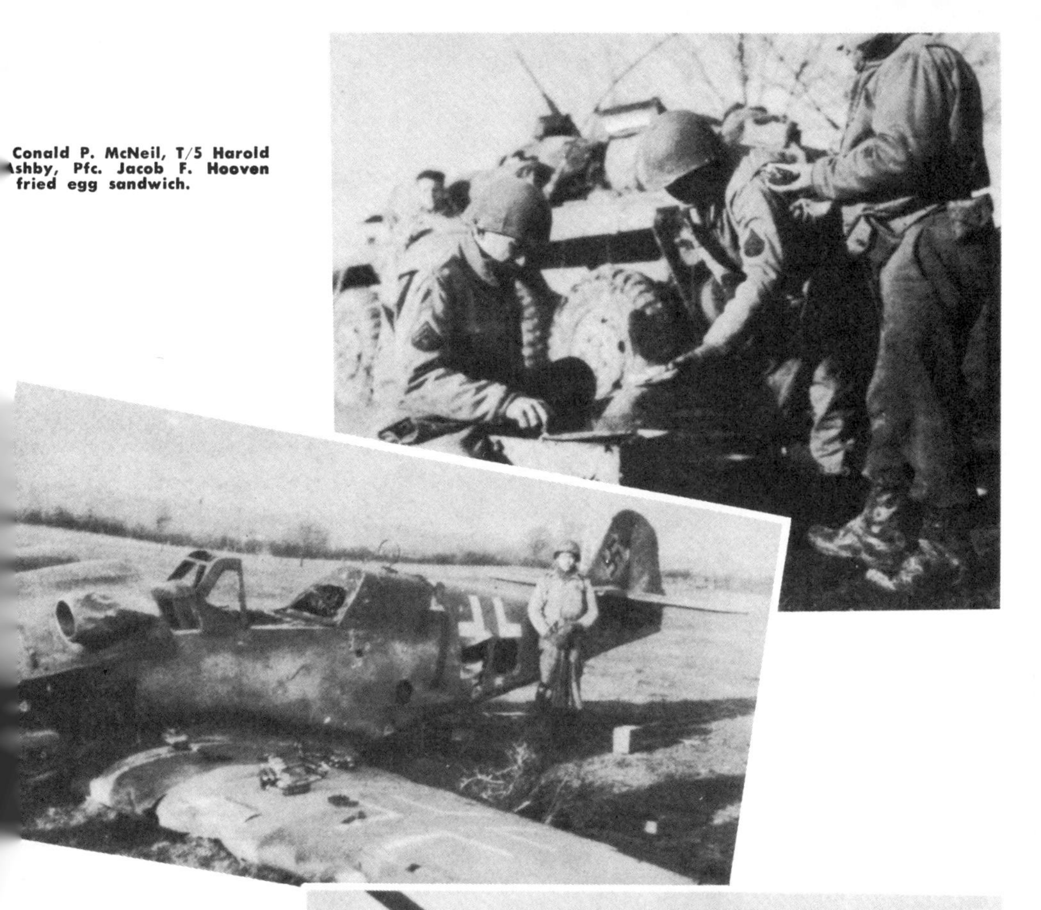

vt. William H. Rhoads helped shoot this down.

Ready for Air Alert.

Pfc. Charles Bavesik of 127th Ord. works on damaged Peep.

Cutting off Munchen-Gladbach.

Gen. Oliver and Gen. Baade are decorated at Munchen - Gladback by French Gov.

Erkeleuz — more PW's

ne were ready to quit.

Lt. James J. Jones Artillery.

On to the Rhin

Some enemy c
by air D-34th

Resistance in Tangermunde.

An enemy Bazooka team which first took its toll.

Paul Hedley painted this at Vorst. R. Gauch, Sgt. V. Noggle, Sgt. Floyd ith.

We turn an 88 around and fire across the Rhine.

Orsoy on the Rhine.

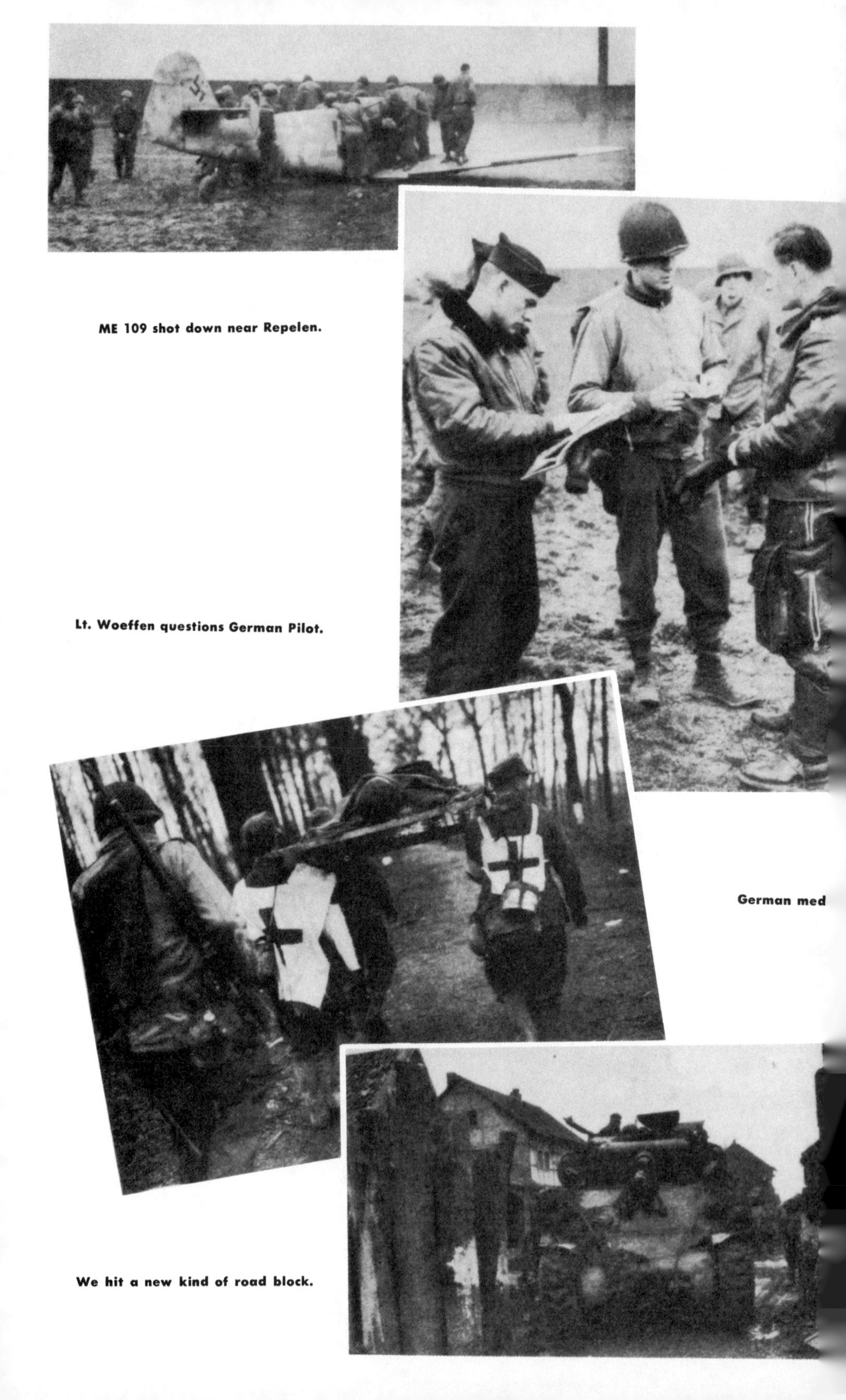

ME 109 shot down near Repelen.

Lt. Woeffen questions German Pilot.

German med

We hit a new kind of road block.

enemy had established himself along the Moers-Utfort-Repelen-Lintfort road.

On the morning of 4 March, Lt. Col. Hamberg's task force moved out. It consisted of the married A and C Cos., supported by the 2nd Platoon of C Co., 628th Tank Destroyer Bn., and the Armored Platoon of C Co., 22nd Engineer Bn. Their mission was to pass through Task Force Boyer, thrust rapidly to Repelen and pave the way for the push to the Rhine by seizing and holding road nets to cut enemy escape routes. The married B Cos. of Task Force Boyer went into CC R reserve.

Under heavy enemy fire, Task Force Hamberg lashed out from Moers, the married A Cos. of the 10th Tank Bn. and the 47th Infantry Bn. leading. An hour later the armored column ran into artillery, bazooka and small arms fire at Sandfor. S/Sgt. William Twilley, in the lead tank, sent 75 mm. high explosive shells crashing into houses along the road as he approached the town.

In the woods to his right Twilley suddenly spotted a group of Germans. He reported them over his radio. "Move out," came the order, and he started into town. A German self-propelled 75 mm. gun was emplaced by a house to the right of the road. Its crew, unable to get to the gun in time, had hidden in the basement.

As Twilley prepared to blast the enemy gun, a bazooka shell hit his tank. The crew bailed out. German infantrymen jumped from foxholes and rushed the crew. Sgt. Twilley eluded them and made his way to the rear, but his assistant driver, Pfc. William Payne, was wounded and was taken prisoner by the Germans. They took him to the basement of a nearby house.

Captured Tanker Is Liberated

Leading a force of 47th infantrymen, Twilley returned, recaptured his wounded assistant driver, and helped him back to the medical aid men. Cpl. William P. Fuller cleared out the remaining bazookamen with his carbine. S/Sgt. Louis J. Ahlin destroyed the 75 mm. gun with a grenade.

The tankers and infantrymen worked through the town with practiced skill, the tanks blasting the houses, the infantrymen digging the enemy out of the cellars. An air raid shelter at the far edge of town yielded many prisoners. An hour later, after taking 200 prisoners, the combat command again headed for Repelen.

Houses lined the road to Repelen, and there were fire trenches at close intervals. The column crawled as the infantrymen walked by the tanks, cleaning bazookamen out of the foxholes and digging Germans out of basements. It was a house-to-house fight all the way. German artillery began to fall on the column, causing casualties among the infantrymen.

While the married A Cos. worked through Repelen, driving out enemy artillery and cleaning the remaining infantrymen from houses, the married C Cos. moved out at noon, pushing up along the right flank to cut the Moers-Rheinkamp road. There they set up roadblocks for the night.

The following morning, 5 March, the C Cos. pushed up the road to Rheinkamp and seized the key highway junction leading from Repelen to Orsoy, the Rhine town four miles to the east. Their mission was to hold the crossroad open for CC R forces driving up from Repelen toward Orsoy.

As the C Cos. waited, a column of men and vehicles appeared, moving toward their roadblock. Believing it to be the CC R column, Lt. Donald Deeter took the 3rd Platoons up the road to meet the approaching force. The platoons were met with a storm of enemy fire. The column was German. Lt. Deeter's tank was hit 11 times by shells from an emplaced anti-tank gun 700 yards away. An infantry halftrack was destroyed. The 3rd Platoons halted. As the enemy prepared to attack, the platoon moved back to its roadblock positions and beat off the assault.

The married B Cos. of Lt. Col. Boyer's task force took the lead that morning. The tanks and halftracks roared out of Repelen at 0845 and began rolling toward their objective: the Rhine. The married A Cos. of the 34th Tank Bn. and 46th Infantry Bn., attached from CC A, came up behind, ready to help if the Germans defending the Rhine should prove tough.

But there was little opposition as the tanks pushed forward, moving faster and faster. The column thundered past the road junction held by the C Cos. and roared over the open country, racing 30 miles an hour toward Germany's greatest river. The tanks and halftracks moved so fast that surprised enemy crews were unable to get their guns into action until after the leading elements had passed, and the attached A Cos. from CC A, bringing up the rear, received more fire than did the B Cos. out in front.

The B Cos. plunged into Orsoy at 1040, just as a column of 15 German vehicles rolled down a converging road on the left flank, heading toward the Rhine ferry. But the Germans missed the boat. Tank guns blasted the enemy column and the tanks and halftracks ground on into the town.

Near the river the leading companies fanned out. The 1st Platoons swung to the left, the 2nd Platoons turned right and the 3rd Platoons headed straight for the river.

Lt. Summerfield brought his 1st Platoon tanks up to an exposed position overlooking the ferry slip. There he caught 35 trucks and 15 sedans, parked bumper to bumper, and two batteries of horsedrawn field artillery pieces, all crowded in the small area, waiting for the ferry. The tank gunners had a field day.

Four self-propelled German guns, moving down from the north, opened up on the platoons. Sgt. Arthur Horswill's tank knocked out two of them; the others were smashed by artillery. German soldiers trapped at the ferry rushed to surrender. Only those who had dug in between the levee and the river kept up the fight. Lt. Edward Muyskens and his infantry platoon began to rout them out. Sgt. Clifford C. Kuntz, his infantry halftrack placed so he could fire over the levee, spattered the enemy positions with his machine gun until he was wounded by a bazooka round.

The 2nd Platoons, moving south along the river, flushed out the remaining Germans in the other half of the town. Sgt. Robert E. Roland ran his 105 mm. assault gun up on top of the levee to knock out a troublesome anti-tank gun firing from across the Rhine.

Meanwhile the 3rd Platoons pushed straight toward the river until they hit heavy enemy fire. The leading tank and halftrack were hit. The others moved to the cover of buildings, then called for the artillery. Shells from the 95th Artillery Bn. blasted the waterfront positions.

Orsoy Yields 300 Prisoners

The bank of the Rhine cleared, the forces set about cleaning out the town. C Troop of the 85th Reconnaissance Sq. moved in and helped dig out the remaining trapped Germans. The bag at Orsoy totaled 300 prisoners. Twenty empty barges and others loaded with military equipment were captured.

Orsoy mopped up, CC R established roadblocks to catch anything being flushed out by friendly units moving in from the west. The B Cos. set up their positions on the northern edge of Orsoy; the A Cos. of the 34th Tank Bn. and the 46th Infantry Bn. blocked to the north along the Rheinkamp-Orsoy road. The rest of the day was spent in shooting up enemy troops as they streamed toward Orsoy, hoping to escape across the ferry and unaware that the town was in American hands.

Meanwhile the married A and C Cos. attacked north of the corps boundary against anti-tank guns and light infantry and artillery fire, linking up with reconnaissance elements of the 8th Armored Division. Several enemy planes were shot down during the drive.

The next day, 6 March, the 95th Artillery Bn. moved up. Resistance within range of their guns on the west side of the Rhine had ended, and they took up new positions from which they could plaster the enemy across the river. On 12 March the artillerymen moved again to Lank Latum, 2000 yards from the Rhine, and continued to rain shells on the enemy despite counter-battery fire which caused casualties among the 95th artillerymen.

The tankers, infantry and reconnaissance men holding Orsoy were relieved by 10 March and went to St. Tonis where they settled down to the routine job of policing the area, maintaining roadblocks and preparing for the final major drive through Germany.

XX

ACROSS THE HEART LAND

Rhine to the Elbe

31 March-14 April

The Fifth Armored's fight from the Rhine to the Elbe is described by tacticians as "exploiting the enemy's rear zones after breaching his frontal positions." The men in the division had a simpler name for it—"rat race." In the Rhine to Elbe rat race the division fought the kind of war it knew best. It was like France all over again, except that white surrender flags flew from the German houses instead of the French Tricolor.

No one slept, no one ate, no one did anything but attack and push on, attack and push on. The tanks and halftracks kept running off their maps as the division spear-headed 260 miles into enemy territory in 13 days. The division ran wild in the German rear areas, isolating great cities, paralyzing communications and overrunning defensive positions before the enemy could man them. Before the division stopped rolling it had reached the Elbe at three points, and was only 45 miles from Berlin. No other American unit fought that close to the German capital.

Crossing the Rhine, CC B and CC R raced abreast to the Weser River, while CC A fought large groups of by-passed Germans in the rear areas.

Across the Weser CC R headed for the Elbe and reached the river in the northern half of the division zone. At Peine, CC A shot to the southern half of the division zone and hit the Elbe at Tangermunde, CC B followed to reach the Elbe at a third point between CC A and CC R.

Combat Command R

On 31 March CC R roared across the Rhine at Wesel and started its drive to the Elbe. Sometimes the column crept, sometimes it raced down the good German highways at 30 miles an hour, but always it kept pushing. CC R ran wild in the German rear areas and 13 days after it started its drive, the German army west of the Elbe was beaten and disorganized and the war was almost over.

First element of CC R to cross the Rhine was a billeting party. Major Rufus M. Wallace was wounded when the party ran into prepared German defenses and was ambushed. Capt. Basquez's C Troop, 85th Reconnaissance Sq., raced toward Senden to stake a claim on a bridge over the Dortmund-Ems Canal. Just short of Senden, Lt. Eastman's 2nd Platoon, which was following the 1st Platoon and Company Headquarters, ran into real trouble. Concealed Germans let the first elements pass, and then opened up on the 2nd Platoon with 20 mm. flak guns, bazookas and small arms. Cpl. Lawrence Sebelius' assault gun roared at the Germans; his gunner, Pvt. John Klinowski, fired as fast as he could. Sebelius went forward under fire to drag back trapped members of the scout section whose vehicles had been hit.

The recon men radioed back information on the enemy and Task Force Boyer moved south to clean out the trouble and then to secure the assembly area, which lay less than two miles south of Munster. Task Force Hamberg shot its tanks and halftracks due east, planning to come into the assembly area from the west.

Married platoons commanded by Lt. Flower and T/Sgt. Glen Cook led the way for the B Cos. of the 10th Tank Bn. and the 47th Infantry Bn. as Lt. Col. Boyer's force marched on the assembly area. The column thundered down a road paralleling the Dortmund-Ems Canal. Lt. Flower's gunner, Cpl. Percy Thunder, spotted German flak gun positions across the canal. Grinding his turret to the right, he knocked out the positions and machine gunned German infantry in the same area.

Lead Tanks KO'ed

The married B Cos. were 1000 yards short of a crossroads in the middle of their assembly area by 1500. As the column rolled toward the intersection, two tanks and a halftrack in the lead suddenly burst into flames. Mark V tanks and self-propelled guns guarding the crossroads, waiting in concealed positions, had destroyed the three vehicles before B Co. could fire a shot. Lt.

Flower was blown out of his turret. Sgt. Cook's halftrack and the second tank, commanded by Sgt. Anthony D. Belletiere, were destroyed.

The road was dotted with buildings, and the buildings were full of Germans who were there to guard the crossroads. Sgt. Cook stayed forward, organized his shaken platoon and started killing and capturing German soldiers in the buildings. Soon more than 50 prisoners were started toward the rear.

Sgt. William A. Skalsky and Sgt. William D. Hardie jammed their tanks against the buildings for protection and traded shots with the German tanks. Between them they knocked out one and drove the others away. The married 3rd Platoons had deployed to the left, the 1st Platoons to the right, and they held positions there. By now it was almost dark and Lt. Col. Boyer's force stayed in position for the night.

Meanwhile, Lt. Col. Hamberg had cleaned out Appelhulsen and turned south. Capt. Marcikowski's C Co., 47th Infantry Bn., received orders at 2100 to move across the Dortmund-Ems Canal in the vicinity of Senden and to hold a bridgehead to protect the engineers who were going to throw a bridge across the canal later that night. There was only one trouble with the orders: They failed to tell C Co. how it was to cross, and there were no bridges. S/Sgt. Bernard Gallagher and Pfc. Israel Stern helped solve the problem by working their way down the dark bank of the canal until they found some two-man boats which they brought back. Lt. Kenneth Webster's 2nd Platoon rowed silently across the canal and dug in a perimeter defense on the other side.

At 0400 Capt. Perlman's C Co., 22nd Engineer Bn., started laying treadway, working swiftly and silently without lights in the black night. Four hours later they had bridged the canal with 300 feet of treadway and the 1st Platoon of C Troop, 85th Reconnaissance Sq., rolled across, leading the combat command. The married 1st Platoon of the A Cos. followed closely behind; Lt. William Johnson was in the lead tank.

Task Force Hamberg ticked off 40 miles to reach Greffen before dark. Near there Lt. Michael Livingston and his 10th Tank Bn. Reconnaissance Platoon caught enemy soldiers tearing planking off a bridge. The platoon opened fire, killing one German, capturing seven and saving the bridge.

The infantry companies and C Troop, 85th Reconnaissance Sq., probed the Ems Canal for bridges suitable for the tanks to cross. The troop finally found a bridge which was later used.

By 1600, A Co., 47th Infantry Bn., had pushed into Greffen and was cleaning out the town. Greffen netted 20 prisoners. Later the A Co. tanks moved into the town.

Next morning, 2 April, all of CC R crossed the Ems Canal. The married C Cos. pushed through the A Cos. and moved on to a bridge over a small stream 1000 yards west of Harswinkel. Here a booby-trapped roadblock, guarded by two machine guns, stopped the column briefly. Tank guns rained high explosive on the German machine guns, the blocks were knocked out of the way, and the column poured into Harswinkel. The town was thick with white surrender flags.

Lt. Deeter's 1st Platoon was leading as the column pushed on through town. Suddenly a German bazooka player stuck his bazooka out the window of a house flying a white flag and fired at Deeter's tank, knocking it out. Infantrymen leaped out of their halftracks, headed for the houses. Lt. Col. Hamberg and Capt. McAuley joined in the hunt for the bazookamen. Two were found by the infantrymen. Germans buried them later in the town.

Lt. Col. Hamberg's force punched on toward Halle. Outside the city the tankers and infantrymen took 20 SS prisoners and wounded others. Sgt. Laurence Detzel's tank picked up a German gas truck loaded with infantry on top, going up a side road. His first round of high explosive blew the truck and the Germans sky-high.

Road Block Halts Column

The column roared through Halle, but was stopped 1000 yards outside the town by another roadblock. Lt. Kleinsteiber nosed his tank up against the concrete drum, gave it a push, and sent it crashing down the mountain side.

The maps showed the road to be a deep, winding cut through the mountains for the next few miles; this was perfect defense terrain. Speed was beginning to pay dividends, however, for the pass was undefended. The column roared on to Werther. Going through the town, Lt. Kleinsteiber's lead tank was bazooked from a building. Lt. Kleinsteiber was instantly killed. Again the infantrymen scrambled out of their halftracks, charged up the incline to the house, and dug out the bazookamen. Tank guns pounded the houses to bits as the column rolled out of town.

Sgt. Dwight Phillips took over the leading platoon in his tank, and for the remainder of the day led a charmed life. Lt. Webster had been wounded in Halle, and T/Sgt. Reece Thornton now led the leading infantry platoon.

The column raced toward Jollenbeck. As Phillips' lead tank entered the town, four bazooka rounds in quick succession were fired at him. Two exploded against trees lining the road, another whizzed by, inches from the tank. The fourth hit the tank and dropped on the road; it was a dud. Thirty German infantrymen and bazookamen fought a short, losing battle to hold the town. Tanks rolled up to houses, fired at point blank range, and C Co. infantrymen dug scared German soldiers from basements and outhouses.

After the town was cleared, Lt. Col. Hamberg pushed his tanks and tracks toward Herford, a large city standing squarely in the command's path. The tanks picked up speed and charged toward the city. On the way, 30 German bicycle troops were overtaken. Some surrendered, others tried to escape up a hillside to the right flank. Tank machine gunners and riflemen slaughtered them as they climbed the hill.

On the outskirts of Herford, Sgt. Phillips' tank was hit by a 37 mm. anti-tank gun, but was not damaged. Phillips' gunner then demolished the enemy position with high explosive shells. The sergeant picked up the microphone to report the destruction of the gun, but his first word was cut off when another German anti-tank gun, this time a 75, hit his tank and knocked it out. Phillips bailed out, but refused to be evacuated. Instead he jumped into another tank and continued to fight.

Lt. Col. Hamberg and Capt. McAuley, who had been forward in their peeps with the lead platoon, hit the ditch when the guns opened fire. Other tanks in the platoon had pulled up against buildings when the firing started, trying to locate the enemy guns.

Lt. Col. Hamberg and Capt. McAuley spotted the German gun off to the right flank, just as a tank which had been shielded by a building started backing up into the anti-tank gun's field of fire. Both officers jumped out of the ditch, waving their arms to signal the tank commander not to move his tank. But it was too late. The tank, as it pulled out from the shelter of the building, was immediately hit. The crew bailed out and crawled into the ditch with Lt. Col. Hamberg and Capt. McAuley.

The mortars had gone into position as soon as the trouble started, and when the enemy guns were located, they began firing, but couldn't register a hit. The 95th Artillery Bn. was also called in and drove away the gun crews. Lt. William Wineman's 1st Platoon of infantry went down, cleaned out the gun crews and destroyed the guns with hand grenades.

Meanwhile, Lt. Col. Boyer had sent Lt. Muyskens and Lt. Thomas F. Zschokke, with their married platoons from the B Cos., together with Lt. Martin's tank destroyer platoon, to cut the Bielefeld-Herford road. Reaching the road, the platoons set up strong roadblocks and during the night shot up six trucks and took 30 prisoners.

Artillery Pounds Hereford

CC R stayed in those positions while the 95th Artillery Bn. pounded away at Herford all night. Shelling the town was a trick, leading the Germans to believe that the town was going to be attacked in the morning. They were out-foxed by Col. Anderson. Big towns were not in CC R's plans as the command pushed off early on 3 April. Col. Anderson had more important things than cities to think of that day; he wanted a bridge over the Weser.

German soldiers waited in Herford for an assault that never came. Col. Anderson flung both his task forces toward the city but split them just before they hit the city limits; as Task Force Hamberg shot to the left and Task Force Boyer to the right, neatly they encircled and cut off the town. The two columns rolled toward the Weser and the vital bridges.

The married B Cos. led by Capt. Pool and Capt. Lewis spurted for the Autobahn east of Herford, made it and raced down the rolling concrete ribbon toward the bridge. Lt. Karda's platoon of the 85th Reconnaissance Bn.'s C Troop sped ahead to check on the last bridge on the Autobahn before the Weser. He found the bridge intact, wheeled around, and rushed back with the good news. A few moments later a C Troop scout section skidded to a halt before the leading tanks, and reported to Lt. Cullin and Lt. Martin, who were working their tanks and tank destroyers abreast on the highway, that a German tank and assault gun were waiting in an underpass to ambush the column. Martin and Cullin slowed down, eased their tank and tank destroyer just barely over the crest of a hill and spotted the German guns. At 1800 yards Cullin's gunner, Cpl. Francis Haslin, blew up the assault gun and Martin's tank destroyer smashed the German tank.

Lt. Col. Boyer's married B Cos. then sailed down the broad highway. Sgt. Lucien Thaxton brought his tank up even with the other tank and tank destroyer. Now three vehicles abreast, two tanks and a tank destroyer, headed the column.

Meanwhile, Lt. Col. Hamberg's force was pushing down to the Autobahn to meet the married B Cos. They by-passed Herford to the left and headed for the super-highway. Capt. Whitley's leading platoon caught a few rounds of high velocity fire which came from the right flank. Capt. Pool was moving up from the right flank, so Capt. Whitley assumed it was this column that was firing on his platoon.

"Hey, Frank, this is Whitley. Damnit, you're firing at my tanks," he shouted into his microphone.

Pool came on the radio, "Hold everything. I'll check," Pool said; then over his company radio channel he called his lead tank. "What are you firing at up there?" he asked.

"Not firing at anything," came Lt. Cullin's prompt reply. "Can't see anything to shoot at."

Back on the battalion radio channel, Pool called Whitley. "You're nuts," he said. "We're not firing at you. Must be Germans."

88's Again

"Roger, out," snapped Whitley, but by now another call was coming in to clear up the mystery. "Found the bastards," Lt. William Johnson, who had the last platoon in column, was shouting over the radio. "It's a slug of 88's way up on a hill to our right. They're shooting at our platoon."

"Coming back!" yelled Whitley as he spun his peep around and headed for the trouble. Picking up Capt. Wersma, he raced back to Lt. Johnson's platoon. Going back, he bellowed instructions over the radio. "Tell the forward observer to get artillery on that hill. Put the assault guns on it. Lay in the mortars. Everybody shoot at it until I tell you to stop."

Reaching Johnson's platoon, Whitley and Wersma laid quick plans for the attack. The 88's were on a high hill looking down on the road. They were dug in and hard to see. The assault on the hill started with tanks and infantry charging up together, the tanks blasting away with their big tank guns and the infantry using marching fire.

Artillery, mortars and assault guns pounded the hill as the tankers and infantrymen pushed forward. Whitley didn't lift the supporting fire until the leading elements were only 40 yards away from the bursts. Now the men could see what had caused the trouble. Ten 88's, not the usual two or three, were dug in on the hill. The heavy fire on the hill had kept the gun crews down, but as soon as it lifted they came up firing. Lt. Neal Franks was killed in the assault. Lt. Johnson's tank was hit by a bazooka and he was wounded. Whitley's peep had been struck and he was walking beside Johnson's tank. He climbed in the turret and took Johnson's place. The attack continued.

Cpl. Clifford Poindexter, gunner in Sgt. Willis Yates' tank, lined his 76 on the first German 88, fired, and scored a direct hit. As he traversed his turret, he fired again several times and his gun blew up eight of the ten 88's. The tanks and infantry were on top of the positions now. The infantrymen charged toward the fire trenches and dug out the stunned Germans. The artillery and other support fire had been right on the target, and many of the Germans had been killed in their trenches.

Sgt. Clayton Pittsinger had led his machine gun squad to the left flank to provide flank protection during the attack, and killed 20 Germans who were trying to escape. The battle for "88 Hill" was over.

While the A Cos. were fighting on the hill, the married B Cos.

were still rushing down the Autobahn, headed for a bridge. Lt. Flower and Sgt. Cook took the lead for the rest of the run. Faster and faster the tanks and halftracks rolled. The bridge was only 1200 yards away now, intact and glistening in the afternoon sun. The tanks were a bare 1000 yards from the bridge when suddenly there was a dull boom as the bridge girders snapped and fell into grotesque positions. The Germans had blown the bridge. Lt. Col. Boyer then recalled his companies.

The morning of 4 April Col. Anderson still hadn't given up hope for a bridge. He shot Task Force Hamberg through the B Cos. at Exeter. With the C Cos. leading, Lt. Col. Hamberg pushed to Hohenhausen, dropped C Cos. there to set up roadblocks and pushed on to Mollenbeck with the A Cos.

Storming and assaulting bridges had failed, so CC R tried another attack. Major Richard F. Wilkins, CC R S-2, accomplished by Lt. Enno R. Hobbing and Cpl. Paul Krekow, passed through the lines into German-held Rintein to negotiate for the bridge over the Weser there.

The German commander listened to their proposals, but arrangements had already been completed for destroying the bridge and it was blown while the envoys were in the town. Major Wilkins had planned to stay only a short time, but the Germans held him overnight on the pretext that the party had not been blindfolded when coming into the town and had seen the defenses.

Col. Anderson threatened to blow up the town if the party wasn't returned safely; at 1045, after staying 20 hours in German territory, the party returned to CC R.

One more futile stab at taking a bridge by storm and speed was made 5 April by Task Force Boyer, which struck toward Hesslingen to grab the bridge there. This time the Germans didn't wait until the last minute. The Cub plane reported the bridge blown before the tanks came within two miles of it. The B Cos. again turned around, got out of the area in a hurry, for high velocity fire was coming in at them from across the Weser and they couldn't stop it.

Engineers Span Weser

Army engineers had built a bridge over the Weser, in the XIX Corps Zone at Hameln, and on 8 April Col. Anderson received orders to take his command across that bridge. C Troop, 85th Reconnaissance Sq., led the way across and was hardly out of sight of the bridge before it ran into a fight, south and west of Springe, the last big town before Hannover. As the recon was destroying the resistance, a Cub plane from the 2nd Armored Division landed near Capt. Pool's tank. He had set down to tell the column that he had spotted German tanks and many German infantrymen in Springe, and that the road to Springe was blocked. The 95th Artillery Bn. doubled the column in a hurry to get in position to fire on the town and the roadblocks. Lt. Kettlehut went forward to a building from which he could observe. By now the Air Corps had reported in and P-47's began working over the town as CC R tore down the roadblocks leading into Springe.

The married B Cos. roared into town after the planes had strafed and bombed and artillery had fired heavy concentrations. The three platoons swept into town and fanned out three ways. One platoon went up the center of Springe, one turned left and the third swung to the right. Prisoners were streaming out of houses and Germans were falling over themselves to give up. Col. Boyer called for help to handle the prisoners. By the time the companies arrived to take over, the B Cos. were mounted up and moving out of town. More than 300 prisoners were collected in Springe.

Three 88 mm. guns and their crews were taken by A Co. an hour after the B Cos. left the town. Sgt. Lewis Ahlin was leading a squad of A Co. on a search of the town when he peeped around a corner, saw the three guns, one with a gunner in the seat, ready to fire. Ahlin killed the gunner with one round from his M-1. That convinced the rest of the Germans. They all surrendered.

The night of 8 April the command stopped south of Pattensen, a bare eight miles from the great city of Hanover. On 9 April CC R planned to cut off Hannover and let it wither on the vine.

Task Force Boyer struck east and north on the morning of 9 April, by-passed Pattensen and crossed the Leine River, with Lt. Zschokke's platoon leading. The column roared on almost to Wulferode when the fog that had blanketed the countryside all morning suddenly lifted. As the fog cleared, all hell broke loose on the column.

"I never saw such continuous heavy fire on a column before," said Capt. Pool. The fire was coming from the heavy flak gun positions around Hannover. Sgt. William Hurley moved his tank into position and knocked out one of the guns. The B Cos. pulled back in the protection of the heavy woods to the rear.

The C Cos. of the 10th Tank Bn. and the 47th Infantry Bn. were working a few thousand yards south on a different route; Lt. Leas in the lead tank was trying hard to snatch a bridge over the Weser-Elbe Canal. The column pushed through Mullingen after disposing of enemy bazookamen there with tank and riffe fire; then it raced for the canal. Lt. Leas saw that the bridge was intact, and thought that for once the Germans were going to leave it that way. But he got only the front part of his tank on the bridge before the Germans blew it. Then he backed off safely. Three hundred Germans were dug in on the other side in strong positions, so the tanks pulled back and blasted away.

C Co. infantrymen deployed behind the tanks and took pot shots across the canal with their rifles. Two C Co. doughboys, S/Sgt. William P. Cadieux and Pfc. John H. Niles, decided the only way to lick the Germans on the other side of the canal was to go after them. Crossing the demolished bridge on the run, they hit the far bank and ran to the nearest German foxhole. Cadieux pulled the pin on a grenade, dropped it in the foxhole and waited for results. Three Germans came out with their hands up. Going from hole to hole, he repeated the process until he ran out of grenades. Cadieux and Niles recrossed the bridge with 25 German prisoners in front of them.

At the same time, a half mile downstream, Lt. Hanf and a patrol of eight men were reconnoitering for bridge crossings. Finding a bridge intact, Sgt. Robert Conner crossed under fire to check it and the opposite bank.

Objective Elbe

At 1600 on 9 April, Gen. Oliver came to Col. Anderson's command post and told him his mission was to drive as rapidly as possible to the Elbe River. At 1630 Task Force Hamberg headed for Peine, with the married C Cos. in the lead. Col. Hamberg ordered the married A Cos. to attack the town of Equord, which lay to the left of the main axis of advance, but had to be cleaned out. The married C Cos. continued north to cut the Autobahn. A Co., 10th Tank Bn., attacked Equord with three platoons abreast in a company line formation, all guns firing. Enemy tanks had been reported in the town, and before the attack was over, four had been accounted for by the A Co. tank guns.

Cpl. Alvin Childress, gunner in Lt. Wagner's tank, knocked out the first German tank by firing down a street in Equord. He scored a hit, forcing the crew to abandon their tank. Two more were knocked out as they fled east toward Rosenthal and the fourth was caught in Rosenthal. One of the German Tanks received 12 hits from Whitley's gunners. Another got 14 hits. None penetrated, but the crews were driven out by fear.

The married C Cos. drove on toward the Berlin-Hannover Autobahn, for if they could cut this highway, the main trunk roads into Hannover would be in CC R hands. As the tanks by-passed Peine to the west, they saw a train, with steam up, in the railroad yards. The entire company battered it with 76 mm. fire, which exploded the locomotive. The companies pressed on to the Autobahn in total darkness. They reached it and Lt. Leas and Lt. Paul Bostic had their platoons set up two roadblocks. During the night wandering German infantrymen coming in from both directions were captured. They refused to believe American tanks were on the Autobahn until they were shown the positions.

During the night the burgermeister of Peine contacted the 10th Tank Bn. and told Lt. Col. Hamberg he wanted to surrender the town unconditionally. Next morning Capt. Daniel A. Grundmann, Military Government office in CC R, went into the town, accepted the surrender, and ordered the streets cleared. When CC R rolled through, the town looked deserted and the shutters were drawn on all the buildings.

The morning of 10 April CC R headed north toward Edmisson, with the A Cos. leading. As the A Cos. approached the town they began to receive high velocity fire. Lt. Early's lead tank was knocked out. Lt. John P. Molnar's platoon then deployed to the right and got two Panthers with the help of the Air Corps.

The Air Corps had come up to work over the town, and the tanks and infantry waited outside while P-47's bombed and strafed. After the planes had set part of the town burning, the 95th

Artillery Bn. began shelling the ruins. As artillery fire slackened, the A Cos. stormed into town, shooting as they rolled. Lt. Wagner and his platoon caught 15 German trucks pulling out of the town and set them aflame with tank fire. That night the command bivouacked in the vicinity of Mienersen.

On 11 April Col. Anderson turned his forces east and struck out for the Elbe. By now the men were very tired. They had fought and ridden 16 hours a day for 11 days. It was only the thought that they were on the final road to victory—the road home that kept them traveling at such a dizzy pace.

Lt. Max Eastman's 2nd Platoon, C Troop, 85th Reconnaissance Bn., raced ahead of the column to Gifhorn the morning of 11 April. Most of the Germans were still in bed. They had no idea the Americans were within miles of the town. Gifhorn collapsed with little resistance. After the town was cleaned out and prisoners started toward the rear, the column roared on toward the Elbe. At Gassondorf Lt. William J. Caroscio helped collect 200 Hungarians wearing the uniform of the Wehrmacht. The Hungarians stumbled over themselves to be the first to give up.

At Gifhorn Col. Anderson split his forces and sent them in to different directions. Task Force Boyer headed straight east for the Elbe; Task Force Hamberg spearheaded to the north on a special "hurry up" mission. Near Wesendorf the married C Cos. overran a huge airport. The tanks shot up three planes on the ground, fired an ammunition dump and then kept moving. Lt. George Shaw's Anti-Tank Platoon, C Co., 47th Infantry Bn., caught some nebelwerfer fire from one flank, whipped their 57's around and picked them off.

While the rear of the column had been stopped by the nebelwerfers, the head of the column had pressed forward so that a two-mile gap lay between the two groups. Col. Anderson started down the two-mile stretch from the head of the column to give a change of orders to Lt. Col. Hamberg. While riding over an open stretch of ground in his peep, Col. Anderson was fired on by an anti-tank gun. The FM radio roared immediately. "Some bastard is shooting at me with an anti-tank gun. Somebody, anybody, come up here and get the sonufabitch!" The Assault Gun

Platoon came on the air and told Col. Anderson they were in position to fire if he could adjust.

"Hell, yes, I can adjust," bellowed the colonel. "Start shooting!" The assault guns opened up and the colonel started adjusting their fire. "Fifty short. Fire for effect," he rasped. The rounds came in. "Fifty short. Fire for effect," he yelled again. "What's the adjustment, colonel?" the assault gun leader asked over the radio. "Fifty short. Fire for effect. You're really running those bastards out of the woods now! That'll teach 'em to snipe at me!" roared the colonel as the German gun crews were smashed.

Late in the afternoon orders were received cancelling the mission to the north. Lt. Col. Hamberg turned his column around and raced after Task Force Boyer. As Task Force Hamberg was fighting north, the married B Cos. led by Lt. Col. Boyer were heading due east and racing for the Elbe. C Troop, 85th Reconnaissance Bn., was in front and spotted enemy tanks in Westerbeck. The tank destroyer platoon laid down a base of fire and one German tank was burning in the town when the B Cos. thundered through at 25 miles an hour. Lt. Graham was in the lead tank. He punched the head of the column through Ehra, Boitzenhagen, Radenbeck and to Jubar. The speed of the drive was completely bewildering the Germans now. Many enemy trucks and supply columns were overtaken and left burning on the road and in the ditches by the tank and infantry guns. At Jubar Lt. Zschokke took over the lead tank and sailed on through Lundenson, Stockheim and into Rohrberg.

General Captured

At Rohrberg Capt. Lewis' company captured a German lieutenant general and his staff. The task force spent the night in Rohrberg and prisoners streamed into the PW cages all night.

At 0530 on 12 April, Task Force Hamberg pulled into Rohrberg, having gone 34 hours without sleep. Soon the column was rolling again.

The married B Cos. led again, with Lt. Flower in the lead tank, all the way to Winterfield. Here the Germans barricaded themselves in a cemetery and tried to fight the tanks. Infantry closed in, assaulted them in the cemetery and smothered the opposition. The B Cos. pushed ahead to Mosinstein, Kallehne, Kerkau, Lohne, Koosebau, Bretsch and to Drusedau. Here they sent platoons out to set up roadblocks on the main Osterberg-Seehausen road.

At 1600 the same day, Lt. Col. Hamberg's force, which had been following, received orders to get to the Elbe and seize the main bridge at Wittenberge. The A Cos., married, led. Before night fell they had run into one of the hardest fights of the drive. The A Cos. rushed through Seehausen; they paused only long enough to check their directions, and then lunged toward the bridge, six and a half miles away. The Anti-Tank Platoon was left to mop up the town.

Lt. Molnar, Sgt. Henry White and Sgt. Jack Bastin rode the first three tanks in column as the tankers and infantry raced for the Elbe bridge. Roadblocks were thick the last two miles. Molnar pulled up before a roadblock, attached a cable to his tank and to the barricade, and heaved away. The huge, concrete-filled drum then toppled into the ditch. Another roadblock a few hundred yards further on was torn down the same way. Then the Germans started to fight. A third roadblock was defended by a hundred SS men and bazookamen. They all opened up from foxholes at point blank range. One bazooka shell glanced off the turret of Molnar's tank, damaging the traversing mechanism.

Every gun of the assaulting tanks shot at once. In Molnar's tank Pvt. Richard Vicknair loaded the 76, then jumped to the .50 caliber machine gun in his turret to spray the Germans. Molnar's gunner, Cpl. Elmer E. Hoffstetter, purposely shot short of the foxholes, which sent projectiles flying into the dirt in front of the holes and down inside them, killing the occupants. T/4 Charles Stoeckeln, Molnar's driver, was doing the work of three men in the front of the tank. He drove, leaned over to fire the assistant driver's machine gun, and handed up ammunition out of the spare racks to the men in the turret behind him.

In the deafening boom and rattle of the battle a telephone at the roadblock began ringing. It rang while infantry dismounted and killed 50 Germans who remained in their holes, and while the big guns roared at other enemy soldiers beyond the roadblock. Finally Pfc. William Austin jerked the phone off its hook and listened. A German officer was talking excitedly from Wittenberge and Austin yelled, "Blow it out your barracks bag! I'll be there in a minute!"

A Hand-to-Hand Fight

The fight turned into utter confusion and became a hand-to-hand battle. First Sgt. Helms, Sgt. Lewis Ahlin and S/Sgt. Jodie Vaughn fixed their bayonets and charged across a small canal to mop up Germans on the other side.

Sgt. Pittsinger took the machine gun and mortar squads along a railroad track which paralleled the road. The mortars under T/5 Perlie Bowman fired in extremely close support of the action.

Capt. Whitley, Sgt. Erwin Welti and S/Sgt. Chester Redding drove through the thick of the fight to the head of the column to bring up ammunition. Molnar's tank was firing so fast they couldn't keep him supplied. Molnar hopped out, jumped into the second tank, and pressed home the attack. In his second tank Molnar pushed past the final roadblock and onward toward the bridge, but SS men began firing from a stone house beside the road.

"Blow it down!" the tank commander shouted.

The tanks opened up and cannon shells boomed through the stone walls. The tanks then ploughed on past the house and turned to the right. The column roared along beside a high railroad embankment, and bazookas opened up from the opposite side. With their machine guns the tankers sprayed the crest of the embankment. A bazookaman raised up to aim his weapon, but before he could fire the tank machine guns got him and he lurched forward on his face.

The column kept ploughing on. Molnar's tank was a half mile from the bridge when a deafening explosion roared above all the noise of the battle. As the tankers and infantrymen looked forward, they saw the boards and girders of the bridge soar into the air and then drop into the Elbe. A cloud of powdered concrete rose slowly where the span had been. The last bridge over the Elbe that the division could hope to get had been blown. Lt. Col. Hamberg called his companies back to Seehausen. The battle for the Elbe was over.

The men in CC R didn't know it then, but their next, and last, battle was going to be toward the same river.

Combat Command B

As Combat Command B approached Munster on the evening of 31 March, it was learned that the bivouac area it was supposed to occupy had not been cleared of enemy troops. The tanks and halftracks, therefore, pulled off in the fields near Appelhulsen. From the assembly area near Anrath, in the Rhineland, the command had come more than 75 miles that day; it had crossed the Rhine on the pontoon bridge at Wesel and had swung past the northern edge of the enemy troops still holding out in the Ruhr pocket. The spearheading drive south of Munster and east to the Weser River was to begin the following day, Easter Sunday.

A light rain fell on the oil-coated steel when the canvas covers were stripped from the machine guns on the tanks and halftracks the next morning. The ground was soft and vehicles had difficulty getting out of the fields and onto the hard-surfaced road. But at 1100 CC B's armor headed east into the German heartland. Leading the push was Task Force Anderson, supported by all of the mobile gun batteries of the 47th Artillery Bn.

The initial mission was to seize and secure a bridge across the Dortmund-Ems Canal to the south of Munster. This was necessary so that the entire combat command could cross the stream, by-pass and get to the east side of the defended city, and then with both task forces abreast, continue to drive east. On the right flank was CC R and on the left were the British 2nd Armored and the American 17th Airborne Division, which were pressing in from the west on Munster.

As the leading married C Cos. of the 81st Tank Bn. and the 15th Infantry Bn. approached the canal, they found their route across a creek block by a bridge that had been destroyed by demolitions. By the time a passable route had been located, however, an order came down for the task force to halt in place. CC R's engineers had been able to bridge the canal near Senden and it was decided to send CC B over this crossing. Task Force Dickenson was now ordered to proceed immediately to the pontoon bridge and lead the command across to the east bank.

After it had cleared this water barrier during the afternoon, Task Force Dickenson, with the supporting batteries of the 71st Artillery Bn. right on its heels, picked up speed and roared unopposed down the highway. By 1900 that evening it had gone more than 23 miles and was entering the outskirts of Warendorf. On a bridge leading into the town, men in the lead vehicles pulled up six demolition charges before the Germans could set them off. From under the bridge they removed eight Teller mines.

When they started to reconnoiter to the southwest of the town, recon men of the 2nd Platoon of the Reconnaissance Sq.'s B Troop, which had been leading the task force, were fired on by a German tank. The enemy shell ripped into the lead peep in which Pfc. Paul M. Vollette, acting scout sergeant, and two other men were riding. Shell fragments punctured two tires, tore a hole in the radiator and floor board, and slightly wounded one of the men.

"We bailed out of the vehicle and scrambled for cover," said the driver, Pfc. Howard D. White. "But later we crawled back, hopped in the peep and got the hell out of there."

As soon as B Troop's 1st Platoon had got across the Dortmund-Ems Canal, it was instructed by CC B's intelligence officer, Major Martin M. Philipsborn, to race north to the town of Telgte, which lies about six miles directly east of Munster. He realized that the enemy troops in Munster would attempt to make this town a key spot in an escape route as soon as they discovered they were being surrounded.

The platoon reached Telgte at 1900 beating an SS column coming from the west, and the German commander offered to surrender his Wehrmacht garrison of 200 men. Later in the evening about 200 enemy SS infantry supported by tanks entered the town from the west and north and the Reconnaissance Platoon was forced to withdraw in the dark.

Task Force Dickenson Spearheads

Task Force Dickenson spent the night in Warendorf while Task Force Anderson coiled near Venne.

At daylight CC B's armor was back on the road again, rolling east in the rain. In the tanks and halftracks men rubbed the sleep from their eyes and took up their vigils, carefully watching to the front and to the flanks for any suspicious signs in the spring-green countryside; they were ready to counter any violent eruptions in these peaceful surroundings.

Task Force Dickenson continued to lead the command the second morning. As it pulled out of Warendorf, it received some fire from the left flank, but the column pushed on toward Sassenberg. Not far behind was CC B Headquarters. After pulling through a stretch of bad road early that morning. Task Force Anderson raced to catch up so that it would be able to knife north into its own zone of action as soon as Col. Cole gave the order.

On the Munster highway southwest of Warendorf a roadblock, consisting of two light tanks from the 81st Tank Bn's D Co., and a squad from A Co., 15th Infantry Bn., was left behind by Task Force Dickenson to protect the left flank. This roadblock, which was in charge of Lt. Kenneth A. McLennon, later that day destroyed a German staff car and captured six enemy trucks, one colonel, six majors and 95 enlisted men.

As the head of the column pulled into Sassenberg at 1000, Lt. Shirley J. Duran, commander of the lead tank, saw a towed 88 mm. gun roll past a T-intersection. When a second 88 started to pass the same intersection, his tank opened up with its 75 and smashed the enemy gun. Then a German tank rumbled into town with guns roaring, but Lt. Duran and his crew knocked that out too.

"Lt. Duran's tank was hit and two men in his crew were wounded by a shell from a second Kraut tank that came into town," said Sgt. Harold J. Strunk, commander of the second Sherman in the column. "We fired one round and knocked out the Kraut tank and around the corner we caught three enemy halftracks."

While Task Force Dickenson continued east from Sassenberg, Task Force Anderson swung north and then east into its own zone of action. It met no enemy resistance until it approached Versmold, where fire from an enemy self-propelled gun disabled the lead tank. The Germans then tried to withdraw their gun from the town, but when it bogged down in a creek, they destroyed it.

As the armored columns slashed east, using secondary roads whenever possible because the Germans tended to concentrate their strongest resistance on the main roads, engineers of the B Co., 22nd Engineer Bn., worked feverishly patching up bad spots in the routes so that the advance would not be delayed.

Supply trucks following the armor were often fired on by bypassed groups of resistance. Four gasoline trucks of the 3907th Quartermaster Co., after stopping to pick up empty gas cans discarded by the tankers, were racing to catch up with CC B's column when they were sprayed with enemy machine guns from the side of the road.

"When I saw the windshield shatter in front of me, I left the vehicle and headed for the ditch," said T/5 John S. Reece, colored peep driver who was leading the convoy.

Just before he reached the ditch a bullet struck him, but did not wound him. It entered the right side of his raincoat, passed through his field jacket pocket, his wallet, fountain pen, sweater, shirt and undershirt. Then, after swinging around his stomach, it came out through his clothes again and into his left field jacket pocket where it stopped when it hit his GI razor.

After pushing past Greffen, Task Force Dickenson pulled up at dusk before the pass through the hills at Borgholzhausen. The lead 81st Tank Bn. A Co. tank, commanded by Lt. Carl W. Schwab, was hit three times by panzerfaust rockets.

"It was the sand bags that we had packed all over the tank before starting this drive that saved us from being killed," said the driver, T/5 Jess E. Arnett.

SS Hold Mountain Pass

Because the pass was of vital strategic importance, it was decided to press forward in a night attack against the 200 SS men who were defending the corridor with panzerfausts and small arms. After winching several of the big guns out of the mud holes in their former positions near Horste, the batteries of the 71st Artillery Bn. went into new positions after dark southwest of Borgholzhausen and proceeded to blast the bazookamen out of the pass. By 0700 the next morning Task Force Dickenson was completely through the mountain barrier and two miles beyond the town of Borgholzhausen, rolling east.

Down out of the woods came more than 3000 foreign slave workers to greet the tankers and infantrymen. One company of Yugoslavian workers stood at attention alongside the road and saluted each vehicle as it passed.

During the night Pfc. Marshal R. Ross and two other men from the 1st Platoon of the Reconnaissance Sq.'s B Troop had set out in a peep in an attempt to make contact with Task Force Anderson to the north. In the darkness they ran smack into an enemy roadblock.

From both sides of the road the enemy troops turned machine guns on the vehicle. But the recon men gunned the peep, sprayed the Germans with their own .30 caliber machine gun and drove through the block. The two men with Pfc. Ross were wounded and the peep was badly shot up.

"When we were a thousand yards on the other side of the block," said Ross, "we tore out the radio, abandoned the vehicle, and on foot circled around the enemy troops to get back to our outfit."

After following Task Force Dickenson through the pass, Task Force Anderson turned north again into their own zone of action. They overran ack-ack positions and captured prisoners, but encountered no serious opposition. About 1200 Lt. Leonard Keene of B Co., 81st Tank Bn., saw a freight train steaming toward his lead tank as the column knifed east. He fired three shots and then, as the train swung off on a spur, fired three more shots and exploded the locomotive.

"I saw another train coming toward us, a passenger train," said Sgt. Wallace Grandmaiter, commander of the second tank in the column. "I fired and my first two rounds missed, but then I hit the engine in the drive wheels and finally in the boiler. Steam started coming out from all parts of it."

Recon men from B Troop's 2nd Platoon, still operating as lone wolves in the area between the two task forces, caught up with a retreating anti-tank gun and its crew. They blasted the gun with the 37 mm. guns on their armored cars. Then they sighted some German soldiers, armed with panzerfausts, speeding east on motorcycles. After a race across the plains, they overtook the Germans and stopped them with machine gun fire.

Early in the afternoon, B Battery of the 71st Artillery Bn. pulled off the road into position, went into action and in a few minutes destroyed two dual-purpose guns which were holding up the head of Task Force Dickenson's column.

When a civilian was hit by a peep along the road near Lohne, T/5 Merlin Halsey and T/5 Daniel R. Williams, medical aid men with the 22nd Engineer Bn.'s B Co., loaded the man into the back of their ambulance and followed another civilian's directions to the nearest hospital.

They had expected to find a civilian hospital, but instead they found themselves in the yard of a big, four-story, 500-bed German army hospital with convalescent soldiers hanging out of all the windows. Out in front was a German colonel.

"Our arrival sort of surprised the colonel." said Cpl. Williams. "I guess he hadn't expected us."

Town Surrenders

Bad Oeynhausen formally surrendered to CC R at 1300. But when Task Force Dickenson reached the approaches to the town at 1600, it received direct and time fire from eight 75 mm. guns. Tank destroyers of the 628th T. D. Bn. went into action and blasted two of the enemy guns. The fire of one of the tank destroyers was directed by Lt. Paul H. McWain of the 71st Artillery Bn. Shermans of the 81st Tank Bn.'s A Co. silenced two more of the guns.

Then, in true western style, a 105 mm. artillery piece commanded by Sgt. Buford L. Smith, slid around a corner into position, opened up and knocked out two more 75's with direct fire. The German crews ran off and abandoned the last two guns. Captured in Bad Oeynhausen was a factory producing 88's and halftracks. Task Force Dickenson pushed past the town and at 1700 reached the Weser River south of Vlotho.

Late in the afternoon Task Force Anderson pulled up into the gap in the Wiehen Mountain Range at Bergkirchen. No enemy fire was encountered as the lead platoon went through the pass and down the steep descent to the broad plain which led to Minden. When they reached the floor of the valley they were fired on from the front and from both the flanks by concealed enemy anti-tank guns. Artillery fire was also thrown at them. The tanks poured counter-fire into the enemy gun positions. Other Shermans that pulled into defense positions behind buildings on the forward slope opened up and knocked out several enemy trucks that were racing toward Minden. During the night the lead platoon remained in the pass and consolidated its positions while the rest of Task Force Anderson coiled south of Bergkirchen.

At daylight a platoon from the married C Cos. was sent to seize and secure another pass west of the Bergkirchen gap. They accomplished their mission without meeting resistance. In the valley on the other side of the pass, however, the observation plane of the 47th Artillery Bn. spotted six 88's near Dutzen. The gun batteries opened up and, following the directions of the aerial observer, neutralized all of the enemy guns. Then, at 1400, the C Cos. outposts reported that a strange column of vehicles was moving down the valley toward Minden.

Meanwhile, Lt. Franklin H. Copp and Pfc. Donald D. Wall had left the headquarters of CC B in a peep and were proceeding toward Minden under a flag of truce to request the burgermeister to surrender the town. With them they took the reluctant and protesting Burgermeister of Bad Oeynhausen so that he would be able to assure the Minden official that the American forces treated the civilians humanely and adhered to the rules of the Geneva Convention.

Here Come the British

But when they started into the town, they met the lead tanks and armored vehicles of the British Third Para Brigade. It was the column which had been seen by the C Cos. outposts as it advanced down the valley on the right flank, and it was now entering the town from the northwest.

The British column's lead tank had just been shot up by an 88, so the Para Brigade commander refused to permit Lt. Copp and Pfc. Wall to continue on their mission.

"He said we would lose our peep if we rounded the next corner," said Lt. Copp. "He was more concerned about our division's artillery which was scheduled to shell the town in a few hours if it did not surrender. He was afraid the barrage would fall on his own troops."

The British commander asked Lt. Copp to race back to CC B Headquarters and have the scheduled shelling cancelled.

During the morning Lt. Col. Dickenson sent patrols to reconnoiter the river banks in his area, to see if any bridges were still intact. No crossing was located, but some German soldiers were spotted attempting to escape across the stream in big river barges.

Sgt. Benjamin Temple, chief mortar observer, radioed back to his 15th Infantry Bn., Mortar Platoon, which started to lob shells into the enemy ferry.

"After we covered the barges with mortar fire, we called on the Assault Gun Platoon for help," said Lt. George H. Richey. "They went into action and sank all 11 of the barges."

Mortar Routs Foe

Some of the enemy soldiers tried to take cover in a factory across the river, but the Mortar Platoon set up a captured 120 mm. German mortar and demolished the building.

The batteries of the 71st Artillery Bn. had moved into position east of Bad Oeynhausen; they were ready to pound Minden into submission if the town did not surrender. When the British moved into the city and the shelling was cancelled, the 71st Artillery Bn. prepared to support the 84th Infantry Division which was preparing to establish a bridgehead across the Weser south of Minden.

The 84th Division pushed across the river and set up its pontoon bridge without meeting too much opposition. They did not find it necessary to call upon the 71st Artillery Bn. for supporting fire. The batteries then undertook some aerial observed missions. One of the objectives they knocked out was an entire flak train, mounting the new German 105 mm. flak gun.

During the next few days both task forces remained on the west bank of the Weser, consolidating their positions and flushing out bypassed German soldiers from the woods around their areas. This mopping-up process from 4 April to 8 April netted CC B 1057 prisoners.

After reaching the Weser, CC B was placed in division reserve and given the mission of supporting CC A and CC R in the drive from the Weser to the Elbe. On the afternoon of 8 April, Task Force Anderson moved into Minden to temporarily garrison the city. The next day the 71st Artillery Bn. was attached to CC A to reinforce the supporting batteries of the 47th Artillery Bn.

On 10 April, CC B pulled up stakes and rolled east again. Task Force Dickenson moved southeast to Hameln to relieve elements of the 30th Infantry Division as the security guard of the pontoon bridge which had been thrown across the river there. Task Force Anderson and the rest of CC B also crossed the river at Hameln, but continued east down the division's main supply route. Out in front of Division Headquarters, clearing the route, were the married C Cos. and one section from the 81st Tank Bn.'s Assault Gun Platoon.

In the air above the speeding tanks and halftracks, a Cub observation plane piloted by Lt. Merritt D. Francies, with Lt. William S. Martin as observer, was spotting targets for the 71st Artillery Bn.'s gun batteries when an enemy Storch observation plane was noticed circling around at three-top level. Diving on the small German craft, Lts. Francies and Martin opened up on it with their pistols and punctured one of the gas tanks. Getting above the Storch, they forced it to the ground where it crashed against a fence. After landing their Cub near the wrecked plane, they captured the two enemy airmen, one of whom had been wounded.

When CC B reached the Weser-Elbe Canal two days later, the married B Cos. relieved elements of CC A as security guards for the canal bridges. Earlier that day, in a woods near Rohrberg, CC B's executive officer, Lt. Col. Edwin M. Coates, set off with two tanks commanded by Lt. Carlo Lombardi of the 81st Tank Bn.'s D Co. and a halftrack of men led by Lt. Curtis L. Ramsey of the 22nd Engineer Bn.'s B Co., and rounded up 440 German soldiers, including 30 officers. The surrender was arranged by Lts. Lombardi and Ramsey, who drove a peep into the enemy-occupied woods and persuaded the Germans to lay down their arms. The enemy force had 26 horses and 12 wagons loaded with equipment. That night CC B coiled east of Thuritz.

Push to Elbe

The next morning the command started clearing the main supply route from Maxenbush to the Elbe. The column was led by the married C Cos. of the 81st Tank Bn. and the 15th Infantry Bn., which started rolling at 0700. As the armor pushed toward the river, one platoon was dropped off in each village to search for enemy soldiers. Near Inden 50 American and British prisoners who had marched 600 miles from Poland and were now being marched back toward Berlin, were liberated and their guards captured.

By 1300 the lead elements had cleared the 26-mile route and were overlooking the Elbe. Beside the river, waiting to cross by ferry to Sandu, were 60 enemy vehicles, loaded with army supplies. The tanks fired on some barges attempting to cross the river and on enemy personnel on the east bank. Before pulling back to take up defense positions for the night around Inden, the C Cos. knocked out the lead vehicles in the enemy column so that the Germans would not be able to get them across during the night.

At 2000 Task Force Dickenson pulled up in Bruneau after an all-day, 122-mile dash from Hameln where it had been relieved during the morning by corps.

The next two days, 14 and 15 April, were spent clearing a corridor six miles wide along the main supply route from Osterburg to the Elbe. Small groups also patrolled the route.

Men in CC B wondered what their next move would be — whether they would jump the river and drive on Berlin, push north toward Denmark, or simply sit and wait for the Russians to move up to the east bank of the Elbe. But none of these guesses was right.

Combat Command A

CC A rolled over the Rhine at Wesel the afternoon and night of 31 March. Tankers and infantrymen gazed open-mouthed at the circus atmosphere around the bridge site. Huge floodlights split the darkness. Boats, bulldozers and huge cranes were working on 24-hour shifts building more bridges across the Rhine. Anti-aircraft guns dotted the approaches. The bridge builders thumbed their noses at the Luftwaffe.

CC A was in division reserve after it crossed the Rhine; it prepared to pass through either CC B or CC R and continue the attack.

Assembling his command in the Senden area, Gen. Regnier gave orders to Capt. Seymour Scott to secure a crossing over the Dortmund-Ems Canal with his A Troop of the 85th Reconnaissance Sq. The recon men pushed off shortly after noon, and an hour later had covered eight miles to reach Hiltrup. Sgt. Kenneth E. Richardson's peep was leading the recon section as it eased into town. Everything looked quiet and normal. But suddenly a German machine gun fired on the peep. Then another machine gun opened up, followed by a bazooka shell. Richardson and his crew bailed out and Lt. Frank L. Thompson, who had followed the lead peep, moved his reconnaissance car up to cover the men as they made their way back to the column.

Capt. Scott immediately brought up the attached E Troop's assault gun platoon and started chopping down German positions. His radio flashed the situation back to CC A. The married A Cos. of the 34th Tank Bn. and the 46th Infantry Bn., hit the road and headed for Hiltrup. Lt. Col. Richard E. Jones checked with Capt. Scott and decided to batter his way through the middle of the town. Tanks of A Co., 34th Tank Bn., deployed around the edge of Hiltrup, blasted the buildings and sent machine gun tracers skipping up the streets. Lt. Horace K. Ward's 1st Platoon of A Co., 46th Infantry Bn., started into town, met dug-in enemy infantry on the town's outskirts and took 150 prisoners.

The mission was to get the bridge. The doughboys didn't stop to clean out the town. Pushing on down the main street and to the far edge of town, Ward's men could see that the bridge was still intact. As they approached the bridge in a skirmish line, a German assault gun opened up at them from across the canal. Pfc. Parvey J. Bourque, a 1st Platoon bazookaman, fired at the German gun and it retreated into a nearby woods.

A Bridgehead is Won

Lt. Ward, S/Sgt. James Callahan, Pfc. Frank Larson and Pfc. George Avett rushed toward the bridge, gained the approaches and started across just as the Germans blew the span. Knocked down and stunned by the explosion, the men crawled back to the bridge approach and waited for the other platoons to arrive. Then Lt. Ward started across the structure again, climbing over the twisted girders. Reaching the other side, he destroyed a German machine gun nest with a hand grenade.

Under cover of S/Sgt. Malcolm Bodarian's A Co., 46th Infantry Bn.'s machine gun squad and Lt. Herbert P. Anesty's headquarters assault guns, the 1st Platoon, then the 2nd and finally the 3rd Platoon of A Co. crossed the canal. Some struggled across the wreckage of the bridge; others used small civilian boats they found on the banks. The company's agressive action soon won a bridgehead on the far bank of the canal.

Meanwhile the married B Cos. of the 34th Tank Bn. and the 46th Infantry Bn., which had been attached to Division Headquarters on 1 April, were having their share of troubles. Headquarters had planned to cut north over a virgin route with the married B Cos. spearheading. Just north of Albersloh, three miles southeast of the point where the married A Cos. were fighting at the Dortmund Canal, they began to receive artillery fire. The column pushed on almost to Wolbeck where it was stopped by fire from self-propelled guns to the front.

Simultaneously, the enemy concealed in woods on both sides opened up with bazookas, machine guns and small arms. The entire point, three tanks and three halftracks commanded by Lt. Thomas W. Burke, was lost. The fourth halftrack in the column received a direct hit and four men were killed and seven wounded.

When the lead halftrack was knocked out, S/Sgt. Edward J. McCarthy, the squad leader, lost a foot, but rallied his men and refused to be evacuated until they were reorganized and returning the enemy's fire.

The men whose vehicles had been destroyed scattered into the woods and found themselves surrounded on three sides. Sgt. Stanley A. Shiverski and Sgt. Fred Roeben moved their tanks up under the anti-tank and bazooka fire to cover the withdrawal of the

Thru Wesel and on.

my vehicles burning.

Across at Wesel
on the Rhine.

Thru Huls.

Cpl. Camdorn — A-34 near Applehulsen.

Over the Dortmund — Ems Canal.

Here they come over.

Near Herford.

Many didn't get to retreat . . . they were cut off.

We liberate French PW's.

Nazi officer attends wounded at Winterfield.

A good Nazi near Bad Osynahausen.

Bombed out German half-track factory.

Near Hamelin — these German Rockets.

Deeper into Germany.

105 Self propelled in Lovenich, Ger.

85 Rcn. takes prisoners.

T/5 Thomas Dimmett near Lovenich.

A P-47 shot down near Peine

Peine surrenders 10th Tankers.

T/f Boyer captures Lt. General near Elbe River.

Caught 'em out in the open.

Our Artillery Air Observer is shot down.

The sack time was short.

DP's get checked, too.

Near Stendal, T/5 Dean Brooke

MsDonald and Grahar
light up.

Men on a 5th Armored Division halftrack pass a blazing barn on a road near Wittenmoore, Germany.

CCA near the Elbe River outside Bismarck.

ur trucks caught hell hen we didn't rid each own of all Nazi.

Some of the German equipment was enormous — A Tiger.

Take that booby trap off that door.

Near the Elbe River we caught a few more.

R Commanders — Colonels
derson, Hamberg and Boyer.

GI non-issue.

ear Wittenberge
ve liberate 500
merican PW's.

CCR captures V-I factory near Dannenberg.

Buzz-Bombs.

T/5 Decicco and Sgt. Wesley E. Drinkard examine this London bound bomb.

Everything begins to surrender.

F. W. 190 lands and surrenders.

A German Jet fighter ME-262 surrenders.

Gen. Oliver, Col. Cole, and Gen. Gillem.

Gen. Oliver meets the Russians on the Elbe River.

Secretary of War Patterson and Lt. Gen. Simson visit Gen. Oliver.

Army Comdr. Lt. Gen. Simpson, 5th AD Cmdr. Maj. Gen. Oliver, 13 Corp Cmdr. Maj. Gen. Gillem, Chief of Staff Col. Farrand.

Division G-3 Staff

Columns converge near the end.

The grave of Carl F. Gross
Neurille in Condroy, L
Belgium.

Lt. Groham, Capt. Pool, 10th Tank.

surrounded men. Lt. Burke and Lt. Charles Stevens helped re-organize them at the edge of the woods.

Medics Surrounded

"Medics! Medics!" the forward men shouted, and Pvt. William S. Knapke and Pfc. Glenn Reynolds hurried toward the front of the column, treated and evacuated eight men under fire. Returning to the front, they went past the forward infantry to check two burning tanks, but the crews had escaped. Further up the road another tank was burning. Knapke raced to it, climbed on and tried to look into the turret, but smoke was pouring out and he could see nothing.

"Anyone in there?" he called. Just then someone yelled from beside the tank. He looked over and saw four Germans. Knapke leaped off the tank and, with Reynolds, jumped in their peep. The engine wouldn't start.

"I looked into the ditch by the roadside and there were four more Jerries," said Knapke. "One was loading a bazooka. I piled out of the peep and hit the opposite ditch from the Germans. Reynolds followed me. The Krauts by then were chasing after us and yelling, "Give up! Give up!"

"We were cornered on three sides. Our nearest troops were 300 yards behind us. Then the tankers started firing over us at the Germans and under this cover we scrambled up the ditch to our lines. Those tankers saved us for sure."

"Several times I thought I'd seen my first and last action," said Reynolds. He had left the States on 10 February, less than two months before.

A Squeeze is Worked

B Co., 46th Infantry Bn., set up a line south of Wolbeck and prepared to hold there for the night. Reviewing the action later, Capt. Raymond Weeks, B Co., 34th Tank Bn., commander, estimated the force opposing him at 200 SS troopers and four to six self-propelled guns or Mark V tanks.

At 1915, Division Headquarters returned the B Cos. to CC A control. Col. Edward G. Farrand, Chief of Staff, remained with Capt. Weeks and Capt. Hewitt until command and fire direction channels had been reestablished with CC A. Messages were sent out to the married A and B Cos., only three miles apart, to maintain contact with the enemy and to attack east and north respectively next morning to join up at Wolbeck.

A Co., 46th Infantry Bn., consolidated its bridgehead and took 200 prisoners during the night. And A Co. patrol led by Lt. Sol. Lubin ranged two miles to the east and before daylight had located a bridge over a small stream which formed the last water barrier before Wolbeck.

At the Dortmund-Ems Canal, A Co., 22nd Engineer Bn., worked all night to build a 132-foot treadway bridge. It was ready by 0615. Two platoons of A Co., 34th Tank Bn., had roared across when a section of the bridge failed. It was repaired by 1100, and the remainder of the force poured across the canal toward Wolbeck.

The married B Cos. pushed off at 1030 toward Wolbeck and found that the previous day's fighting and all-night artillery pounding had dissolved most of the resistance. The married A and B Cos. met in Wolbeck at noon.

In these two actions, fought only three miles apart and only six miles south of the city of Munster, CC A took more than 600 prisoners, killed 200 more of the enemy and destroyed three flak batteries.

Following CC R's route, CC A raced to the vicinity of Herford; it reached the city 4 April. The combat command then stayed near Herford, for the next five days, waiting for bridgeheads to be made over the Weser.

Over the Weser

CC A streamed across the Weser River at Hameln on 9 April, close on the heels of CC R's flying column. CC A's original mission was to cut south of Hannover, then swing northeast and work in the northern part of the division's zone. The 71st and 47th Artillery Bns. were in support.

Shortly after midnight the command bivouacked south of Hannover and Capt. Scott's A Troop, 85th Reconnaissance Sq., streaked northeast and seized the first of two bridges over the Weser-Elbe Canal at Sehnde. Task Force Burton was ordered to secure both bridges, and a married platoon led by Lt. Walter E. Williams and Lt. Morris Goldberg rumbled to the first bridge before dawn. Two infantry squads were rushed to the second bridge, but were beaten back by heavy automatic fire and artillery.

While the married platoons captured the bridge, CC A had received a change of orders which gave them the southern half of the division zone instead of the northern half and ordered them to attack all the way to the Elbe. The platoons held their one good bridge and protected CC A's northern flank as it moved out.

CC A moved at noon on 10 April and passed through Peine at 1630. The 85th Reconnaissance Sq.'s A Troop snatched another bridge from the Germans over the Oker River at Didderse. Sgt. June R. McCloud and his recon section raced to the bridge. He called back over the radio, "Hello, Able 31 to Able 5. I'm at the bridge. It's intact. Wait. I'm going to cross." Just then the Germans blew the bridge. McCloud came back on the radio. "Hello, Able 5. They just blew the bridge! Stand by. I'm going to take a look." Two minutes passed, and then, "Hello, Able 5. Bridge is okay. All of the charge didn't go off. I'm cutting the rest of the wires!"

By 2040 Task Force Burton had the A Cos. astride the main Brunswick-Gifhorn road. By 2300 the entire combat command was across the Oker and a married A Co. platoon led by Lt. Mouse P. Maurer and Lt. Joseph Clifton had secured the Wedelheine bridge over the Weser-Elbe Canal. As the married platoons rushed to the bridge, they caught heavy small arms and bazooka fire and saw the Germans feverishly preparing to blow the bridge. S/Sgt. John N. Schaeffer of A Co., 34th Tank Bn., deployed his tank section and placed such withering fire on them that the Germans withdrew, leaving the bridge undamaged. The 46th Infantry Bn.'s Assault Gun Platoon also laid down heavy fire to help drive the Germans away.

Armor Breaks Loose

CC A started to roll toward the Elbe at first shooting light on 11 April, and before the day was over they had hung up a new record for combat distance traveled in one day. The C Cos.

hurried to seize the bridge over the Fallersleben Canal, but took a wrong turn in the town because of a faulty map. In Fallersleben, Capt. Otto K. Georgi reconnoitered on foot, found the bridge and put the C Cos. on the right road. By 1200 the speeding C Cos. had crossed both the Weser-Elbe and Aller Canals and reached the crossroads east of Weyhausen. Here a Tiger tank stuck its nose over a hill in the distance and Lt. Donald E. Daniels and S/Sgt. Robert E. Mennow sniped at it with their 76 mm. guns. The German tank backed off the hill and disappeared.

The combat command thundered down the main roads; it probed its route with splattering machine gun and tank fire and stopped only to clear roadblocks. The column ploughed on, mile after mile. Roadblock after roadblock was smashed as the churning column kept punching toward the Elbe.

More than 400 prisoners were taken during the day by the speeding tankers and infantry. A hospital with 500 more prisoners was found at Klotze.

The weather was clear and perfect for air support, but the ever-welcome P-47's were mysteriously absent in the afternoon. The men didn't learn until later that their lunging drive had carried them completely out of the planes' effective fighting range.

German supply columns were overtaken on the road and riddled with machine gun bullets. German vehicles rounded corners to find themselves faced with a 20-mile-long tank column. Burning German trucks, wagons and cars lay gutted in the ditches as CC A plunged on.

Task Force Jones was ordered to guard the road over which CC A traveled, and it started dropping off small groups to guard bridges and intersections. Only Task Force Burton, with two married companies and the supporting artillery, was left when CC A reached Bismarck.

At 1700 Gen. Oliver came to Gen. Regnier's command post. He was elated with the command's phenomenal progress and assured the CC A commander that he would relieve Task Force Jones and sent it back to CC A; he also said that he would get gasoline to the command, for by now gas supplies were dangerously low.

At 2200 CC A closed in bivouac for the night after a 63-mile fighting run in 13½ hours. CC R was fighting on the north flank, but was 25 miles to the rear. The 2nd Armored Division was 50 miles to the south. CC A had struck deep into the heart of Germany and was surrounded on three sides. The time was ripe to attack.

Next morning, 12 April, the tankers and infantrymen struck toward the Elbe. Lt. Charles H. Taggert's light tank platoon of D Co., 34th Tank Bn., roamed the side roads, mopping up Germans fleeing from the bristling column. Lt. Glenn O. Garber's 628th Tank Destroyer platoon set up roadblocks at main intersections, pointing their long 90 mm. guns hopefully to the flanks and waiting for a blundering German column to come into their sights.

The roaring column churned on toward Tangermunde. The men did not have to be told that the Elbe River bridge at Tangermunde was one of the most important bridges in the world that day. They knew that if the bridge could be taken, the Fifth Armored would roll into Berlin without waiting for orders or strategy.

The married C Cos. with Lt. Robert E. Nicodemus' platoon leading, trundled into Tangermunde at noon, shooting as they rolled. The town was defended by four German battle groups, totaling 800 men with hundreds of panzerfausts. These groups were supported by heavy flak guns firing from across the river. One of the battle groups came from the German officer candidate school at Brandenberg and had been personally briefed by Hitler to penetrate American rear areas and harass supply lines. When cornered they were fanatical fighters.

Germans Open Up

The tanks thundered through the first four blocks in Tangermunde without a shot being fired at them. Suddenly the town's sirens began to wail. It was the signal for the Germans to start shooting with everything they had. Panzerfausts rained on the tanks, some hitting, others exploding against buildings and in the streets. German burp guns splattered against tank turrets. Sgt. Charles H. Householder, C Co., 34th Tank Bn., was in the lead tank, followed by Sgt. Leonard B. Haymaker's tank. As the Germans lobbed panzerfausts at them, the two sergeants started blasting the buildings with their tank guns. Their machine guns poured tracers into basement windows and through doors. Sgt. Householder stood high in his turret, firing his tommy gun while his gunner operated the machine gun and 76 mm. While thus exposed, Sgt. Householder was mortally wounded by sniper fire and his tank was disabled by a panzerfaust.

Sgt. Haymaker moved up and took the lead. His tank, too, was hit by a panzerfaust and burst into flames. The sergeant bailed out and then realized his crew could not escape under the heavy fire. Firing his tommy gun in short bursts, he moved toward the enemy, covering his crew while they withdrew, letting the Germans concentrate their fire on him. Sgt. Haymaker was killed as his crew escaped.

The medics ran to the knocked-out tanks when they were hit. T/5 John A. Dunleavy left the shelter of a building and dashed up the street to Sgt. Householder's tank. He dragged a wounded tanker to the rear of the tank and administered first aid. Picking up the wounded man, he started down the street. As he crossed an intersection Dunleavy was severely wounded by an enemy sniper. The medic was wounded a second time as he continued to drag the tanker to safety.

Pvt. Robert G. Milliman also went to Sgt. Householder's tank, pulled two wounded tankers from the turret and carried one to the safety of a building. He returned for the second man and was carrying him to safety when he was mortally wounded by sniper fire. Meanwhile, Lt. Nicodemus' tank moved forward. At an intersection the cross street was jammed with German infantrymen with rifles and bazookas. Pfc. Luther A. Parham, firing the machine gun mounted in his tank, killed or wounded 75 Germans, relieving most of the enemy pressure in that area.

C Co., 46th Infantry Bn., had dismounted and had begun cleaning out the building one by one as they moved toward the bridge. Reaching an intersection, the 2nd Platoon was stopped by sniper and bazooka fire from a house facing them. The platoon leader, Lt. Edgar D. Swihart, worked his way toward the house 150 yards away. S/Sgt. Raymond J. Caplette covered him from the other side of the street. Dodging from doorway to doorway, they both got within 50 yards of the house. Caplette fired four bazooka rounds into the house and Lt. Swihart rushed the remaining distance, entered the house and killed one German bazookaman and two riflemen.

A 47th Artillery Bn. observer, Lt. John E. Millett, Jr., came up to direct the fire of the three supporting artillery battalions. Sgt. Patsy A. Flaminio and Pfc. Preston E. Hutchcraft volunteered to take the observer to the observation post, a tower 300 yards away. Moving out ahead of the observer, these two men advanced toward the tower. They had gone a block when Hutchcraft, rounding a turn in the street, was instantly killed by a sniper. Flaminio, instead of turning back, continued to lead the observer forward. A moment later he was mortally wounded. Lt. John A. Reed then went forward and led Lt. Millett the remaining distance.

The Fight from Outside

Capt. Henry P. Halsell, CC A S-3 Air officer, watched the fight from outside the city and wrote this description:

"I was with CC A's command post about a mile and a half outside Tangermunde. We were off the road on both sides, and my halftrack was on the left and nearest the town. The 47th Field Artillery Bn. was across the road from me and the 71st Field Artillery was behind me. The 557th Field Artillery's 155 mm. self-propelled guns were going into position further back. The weather was beautiful, with the sun shining brightly.

"The artillery was firing every 30 seconds and I could see the time fire burst over the bridge site and the red dust of brick rise from the town after each volley. Some of the artillerymen were digging foxholes, for two planes had come over us very low during the morning and some artillery had landed near the engineers, on the right of the road nearer the town. The vehicles and guns, deployed in the flat fields, reminded me of desert maneuvers.

"I looked toward the town, clearly visible, and noticed a commanding rise of ground on the left of the road and the headquarters of the 46th Infantry Bn. on the road. I saw several people come over the hill and picked up my field glasses to watch. It was hard to tell what was going on, for there was little traffic on the radio. Gen. Regnier was in the town with Lt. Col. Burton at this time.

"The people on the hill proved to be German soldiers waving white handkerchiefs. As I watched, four men from the 46th Infantry Bn. detached themselves and went across the wheat field toward the Germans. As they went, more and more Germans popped out of foxholes, wanting only to surrender. I guess this must have gone on for at least an hour and that as many as 120 surrendered. The assault guns were in position at the base of the hill, firing over their heads. Perhaps they had a lot to do with the Germans' surrender.

A. A. Blasts Luftwaffe

"I was not able to watch continuously, for Heinie planes began to come in over us. I have never seen anything like it. They were not more than 50 to 100 feet off the ground. They came in from the north and from the south. We learned later that they were flying from nearby airfields. The first one I remember came from the north. Everyone opened up on it and it crashed near the engineers, shearing off a telephone pole beside the road as it bellied in. Shortly thereafter three more came from the same direction. We got two of these. The one that got away went off to the southeast so low that he had to climb to clear the hedges. A 387th Anti-Aircraft halftrack moved over to my side of the road to get in on the good shooting.

"Standing beside me was an Air Corps liaison officer and he could hardly contain himself. A pilot, he had flown 16 missions and had never seen a German plane. Today he had already seen six. He was listening to the VHF radio and could hear fighter-bombers working for the 2nd Armored Division somewhere near Brunswick, yet we could get no planes for ourselves. The pilot remarked to me, 'I'm not a very good pilot, but if I had my old T-bolt here, I'd be an ace inside of 10 minutes.'

"Planes continued to come in and be shot down. One jet plane appeared. Our guns opened up, but the pilot turned on the juice and was gone before you could blink an eye. Later in the afternoon the Germans got smart. Instead of coming over the Artillery battalions with all their anti-aircraft protection, they beat it down the Elbe so low that we couldn't shoot at them.

"Late in the afternoon, however, one pilot came in from the south. He was flying a big, two-motored bomber about 60 feet off the ground. They got him very quickly, for he did a slow bank. His left wing hit the ground and the plane crashed, throwing flaming gasoline over about an acre of ground. It was a beautiful sight, but awful, for two men in a 387th anti-aircraft halftrack were burned."

Back in town, as the married C Cos. of the 34th Tank Bn. and the 46th Infantry Bn. continued to fight their way from house to house, the married A Cos. moved up, circled and attacked the town from the northwest, with two platoons of infantry supported by tanks. Panzerfausts exploded around the tanks and German snipers kept heavy fire on the surging infantry, but nothing could stop the drive. The married A's pushed into the town, and were halfway into the center of the city when two German officers were captured. They told Capt. Devault that the garrison wished to surrender. All firing ceased, except for occasional sniping shots by the fanatic SS, and negotiations began between Lt. Col. Burton and the German commander, with Capt. Georgi acting as interpreter. Agreement was made for the garrison to surrender at 1745.

SS Hinder Negotiations

"When the German officer went back through the city, he kept telling civilians that it was all over. The people cheered and cried with joy," Capt. Georgi said.

The entire problem of attacking the town had been made extremely difficult because of 500 American prisoners of war the Germans were holding in the city. They were in two groups. One group of 300 had been liberated by the married A and C Cos. when they drove into the town, but 200 more were still in the city under SS guard. The SS troops were making their stand in the very area where the Americans were imprisoned.

While the officers awaited an answer to their surrender terms, they heard the mighty roar of explosions. During the negotiations the word came to them that the Tangermunde bridge, the span that they had hoped would carry them on a last lap to

Berlin, had been blown. Haste was no longer necessary now, and the most important consideration was to get the American prisoners to safety.

The surrender negotiations hit a snag, however. "The German colonel in charge of the city wanted to surrender," Lt. Col. Burton said. "He went to his subordinates, and most of them wanted to surrender too. But some of the SS troops said no, that they would defend the city. The mayor pleaded with them, but they still refused. When the German colonel demanded that they follow his orders to surrender and turned to leave, one of the SS men shot him. The colonel hit the ground, crawled along the ditch and escaped. Lt. Ellis R. McKay, Sgt. Woodrow Wilkinson and T/Sgt. Harry Gannon went forward and helped bring him to safety."

The men wanted nothing better than to blow down the town, for two tankers had been shot while negotiations were in progress, but the American prisoners were the deciding factor in reopening negotiations for the last time. The SS were contacted once more and firing ceased again at 2100. Lt. Col. Burton, Major Fuller, Capt. Georgi and Lt. Anesty made up the American team.

"The SS captain was arrogant," said Capt. Georgi. "He said he refused to surrender the town because he held the 200 Americans and he knew we wouldn't attack for fear of killing them. I reminded him that the town was also full of civilians and that he was in no position to bargain for anything. Lt. Col. Burton told him flatly to deliver the Americans safely to our lines by 2230, and in return we would allow the civilians until 2300 to clear the town. Then we were going to blow it apart."

American PW's Liberated

This agreement was made, and at 2230 on the dot the Americans were brought to the combat command's lines. Civilians were streaming out of the town to the outlying hills. The SS still wanted to fight, and CC A was glad of it.

At 2315 the combat command was to begin its systematic destruction of the city with its big guns. Every gun and mortar was turned on the town. The tank companies—34 tanks—were lined up outside the city. Mortars and assault guns were put in place.

The tank destroyers brought up their big 90 mm. guns. Three battalions of artillery, the 47th and 71st battalions of 105 mm. howitzers and the 557th battalion of 155 mm. self-propelled guns were alerted to fire.

The destruction started on schedule. For almost an hour the earth trembled as the combined guns tore the city apart. Houses caved in and streets erupted. By 2400 the city was dead. The men firing the guns thought with grim satisfaction of the SS troops still in the city. Everyone else had fled.

During the barrage Capt. Biederman, A Co., 34th Tank Bn., commander, was wounded for the third time during the division's campaign and was evacuated. Lt. Otho Thomas took charge of the company.

Meanwhile, Task Force Jones was waging another fight for a railroad bridge north of Tangermunde; it was the sole remaining Elbe River bridge in the division's zone. By 1800 the married B Cos., under Lt. Col. Jones, had started their attack on the railroad span. It was the start of a dramatic, beautifully executed fight by the married companies.

Lt. Col. Jones moved his companies rapidly through Ostheeren, Miltern, Langensalzwedel and Staffelde to the main road junction west of the bridge. A German infantry company, well dug in, was waiting for the married B Cos. as they moved toward the bridge.

The tanks deployed and started blasting the dug-in Germans. The 46th infantrymen piled out of their halftracks and began to work their way forward. The area above the bridge was white with air bursts as the artillery laid time fire to drive the Germans away and prevent them from blowing it. The infantry ploughed on, using marching fire to clear out the defending Germans. Lt. Champ Montgomery's leading platoon had the bridge almost within their grasp and were only 60 yards away when it exploded in their faces. Lt. Col. Jones immediately recalled his forces and pulled back to Staffelde and Langensalzwedel.

In the fight the German company defending the bridge was completely destroyed, with 110 killed and 24 taken prisoner.

Airport Taken Intact

During the night the large town of Stendal had asked to surrender, and the next day, 13 April, the combat command moved in. Near Stendal a large airport with 80 planes, all in operating condition but lacking fuel, was overrun.

The married A and B Cos. started to work north up the Elbe River, cleaning out Germans in CC A's assigned zones. The B Cos. worked closest to the river and ran into the toughest fighting. They cleared the large forest east of Stendal and then approached the ferry site at Arneburg in three columns of one married platoon each. The right platoon, working up the river road a mile south of Arneburg, caught bazooka, 20 mm. and artillery fire. It was here that S/Sgt. Frank Wheeler's tank was hit. He was injured by a shell fragment. He bailed out, but when he looked around, he saw that one of his tank crew was missing. Running to the burning and smoking tank, he started to climb up on the tank when he was killed by a sniper.

At the same time the center platoons received small arms and heavy anti-tank fire, which came from 150 mm. railroad flak guns. Lt. Clint de la Houssaye put his assault guns into position to fire on the railroad guns, and then he captured a hill by himself so he could observe the fire. In taking the hill he drove off three Germans who were also using it as an observation post. Assault guns, mortars and direct tank fire pounded the heavy railroad guns and knocked them out.

The two flank platoons assembled on the center platoon for an assault on Arneburg. Task Force Jones deployed over a wide front and took the town under fire.

During a lull in the shelling, a white flag was hoisted in the town and Lt. Col. Jones gave the order to cease firing. A German medic came out of the town with 40 men and said the remainder of the garrison would surrender if given the opportunity. Lt. Col. Jones sent him back into the town with instructions that all who would surrender must give themselves up in 30 minutes. At 1830 he returned with 40 more prisoners, but said he lacked time to contact the whole garrison.

Heavy Fire from Hospital

It was growing dark, and Lt. Col. Jones decided to attack the town immediately. He gave instructions to attack at 1846, but to withdraw if fighting grew too heavy. The attack was made with two dismounted platoons of infantry moving abreast, covered by combined assault fire of the tanks and mortars. The advancing force was met by small arms, machine guns and bazooka fire. A large hospital was in the town and explicit instructions had been given to the men to avoid firing on it. It was from this hospital that the heaviest German fire came.

The leading platoons had penetrated into the middle of the town without the loss of a man when the decision was made to withdraw. The task force assembled in the woods near Wischer and throughout the night guns of the 34th Tank Bn., and 47th Artillery Bn. fired on Arneburg.

On 14 April Task Force Burton moved west and met the 102nd Infantry Division coming up the river. The C Cos. remained in Stendal, guarding supply installations and controlling the large numbers of displaced persons.

At dawn Lt. Col. Jones moved his task force on Arneburg again, and after a 15-minute mortar and artillery concentration, launched an attack starting at 0830, with dismounted infantry supported by tanks. Resistance was light and the town was clear by 1140. In the attack Pfc. Robert E. Schierholz, a B Co. rifleman, saw a German bazookaman come up out of his foxhole, fire a round at a tank and miss. Schierholz nailed him with his M-1, putting eight rounds into the German before he could fall to the ground. Lt. Thomas Burke helped coordinate and direct most of the supporting fire.

The town netted an additional 52 prisoners and the German material losses amounted to four 150 mm. railroad guns, four 20 mm. flak guns, a military train, an ammunition dump and 10 American 2½-ton trucks.

Task Force Jones continued north after cleaning out the town and cut the last escape route for the Germans in the command's zone. The Germans were desperately trying to cross the river on ferries and barges at several points and the mortar platoons kept busy taking pot shots at them.

For the next week CC A scoured rear areas, looking for German forces which were harassing the division's supply lines. The 46th Infantry Bn.'s Reconnaissance Platoon and a CC A billeting detail were captured by a large German force near Kobbelitz. One man, Pfc. Perry Watkins, escaped and the others were held prisoner in the woods. Their German captors knew it was only a matter of time until they themselves were captured, and treated the Americans with the greatest respect, offering them cigarettes and finally releasing them the following night.

XXI

THE LAST FIGHT

15 April–23 April

After its spectacular drive to the Elbe the Fifth Armored turned around, cleaned out by-passed rear areas, destroyed a newly-formed German division, and for the second time, fought to the Elbe River.

CC B raced 55 miles to the rear to trap and destroy the Von Clausewitz Division. CC A drove north to the Elbe and made contact with the British, CC R, keeping abreast of CC A, also drove to the Elbe.

Combat Command B

CC B's final appearance on the Western Front came as an encore. But it was an encore which almost surpassed an already brilliant and spectacular main performance. Appropriately, it was a battle between American armored and German panzer forces. And it was CC B's most decisive engagement.

When the combat command reached the Elbe on 13 April, it appeared that CC B's job on the continent had been completed. But on 15 April, when word was received that marauding enemy groups were endangering the division's supply lines far to the rear, CC B was ordered to meet this new threat. At 1730 that day, less than an hour after they had rejoined the rest of the command on the Elbe after being relieved of their security mission at the Weser-Elbe Canal, the married B Cos. of the 81st Tank Bn. and the 15th Infantry Bn. were sent racing back to Winterfield. The entire command prepared to make the 50-mile run the following morning.

While the column was on the road, rolling west during the morning, Col. Cole was notified that a convoy of supply trucks had been ambushed near Ehra. He immediately sent the armored fingers of the reconnaissance elements probing the area north of the main supply route between Ehra and Klotze. Task Force Anderson combed the area in the vicinity of Donitz, while Task Force Dickenson worked from Brome to Millin and the 85th Reconnaissance Sq.'s B Troop from Brome to Jubar. But no enemy force was encountered.

Forest Combed for Krauts

The forests in the area were combed again the next morning and roadblocks were strung out along a 25-mile front facing north from Wittingen through Zaesenbeck to Ruhrberg. Thirty minutes after tankers and infantrymen from the married A Cos. had set up a roadblock near Ohrdorf they spotted a column of vehicles sneaking along the edge of a woods southeast of Wittingen.

"We could just about make them out because they were about 2600 yards away," said S/Sgt. Harold J. Strunk, sergeant of the 2nd Platoon. "There were five tanks and two halftracks."

"Right after we caught our first glimpse of the column, it disappeared behind another clump of trees," said Sgt. Salvatore Candito, a tank commander. "But when it came out on the other side of the trees, we started tossing shells at it."

Sgt. John Ivers, tank gunner, targeted in and, at the 2600-yard range, knocked out a tank and a halftrack.

That evening Col. Cole summoned his task force commanders for a meeting at CC B Headquarters. On his way there, Lt. Col. Dickenson was thrown out of his peep and injured when the vehicle hit a bomb crater in the road. He was evacuated to a hospital and Major Emerson F. Hurley took over command of the task force.

That night Task Force Anderson established roadblocks at Mehmke, Ruhrberg and Stockheim, while Task Force Hurley set up roadblocks at Zaesenbeck, Ohrdorf and Wittingen.

About noon on 18 April the 71st Artillery Bn.'s observation plane reported that strange vehicles were moving southeast out of Lindhof. A section from the married B Cos. was sent to investigate, and when the men reached Jubar they noticed what appeared to be a column of enemy tanks heading into the woods north of Ludelsen.

More Road Blocks Established

Task Force Anderson moved quickly to surround this enemy force. The married B and C Cos. set up strong roadblocks at Jubar, Borsen, Mehmke and Stockheim, while a tank destroyer platoon from the 628th T.D. Bn.'s B Co. and the Anti-Tank Platoon from the 15th Infantry Bn.'s B Co. put in a roadblock at Ludelsen.

After all of the exits from the forest had been sealed off, the gun batteries of the 71st Artillery Bn., which were in position at Gladdenstadt, started pounding the woods. Fire was adjusted by the Cub observation plane, and then the 47th and 555th Artillery Bns. joined in the serenade.

When the clouds of billowing smoke and dust started to clear, a platoon of infantrymen with a tank destroyer and a new M-26 tank went down one of the firebreaks to develop the situation.

"Our first shot got an American truck which the Krauts had captured and were using," said Sgt. Herbert A. West, commander of the tank destroyer. "After our second shot set the truck on fire, our third round also went through the truck, set fire to a halftrack that was behind it, and then knocked out an armored reconnaissance car."

Small arms fire was heavy, but the M-26 tank opened up with its powerful 90 mm. gun and destroyed two more armored vehicles. Then the small probing force was instructed to pull back out of the forest immediately. Supporting fights of Thunderbolts had arrived to deliver a final, crippling blow to the remaining enemy resistance in the woods.

Six flights of four planes each descended on the woods. Following the radio directions of the slow-flying but sharp-eyed Horsefly (air-ground liaison observation plane), they bombed and strafed and sent rockets smashing into the trapped enemy force. The roar of the explosions could be heard for miles across the German heartland and by dusk every German vehicle beneath the huge clouds of dust and smoke had been destroyed.

The Horsefly, a recent innovation to aid fighter-bomber observation, had been developed some time earlier, but ideas for its further development had been added by Major Ernest Briggs, division G-3 air officer. Lt. Edward F. Little, of CC A Headquarters, did the observing during the action; he helped the fighter-bombers locate their targets and then radioed back the results.

Survivors of the attack came out of the woods. Sick of war and shaken within an inch of their lives, they surrendered readily.

Just before dark the 3rd Platoon of the married A Cos. went up from Ohrdorf through Haselhorst and set up a roadblock in the little village of Lindhof. They were sent there to prevent any elements of the battered enemy force to their right from moving west and also to protect the 71st Artillery Bn.'s batteries which had taken up positions to the south of Haselhorst. They did not know what was north of them and had been informed that friendly troops might be in the area.

About 2130 that night a powerful force of tanks and armored vehicles descended from the north and rolled into the village.

"We held our fire and let them get up close to us because their column was led by three American halftracks," said Cpl. Vincent Stolarczyk of the 15th Infantry Bn. "We didn't know they were Heinies until they started talking German."

"Before we knew it, they had hit our tank and set it on fire," said Cpl. Stacey Dickson, a tank commander of the 81st Tank Bn. "We were lucky and we all managed to get out of it all right."

When the Germans started to surround the roadblock, the GI's fought their way out of the encirclement and pulled back toward Haselhorst. Ten infantrymen and two halftracks got caught in the enemy trap. The wounded infantry platoon leader, Lt. William M. Capron, was evacuated on the back of one of the tanks.

From the ridge near Haselhorst, the tankers, acting as observers, started directing artillery fire on the enemy vehicles and temporarily halted the advance.

"We used our knocked-out tank, which was burning brightly in the darkness, as a reference point and laid down the artillery barrages all around it," said Sgt. Wilbert Hufman.

When the shells started whining in on the enemy force and scattering the German soldiers, the A Co. infantrymen who had been encircled took the opportunity to make a break from their captors. Cpl. Stolarczyk and Pvt. Glen Byrd got up and ran while the Germans had their heads down and rejoined their platoon at Haselhorst. Then Pfc. Robert E. Scharon and Pfc. Charles G.

Harrison climbed out of the foxhole where they had concealed themselves and made a dash to one of their abandoned halftracks. While Scharon guided him from the front of the vehicle, Harrison drove the halftrack back to American lines.

Enemy Plans Revealed

"They captured me and I was put in a halftrack with 12 Germans," said Pvt. Basilo Contrares. "But when our shells began whistling in, they all jumped out and headed for cover—all except my guard. So during the excitement I grabbed him and threw him out of the vehicle; then when a shell blew his head off, I took off and got back to my outfit."

When the enemy assault wave first hit the roadblock at Lindhof and started to overrun it, the 85th Reconnaissance Sq.'s B Troop, which was holding a block on a road that ran northeast out of Lindhof, captured one of the attackers. Pfc. Ray F. Burke took this soldier and rushed him back to CC B Headquarters through territory that had now been overrun by the Germans.

Interrogated by Lt. Franklin P. Copp, this prisoner revealed not only the identification of this enemy force, but also its strength, mission and operational plans. He stated that it was the Von Clausewitz Panzer Division, and that it was attempting to push south across the Weser-Elbe Canal and then head for the Harz Mountains. The recon party that had been sent out to find a clear route south out of Jubar was the force that had been destroyed in the woods that afternoon.

The main body of the panzer division, he said, consisted of three task forces. Each task force, approximately 1000 men strong, was equipped with one Mark V tank, two tanks mounting 75 mm. guns, one Mark IV with 75 mm. rifle, one tank destroyer mounting an 88, 25 halftracks, four 105 mm. self-propelled howitzers, three tractor towed 105 mm. guns, many cargo trucks, and several American peeps, trucks and halftracks. The division also had attached to it a special signal company so that it could remain in direct contact with its army group.

Said CC B's S-2, Major Martin M. Philipsborn, who had also served as an intelligence officer in North Africa, "This is the first instance in operations against the enemy, that I can recall, when we knew his strength, objective and tactical plans while they were still being executed."

This invaluable information was immediately dispatched to all units. They now knew what faced them and could prepare to counter the enemy plans. On the road that led west out of Lindhof, Headquarters Platoon of the 85th Reconnaissance Sq.'s B Troop held a roadblock with two halftracks, one armored car and three peeps. When the B Troop commander, Capt. Loran L. Vipond, read the message from CC B, he immediately sent back the following message: "If the attack is diverted in this direction, we may need a little help."

While one enemy column was pushing from Lindhof to Haselhorst that night, another started south down a second route which led to Hanum. Out in front was a truck and an American halftrack with all guns blazing. When a 628th T. D. Bn. Tank Destroyer smashed both vehicles as they approached the town, the remainder of the column deployed into the woods and did not attempt to advance any further.

Throughout the night the enemy vehicles could be heard moving about and getting into position for an attack in the morning. At the A Cos. command post the tank company commander, Capt. Robert M. McNab, and the infantry commander, Capt. George W. Kellner, organized their men and prepared to meet the full weight of the enemy thrust. The married 1st Platoon was sent to Haselhorst to reinforce the 3rd Platoon. Then, after the 71st Artillery Bn. batteries had displaced from Haselhorst to Ohrdorf, the two platoons also pulled back to Ohrdorf at 0500 and set up defense positions in a semi-circle around the town.

"As we were withdrawing to these new positions, a German self-propelled gun and a halftrack started down the road toward us," said Lt. Robert P. Lant, the 1st Platoon tank commander. "Our tanks opened up and got the gun and our infantry shot up the personnel in the halftrack."

Germans Try Again

At daybreak the German tanks and self-propelled guns rumbled to the edge of the woods and started blasting the defense positions around the town. Two medium tanks were hit and the building in which the 71st Artillery Bn. fire direction center was located was also hit and set on fire. The rest of the Shermans swept the advancing enemy tanks and guns with fire and the artillery batteries put down a barrage of shells on them.

"We pumped five shots into a Mark IV and finally stopped it," said Sgt. Charles Petersen, tank commander.

The enemy attack got no further than the edge of the woods.

To the west, tank destroyer men on a roadblock near Wittingen saw two German vehicles come out of the forest behind them.

"Our gun was pointed in the opposite direction when we spotted them through binoculars," said Sga. Mike Gazdaka. "We swung it around quickly and at a range of 1500 yards knocked out both of them. We later discovered that one was a halftrack and the other a German tank destroyer."

At Lindhof Pfc. Grover Peffers and Pvt. Paul Dempsky had remained in their foxholes all night while the artillery pounded the enemy-held village. Then, at daybreak, they crawled out and were taken prisoner.

"We got to talking to this Heinie tech sergeant who spoke very good English," said Dempsky. "He had lived in the States for several years and we talked about Boston and New York and the World's Fair. And then he told us he was fed up and wanted to surrender. So during the next barrage the three of us took off for our lines."

All day the artillery continued to smash the bottled-up enemy vehicles which had deployed in the woods. Waves of Thunderbolts roared in and, working through the Horsefly, mercilessly strafed and bombed the German force.

During the afternoon six enemy ambulances, loaded with wounded, pulled down to American lines and surrendered. Out of the woods came streams of nerve-shattered prisoners, including all of the division's staff except the division commander, Gen. Unrein, and his chief of staff who managed to slip through to the south and were later captured in the Harz Mountains.

When one of these prisoners declared that a GI lay wounded in a house at Lindhof, the report was radioed to Task Force Hurley and was overhead by Pfc. George S. Kehm and Pvt. Herman Kaplan, medical aid men.

Although the village was in German hands and was being leveled by artillery and fighter-bombers, Kehm and Kaplan left immediately in their peep and entered Lindhof. The peep was seen by the planes from the air, but task force headquarters could not assure the pilots that it was one of their vehicles, so the planes continued to bomb and strafe.

"After we picked up the wounded man and started back out of town," said Kaplan, "six Germans who said they wanted to surrender jumped on the peep and came back with us."

On the right flank Task Force Anderson combed the woods in which the recon elements of the Von Clausewitz Division had been trapped, but no further resistance was encountered. Later in the afternoon the roadblocks south of Jubar were strengthened, as it was believed that the Germans would make an attempt after dark to break through there.

The remnants of this debacle did make the desperate attempt to escape through the steel cordon that had been tightened around them, but they were unsuccessful.

"Our battery was still in position near Ohrdorf and about 0230 that morning we heard their vehicles start milling around, and then about 0400 they started coming toward us," said Lt. Norman E. McNees, reconnaissance officer for the 71st Artillery Bn.'s B Battery. "We started firing point blank, but we didn't hit anything in the dark."

"When it got light," said Sgt. Philip L. Henderson, third section chief, "we knocked out a radio truck with direct fire and captured the occupants of an armored recon car and a motorcycle rider."

Sgt. Gazdayka and his tank destroyer crew, after firing without success in the dark, went into action again at dawn and destroyed a halftrack and a cargo truck.

At 1000 that morning the married B Cos. started clearing the Klotze Forest from the east, pushing west toward Lindhof and Haselhorst. The fighter-bombers and artillery worked the woods over again about noon and by 1400 both towns had been taken. On the west side of the forest a tank equipped with a loudspeaker urged the Germans to surrender. Twenty men and one officer responded immediately.

CC B had trapped two task forces of the Von Clausewitz Division in this pocket. The third task force had turned west and then south and was being destroyed by XIII Corps troops. By the morning of 21 April, all of the enemy vehicles which had attempted to slice through CC B had been knocked out and all but a few of the German soldiers had been killed or captured. CC B's losses in annihilating these two task forces were five men killed, two wounded, two missing.

Since 1 April the command had taken 3150 prisoners, killed 800 Germans and wounded 800 more. And it had destroyed or captured 72 miscellaneous assault guns, 110 miscellaneous vehicles, 10 tanks, 21 locomotives, a trainload of ammunition, 11 barges and two flak radar stations.

On 24 April the order came down for CC B to leave the Klotze Forest and move to another area a few miles west. Men in the command did not know it then, but for them the war in Europe was over.

Combat Command A

On 20 April, CC A was alerted for a move to clear out German pockets north toward the Elbe. That afternoon A Troop, 85th Reconnaissance Sq., and Task Force Jones moved north, clearing the woods north of Rohrberg and seizing the line of departure for the attack.

At 0100 the forces manning the line of departure reported vehicular movement to their front. From prisoners it was learned that two battle groups of 100 to 200 men each, with 12 assault guns or tanks, were attempting to move south through the outpost line. Enemy pressure increased, and soon the married 2nd Platoons of the B Cos. of the 34th Tank Bn. and the 46th Infantry Bn. were heavily engaged in the darkness against an aggressive enemy. The platoons were only at half strength as a result of the previous heavy fighting at Wolbeck, the railroad bridge and Arnsburg.

Lt. Alfred Richter, B Co., 34th Tank Bn., platoon leader, called for permission to withdraw from the town of Wistedt and move back across a small stream 50 yards from the town. By 0500 enemy infantry had infiltrated across the stream and superior forces were closing in on the platoon from three sides. The married 2nd

Platoons withdrew across the stream and reinforced the 3rd Platoons in Langenapel.

At 0630 Lt. Col. Burton arrived at Langenapel with the married A Cos. The presence of this force effectively discouraged the enemy from making further attacks. Gen. Regnier arrived shortly afterwards and made plans for the 2nd and 3rd Platoons to retake Wistedt. The married platoons attacked the town again and by noon had retaken it. Gen. Oliver had come forward to confer with Gen. Regnier and watched the fight as Wistedt was recaptured.

In Wistedt the married platoons found ample evidence of the effectiveness of the fight they had been waging. A total of 171 prisoners was taken, and 24 trucks, 10 trailers, two halftracks, six scout cars and two assault guns were destroyed.

Meanwhile the married A Cos. had deployed over a wide front and, as soon as Wistedt was taken, launched a full scale attack on Hennigen. The town was quickly taken, together with large numbers of prisoners. Most of the prisoners were from the Panzer Brigade Feldhernhalle, the same outfit which had given CC A such a fierce fight outside Luxembourg City back in September.

By now the backbone of the enemy's defenses had been broken and CC A advanced rapidly. In Gergan Task Force Burton came under mortar and anti-tank fire. The infantrymen of A Co., 46th Infantry Bn., dismounted and mopped up the resistance. By nightfall, leading elements had reached Gaddau.

Resistance was lighter on 22 April. In the morning the A Cos. received two concentrations of nebelwerfer fire and suffered casualties. The command advanced rapidly north through a large forest, meeting scattered small arms and rocket fire.

Tallyho!

The afternoon of 22 April, the A Cos. made contact with the British. The meeting almost ended in disaster. American, British and German forces were so intermingled throughout the area that it was impossible to decide whether to fire if a strange vehicle were sighted.

Cpl. James E. Mathies, tank gunner of A Co., 34th Tank Bn., was all set for anything as his tank rounded a corner and he saw an unfamiliar vehicle 400 yards away, its gun pointed straight at

Mathies' tank. Mathies' 76 roared twice in rapid succession and the rear of the strange vehicle disappeared. It was a British scout car. The British soldiers manning it piled out and were recognized before further damage was done.

The Britsh commander of the car afterwards came up looking for Mathies. "That was fast shooting, old chap," he told the 34th Tank Bn. gunner. "We had been there an hour, waiting to shoot anything that moved around that corner, and when you came around it you hit me twice before I could lay my hand on the trigger." With that he patted the startled Mathies on the back and went to see what he could salvage out of his scout car.

The combat command continued to push north, cleaning out objectives one by one during the day. Major Fuller, leading the married C Cos., reached the last corps objective on the west.

During the night the C Cos. sent out a patrol to make contact with the A Cos. on their right. An enemy column was discovered, caught between the two married companies. Lt. Walter Williams, commanding the 2nd Platoon of A Co., 34th Tank Bn., with tank destroyers of A Co., 628th T. D. Bn., knocked out two German tanks at a roadblock and the patrol was burdened with so many prisoners that it had to return without making contact.

The last day of the fight, 23 April, the married A Cos. of Capt. De Vault and Lt. Thomas attacked the town of Hitzacker and seized the high ground nearby. The 85th Reconnaissance Sq. set up an observation post there. Hitzacker was defended by a company of dug-in infantry on the western edge, a roadblock, a flak gun, a Panther tank and many panzerfausts. The infantrymen of the 46th Infantry Bn. attacked the town on foot, supported by tank and tank destroyer fire. As they moved in they received heavy fire from German machine guns and the Panther tank. The machine gun positions were chopped up by the heavy tank fire, and the Panther tank was blasted with three direct hits by Cpl. Samuel Kubisco, Lt. Williams' gunner.

By 1300 the town was taken and the high ground to the north secured. A total of 200 prisoners was taken in the town.

From the high ground the infantry spotted a barge loaded with Germans trying to escape with their equipment across the Elbe. Tank guns fired at it, but it floated out of range down the river.

A Cub plane arrived and laid in the command's artillery, knocking out the heavily loaded barge.

On the north the married C Cos. pushed patrols down to the Elbe at numerous points. Task Force Jones took prisoners in the Dannenberg Forest and at Schmardau the 34th Tank Bn.'s Reconnaissance Platoon forced the surrender of an entire German company. At a large oil dump near the river, Capt. Seymour Scott, commanding A Troop, 85th Reconnaissance Sq., captured another 170 Germans with their officers.

By a coincidence, a German maintenance unit surrendered its complete equipment, including a large stock of tires and tubes, to the 34th Tank Bn. maintenance officer, Capt. Armand E. Cabrel. The German unit had heard a rumor that it was to be used to defend Berlin, and had decided to reassemble on the American side of the river and surrender.

On 24 April the 29th Infantry Division relieved CC A and the command moved to occupy an area further west.

V-E Day found the command peacefully caring for displaced persons, the war having ended for them almost two weeks before.

Combat Command R

CC R had ended its first battle for the Elbe River, but the combat command had still another mission ahead of it before its war role was over.

The combat command was mopping up scattered resistance in the vicinity of Winterfeld when, on 18 April, it was ordered north of Salzwedel, in the British Zone of Occupation. From there it was to drive north, smash strong enemy forces still holding the area, and take the Elbe River town of Dannenberg. For the second time in a month its objective was the historic Elbe.

On 20 April, C Troop of the 85th Reconnaissance Sq. set out from Salzwedel to reconnoiter routes toward Luchow and ran into enemy roadblocks and infantry in the woods west of Salzwedel.

The order for the attack came 21 April. The married A and C Cos. of the 10th Tank Bn. and the 47th Infantry Bn. under Lt. Col. Hamberg were to clean out German forces from the woods to the west, while the married B Cos. were to push toward Luchow and await the rest of the combat command there.

Clearing the woods was no simple mopping up operation for Task Force Hamberg. The enemy armored and infantry forces holding the area were augmented by Germans who had been pushed back into the woods by CC A's advance on the left of CC R.

While one married company thrust south from Salzwedel to a railroad line, the other struck north from the southern edge of the woods. The 95th Artillery Bn. smashed enemy troops and material caught in the trap, blasting eight dual-purpose 88 mm. guns, nine nebelwerfers and a number of machine gun nests.

Near Seeben, Pvt. Hugo D. Musgrove, of the 47th Infantry Bn., set off into the woods after four German soldiers and found himself face-to-face with an enemy tank. He ran back to his halftrack, snatched up a bazooka, returned, and with his second round destroyed the retreating tank at the range of 300 yards.

By 2100, when the task force bivouacked for the night, they had flushed out and destroyed nine long-barreled 75 mm. guns mounted on Czechoslovakian tank chassis, as well as three armored vehicles, a Volkswagon and a dozen trucks.

The married B Cos. attacked north at 1430 and ran into heavy enemy fire from their left flank as they neared Saase. Lt. Howard K. Kettlehut, 95th Artillery Bn., forward observer, moved with the forward elements, directing artillery fire from his batteries on anti-tank guns and nebelwerfer positions. A half hour later the armored column hit a roadblock protected by mines. The C Co. engineers went forward to clear the mines while the task force went into bivouac. In a day of hard, bitter fighting the combat command had taken 300 prisoners.

After their mission of clearing the woods was completed, the married A and C Cos. of Task Force Hamberg moved out at 0645 the next morning, 22 April, in two columns pushing toward Luchow. The C Cos. moved through Salzwedel and Luckau; the A Cos. through Brietz, Wustrow and Dolgow.

South of Luchow the B Cos. ran into a hasty minefield. Lt. Stephen E. Allen, Jr., and his 22nd Engineer platoon cleared away the mines and the column ground on toward the town.

The two columns of Task Force Hamberg joined near Luchow and the C Cos. led the way into the town. The B Cos., on a parallel route across the Juetze River, entered Luchow from the opposite side. The town surrendered unconditionally at 0815.

The two task forces pressed on, the A and C Cos. of Task Force Hamberg striking north through Grabow; the B Cos. thrusting through Seeraw toward Zadrau. As they advanced, all three companies came under heavy nebelwerfer fire north of Luchow. The columns halted while the 95th Artillery Bn. went into position. Because of the difficult terrain, however, placing the howitzers into position to bring fire on the nebelwerfers proved to be a long, tedious task.

While the column was halted, Lt. Robert Stutsman led a dismounted patrol from B Co., 47th Infantry Bn. through the Luchow Forest toward Zadrau where the enemy was reported to have set up its regimental command post. Moving through the woods, the patrol encountered heavy sniper fire. The infantrymen continued mopping up the area during the halt, and C Cos.' engineers pulled mines from the road shoulders.

Fight to Dannenberg

It was 1400 before the columns moved out again. Lt. Col. Hamberg's troops met with little resistance as they pushed through Tramm and on toward the outskirts of Dannenberg.

The married B Co. under Lt. Col. Boyer found Zadrau bitterly defended by Hitler Jugend troops, some only 14 to 16 years old but fighting with fanatical tenacity. Their sniper fire was unusually accurate, and they continued to fire even when the houses where they had barricaded themselves burned down around them.

Roadblocks and tank traps around Zadrau added to the difficulty of taking the town. The 95th Artillery Bn. and the supporting fighter-bombers took over. Zadrau was a mass of smoking rubble when the task force again churned on, turning west toward Heide.

In Heide a Cub plane pilot, flying in the rain ahead of the armored colunm, spotted six heavy German 88 mm. guns, being towed by prime movers. He radioed the position to the 95th Artillery Bn. The batteries let loose with a barrage on the enemy column. When the tankers and infantrymen of the married B Cos. entered Heide and turned east toward their original route, they found the six demolished 88's, the crews still in their seats where they had been caught by the deadly accuracy of the 85th Artillery Bn.'s shellfire.

Outside of Heide, Task Force Boyer ran into a column of 10 towed nebelwerfers. First encountered by the married A Cos. as they had moved off on the left to contact CC A to the west, the German column had fled east, cut in front of the C Cos. and would have made good their escape had not the B Cos. come thundering up the road at that moment. The tanks blasted the six-barreled mortars, smashed the entire column, and ground on toward Dannenberg.

As the A and C Cos. of Task Force Hamberg moved through Shaafhausen toward the outskirts of Dannenberg, the 2nd Platoon of the C Cos., led by Lt. William J. Caroscio and Lt. Paul Vostic, turned down a side road and came upon a huge, carefully concealed assembly plant for V-1 and C-2 robot bombs. So well camouflaged that it blended into the woods and was almost invisible from the road, the plant consisted of more than 60 separate buildings, roads and railroad sidings. There the men discovered a new and untried German secret weapon, a piloted V-1 bomb complete with cockpit, instrument panel and controls, and a parachute so the pilot could drop to safety after he had trained his bomb on the target.

Lt. Col. Hamberg's A and C Cos. were closing in on Dannenberg from the west when anti-tank shells from the vicinity of the town came slamming into the column. The lead tank and two halftracks were knocked out. The armor drew back while infantrymen of the 47th Infantry Bn. dismounted and made their way through the forest toward Dannenberg, looking for the gun positions. They found three 88's and two 20 mm. guns, and directed 95th Artillery Bn. fire on the positions.

The two task forces remained overnight outside of Dannenberg and prepared to assault the town in the morning. The A and C Cos. bivouacked at Shaafhausen, while the married B Cos. halted at Nebenstedt.

That night the report came that the Germans were hurriedly ferrying reinforcements across the Elbe for the defense of Dannenberg. All available artillery was turned on the town and the ferry sites on the river.

On the morning of 23 April, the two task forces moved into Dannenberg; the two married companies of Task Force Hamberg pushed in from the west, and the married B Cos. of Task Force Boyer entered the town from the east. After a brief fire fight, the town put out white flags at 0830.

Now the ferries that had been bringing reinforcements were evacuating the Germans back across the Elbe at Domitz. The 95th Artillery Bn. batteries turned their fire on these ferry sites.

During the remainder of the day, CC R accepted the surrender of a number of communities in the area. The A and C Cos. cleared the area through Prisser, Riskau and Kabmen; the B Cos. mopped up around Quickborn and Susborn. By late evening, CC R's second drive to the Elbe and final mission in Europe had been completed.

Division Staff *and* Unit Commanders

5TH ARMORED DIVISION

ORGANIC UNITS

Headquarters Company, 5th Armored Div.
Combat Command A
Combat Command B
Combat Command R
10th Tank Battalion
34th Tank Battalion
81st Tank Battalion
15th Armored Infantry Battalion
46th Armored Infantry Battalion
47th Armored Infantry Battalion
5th Armored Division Artillery
47th Armored Field Artillery Battalion
71st Armored Field Artillery Battalion
95th Armored Field Artillery Battalion
85th Cavalry Reconnaissance Squadron (Mecz)
22nd Armored Engineer Battalion
145th Armored Signal Company
127th Ordnance Maintenance Battalion
75th Armored Medical Battalion
Military Police Platoon
5th Armored Division Trains
5th Armored Division Band

COMBAT COMMAND A

Brig. Gen. Eugene A. Regnier
COMMANDING

COMBAT COMMAND A plunged into the fight south of Fougeres, France, to lead the Division in the encirclement of the city of Le Mans. Striking north, Gen. Regnier's columns forged the inner ring of the steel circle which trapped the Germans in the huge pocket behind the Argentan-Falaise gap. The fighting men of Combat Command A saw the city of Argentan on the night of 12 August, eight days before the trap was closed. In the Eure-Seine corridor bitter resistance was crushed to create the second pocket in France.

Crossing the Meuse south of Sedan, the tank-infantry teams caught the Germans by surprise and liberated Luxembourg City and captured intact the powerful transmitter of Luxembourg Radio at Junglinster. Shaef Psychological Warfare Section regarded this as the "greatest single stroke of luck in the war."

Beyond the Hurtgen Forest in the mud and cold of December the enemy was cleared to the Roer River by taking the high ground overlooking Winden and the capture of the towns of Kufferath and Schneidhausen. Across the Roer in February the battle was carried from Rheindahlen to the Rhine at Krefield.

In the final chapter of World War II this fighting team crossed the Rhine River on the last day of March and reached the Elbe River at Tangermunde at noon on 12 April 1945.

Gen. Regnier joined the Fifth Armored Division in December 1942 at Camp Cooke, Calif., and was assigned to Combat Command B. In September 1943 he was transferred to Combat Command A, which he commanded throughout the war.

He began his military career in May 1917, when he was commissioned a Second Lieutenant in the Infantry. Serving overseas in World War I he participated in the St. Mihiel and Meuse-Argonne campaigns.

Following the war Gen. Regnier served two tours of duty with the 1st Cavalry Division. During the period 1929-1933 he was Aide-de-Camp to the Honorable Henry L Stimson when he was Governor-General of the Philippines and Secretary of State.

He attended the Cavalry School in 1921 and the Command and General Staff School in 1938. He was an instructor in the tactics department of the Cavalry School in 1939.

In March, 1941, he returned to the 1st Cavalry Division and commanded the 91st Cavalry Squadron. Transferred to the 6th Armored Division in July, 1942, he commanded the 68th Armored Regiment. He was promoted to Brigadier General 3 December 1942 and joined the Fifth Armored the same month.

Combat Command A's Fighting Team

34th Tank Battalion
46th Armored Infantry Battalion
47th Armored Field Artillery Battalion
Troop A, 85th Cavalry Recon. Squadron
Co. A, 22nd Armored Engineer Battalion
Co. A, 628th Tank Destroyer Battalion
Battery A, 387th AAA AW Battalion

COMBAT COMMAND B

Col. John T. Cole
COMMANDING

COMBAT COMMAND B engaged the first enemy troops near Vitre, France, as the columns rolled east to block the escape routes from the city of Le Mans. Following the drive to Argentan, the tanks raced to the city of Dreux to capture the Eure River line as German tank reserves approached from Paris.

After clearing the enemy between the Eure and Seine Rivers, Combat Command B streaked north through the Compiegne Forest to the Belgian border at Conde. Then, after clearing a sector through Luxembourg 150 miles to the east, Col. Cole's troops were the first Allied soldiers to cross the German border. A small patrol from Troop B, 85th Cavalry Reconnaissance Squadron crossed the Our River boundary at Stalzemburg at 1630 on 11 September 1944. Five days later the whole combat command penetrated into the pillbox area beyond Wallendorf to draw large German forces from the Aachen area.

In the crossing of the Roer in February, Combat Command B lashed out across the flat country to cut off Erkelenz and capture to key city of Rheindahlen. Four days after crossing the Rhine in April the Weser River was reached at Minden and Bad Oeynhausen. Stopped at the Elbe on 13 April, Combat Command B returned 75 miles to open up the XIII Corps supply route. The fighting ended with the complete destruction of the Von Clausewitz Panzer Division in the Klotze Forest.

Col. Cole was assigned to Combat Command B in September 1943 when the Fifth Armored Divison was stationed at Pine Camp, N. Y. He took the combat command overseas and commanded it throughout the fighting in Europe.

A graduate of West Point's 1917 class, Col. Cole served overseas in World War I with the 3rd Cavalry and the Tank Corps. From 1924 to 1928 he was an instructor in the techics department at the United States Military Academy.

Col. Cole was a member of the Army Horse Show Team and the U. S. Olympic Equestrian Team from 1930 to 1934. Following the Olympic Games in 1936 he was Captain of the Army Horse Show Team in 1936-37 and again in 1938-40. He was Captain-elect of the U. S. Olympic Equestrian Team in 1940 when the games were cancelled due to the war.

He graduated from the Cavalry School Troop Officers' Course in 1923, Advanced Course in 1929, and Advanced Equitation Course in 1930. He completed the Command and General Staff School in 1938.

From 1934-36 he commanded the 2nd Squadron, 7th Cavalry, 1st Cavalry Division. Assigned to the 2nd Cavalry at Ft. Riley in 1940, Col. Cole assumed command of that unit in April 1941. He was transferred to the Armored Force in July 1942 and assigned to the Fifth Armored Division the following September. He commanded the 81st Armored Regiment until September 1943.

Combat Command B's Fighting Team

81st Tank Battalion
15th Armored Infantry Battalion
71st Armored Field Artillery Battalion
Troop B, 85th Cavalry Recon. Squadron
Co. B, 22nd Armored Engineer Battalion
Co. B, 628th Tank Destroyer Battalion
Battery B, 387th AAA AW Battalion

COMBAT COMMAND R

COL. GLEN H. ANDERSON
COMMANDING

THE HISTORY OF COMBAT COMMAND R really began in June 1944 when Gen. Oliver designated Col. Anderson's Reserve Command as a fighting combat command. Augmented with personnel from the 47th Armored Infantry Battalion, the staff was complete when the command assembled in Normandy.

Pacing Combat Command A in the drive to create the Falaise Gap, Combat Command R awaited orders on 12 August 1944 to advance and meet the British north of Argentan. When the Division stopped on the Belgian border, Col. Anderson's forces streaked 100 miles in eight hours, to make the first crossing of the Meuse River in the First Army sector.

On 14 September the combat command completely penetrated the Siegfried line and had crossed the Prum River on the route to Bitburg when orders stopped the advance. In the muddy battles in the Hurtgen Forest in December, Combat Command R received the Distinguished Unit Citation for the capture of the towns of Kleinhau, Brandenburg, and Bergstein.

In late February Combat Command R passed through the other combat commands, to carry the advance of the Division to the banks of the Rhine River at Orsoy. Col. Anderson's troops spearheaded the Division's advance to the Weser River. After a three-day halt, Combat Command R continued to drive to the Elbe, reaching its bank opposite Whittenburg, 12 April 1945

Col. Anderson's service with the Fifth Armored Division started in the middle of the desert maneuvers in September 1942 He commanded the 46th Armored Infantry Regiment until September 1943. From that date, as commanding officer of the Reserve Command, he supervised the training of the three armored infantry battalions.

Col. Anderson's military career started in 1917 when he graduated from West Point with a commission in Infantry. He served as a captain during the first World War.

He graduated from the Infantry School in 1933 and completed the course at the Command and General Staff School in 1936 He is also a graduate of the French Tank School in Versailles, France.

Col. Anderson had various assignments with infantry units following the war. From 1936 to 1940 he was an instructor at The Infantry School. Two years prior to joining the Fifth Armored Division he commanded the 752nd Tank Battalion at Ft Lewis, Washington.

The title of "Foghorn" was given Col Anderson by the soldiers of Combat Command R because of his deep, mellow voice

Combat Command R's Fighting Team

10th Tank Battalion
47th Armored Infantry Regiment
95th Armored Field Artillery Battalion
Troop C, 85th Cavalry Recon. Squadro
Co. C, 22nd Armored Engineer Battalio
Co. C, 628th Tank Destroyer Battalion
Battery C, 387th AAA Battalion

DIVISION ARTILLERY

COL. DOUGLAS J. PAGE
Commanding

THE FIFTH ARMORED DIVISION ARTILLERY included three organic self propelled battalions; the 47th, 71st, and 95th Armored Field Artillery Battalions. The 387th Anti-Aircraft Artillery AW Battalion operated under "Divarty" and, at times, the 628th Tank Destroyer Battalion fired under the artillery control.

The armored artillery M7s were designed to keep closely behind the fast-moving tank columns and answer requests for fire from positions on the roads or in the fields. The quick response from the artillery battalions was outstanding in the Fifth Armored Division.

The 47th claims the distinction of having fired the first artillery at the Germans in Argentan and to have said "On the Way" for the first shells that landed in Germany.

Most exciting action for the 71st occurred in April 1945 at Hazelhorst, Germany, when 88mm shells ripped through the building housing the fire direction center. The M7s returned with direct fire while the headquarters moved.

The 95th's most thrilling action came during the first penetration of the Siegfried Line through Wallendorf. At Hommerdingen the 105s fought off tank-infantry assaults to defend their position area.

Prominent among the attached artillery units were the 400th Armored, 987th, and 557th Field Artillery Battalions.

The first Artillery officer for the Division was Col. Harold W. Blakely. He was succeeded by Col. Roy L. Dalferes, who remained in that position until June 1944. At that time Col. Douglas J. Page joined the Division in England and continued until the end of the war as Artillery Officer.

Col. Page graduated from the United States Military Academy in 1916 as a Second Lieutenant in Infantry. He transferred to the Cavalry in 1917 and to the Artillery in 1920. During World War I he was promoted to the rank of Major. Colonel Page's military career includes many artillery assignments. In 1940-41 he commanded the 34th Field Artillery Battalion. In the fighting in North Africa he was executive officer of the 9th Infantry Division Artillery.

CHIEF OF STAFF

COL. EDWARD G. FARRAND

IN AN ARMORED DIVISION the Commanding General has in his headquarters the General and Special Staffs to handle the details in planning and carrying out operations of the division.

The General Staff is responsible for the management of the personnel, intelligence, operations, and supply of the division, while all other activities in the headquarters are performed by the Special Staff members.

Col. Edward G. Farrand, as Chief of Staff, directed and coordinated the work of both staffs and acted as the adviser to the Commanding General from August 1943 until the end of the war. The personality of Col. Farrand is woven deeper into the record of the Fifth Armored Division Headquarters than any other officer since he was present at the origin of the Division as assistant G-3. He became G-3 in January 1942 at Camp Cooke, Calif., and Chief of Staff at Pine Camp, N. Y. Tall, energetic Col. Farrand was known to everyone as "The Chief."

He graduated from the United States Military Academy in 1927 with a commission in Artillery. After several assignments with artillery units he returned to West Point as a language instructor from 1934 to 1938. Shortly before joining the Fifth Armored in October 1941 he attended the Command and General Staff School at Ft. Leavenworth.

LT. COL. FRANCIS W. MARKS
ASSISTANT CHIEF OF STAFF G-1

LT. COL. FRANCIS W. MARKS was the personnel manager for the Division. His duties included the requisition and assignment of replacements, processing of the recommendations for decorations, promotions and transfers of individuals, and the evacuation of prisoners of war. He joined the Division at Camp Cooke, Calif., as adjutant of the 81st Armored Regiment, and became G-1 in December 1943. A lawyer in civilian life, Lt. Col. Marks is a graduate of Boston University.

Assistant Chief of Staff G-2

LT. COL. LONSDALE P. MACFARLAND, JR., directed the Division's intelligence activities. He evaluated and disseminated enemy information and furnished terrain studies for the combat elements. From troop reports and the interrogation teams he furnished the Commanding General detailed reports of the enemy's capabilities. Lt Col. MacFarland joined the Fifth Armored Division during activation in August 1941. He is a graduate of Virginia Military Institute and Cumberland University. A native of Tennessee he practices law in civilian life.

Assistant Chief of Staff G-3

LT. COL. F. BOYNTON BUTLER, JR., was responsible for the preparation of field orders and keeping higher headquarters informed of the location of the flying tank columns. His section also coordinated the air support for the Division. An original cadreman at Ft. Knox, Ky., Lt. Col. Butler was executive officer of Combat Command A prior to becoming G-3. He is a graduate of New Mexico Military Institute and Northwestern University. In civilian life he is the business manager of the Wisconsin Alumni Research Foundation at Madison, Wisc.

Assistant Chief of Staff G-4

LT. COL. HARRISON R. ENTREKIN was responsible for the supply of the Division. Whether it was exploiting across France and Germany or slugging it out in the Hurtgen Forest, Lt. Col. Entrekin coordinated the flow of food, clothing, gasoline, and ammunition with the battalion supply sections. He joined the Division on October 1, 1941 as a member of the Division staff. Born in Indiana and a graduate of Purdue University, he is a telephone engineer and lives in Oak Park, Illinois.

Combat Command A's Married Team

Lt. Col. Thomas B. Bartel

Lt. Col. Richard H. Jones

34th TANK BATTALION

THE 34th TANK BATTALION was activated at Pine Camp, N. Y. on 20 September 1943 by the redesignation of the 2nd Battalion, 34th Armored Regiment. The light tank company, (D), was formed by the transfer and redesignation of Company A, 81st Armored Regiment. Lt. Col. Thomas B. Bartel commanded the battalion on activation and went with it overseas. He was wounded 1[?] August near Argentan, France. Major Glen L. Foote led the battalion to the Seine River. Lt. Col. Karl L. Scherer commanded from 30 September to 8 November when Lt. Col. William L. Cabaniss arrived. On 30 January Lt. Col. Cabaniss was wounded Lt. Col. Richard H. Jones assumed command on 15 February 1945 and remained until the war ended.

46th ARMORED INFANTRY BATTALION

Lt. Col. William H. Burton, Jr.

THE ORIGIN of the 46th Armored Infantr Battalion dates back to 1 January 194 when the 3rd Battalion, 46th Armored Infantry Regiment was formed from the 1s and 2nd battalions of that unit. On 2 January 1943 it received the separate battalion designation. The list of commanding officers includes Maj. Dee R. Ellis, Lt Col. Leo F. Kengla, Lt. Col. Edgar A. Gans and Lt. Col. Burton. The 46th was taken overseas by Lt. Col. Earl S. Gibson. Receiving command of the 46th again in April 1944 Lt. Col. Burton led it throughout the war except for a week in Augus when he was wounded.

Combat Command B's Married Team

81st TANK BATTALION

LT. COL. LEROY H. ANDERSON

PERSONNEL of the 81st Tank Battalion trained for two years as the 2nd Battalion, 81st Armored Regiment. On 20 September 1943 personnel from Headquarters and Service Companies of the 81st Regiment were added when it became a separate battalion. Company B of the Regiment was redesignated Company D and became the battalion's light tank company.

The first commander was Lt. Col. Hollis B. Hoyt. Maj. Jesse M. Hawkins, Jr. succeeded Lt. Col. Hoyt upon arrival at Camp Cooke. In July 1942 Lt. Col. LeRoy H. Anderson became commanding officer and remained with the battalion through the remainder of the training and all of its combat in Europe.

15th ARMORED INFANTRY BATTALION

THE 2ND BATTALION of the 46th Armored Infantry Regiment was redesignated as the 15th Armored Infantry Battalion on 20 September 1943. Lt. Col. Earl S. Gibson commanded during the first two years of training. Lt. Col. Wintermute took the battalion overseas and was wounded 10 August north of Le Mans, France. Major Toney Giorlando assumed command until 28 August. Lt. Col. Kenneth P. Gilson led through north France and Luxembourg and was wounded near Niedersgegen, Germany on 20 September. Lt. Col. Dickenson joined on 23 September and commanded until the last fight near Wittingen, Germany, the middle of April 1945, when he was injured in a vehicle accident.

LT. COL. GLENN G. DICKENSON

LT. COL. JOHN S. WINTERMUTE

Combat Command R's Married Team

10th TANK BATTALION

Lt. Col. William A. Hamberg

WHEN THE tank regiments gave way to the administrative battalions on 20 September 1943 at Pine Camp, N. Y., the 3rd Battalion of the 34th Armored Regiment was redesignated as the 10th Tank Battalion. Personnel for the headquarters and medical detachment also came from the 34th. Company C, 81st Armored Regiment, was transferred and redesignated as Company D, 10th Tank Battalion. The list of commanders includes Lt. Col. Paul C. Febiger, Maj. Joseph J. Baker, and Maj. Thomas H. Dowd. Lt. Col. Hamberg became commanding officer in the desert maneuvers and remained in that position throughout all the fighting in Europe.

47th ARMORED INFANTRY BATTALION

THE PERSONNEL of the 47th Armored Infantry Battalion spent the first two years training as the 1st Battalion of the 46th Armored Infantry Regiment. The 47th title is the result of the redesignation when the Division was streamlined at Pine Camp, 20 September 1943. The commanding officer at Ft. Knox on 1 October 1941 was Maj. Maurice F. Brothers. He was succeeded by Lt. Col. James W. Newberry. Just before the move to the desert from Camp Cooke, Lt. Col. Howard E. Boyer was assigned to the battalion and remained as its commanding officer throughout the training and all of the combat period.

Lt. Col. Howard E. Boyer

47th ARMORED FIELD ARTILLERY BATTALION

Lt. Col. John B. Rosenzweig

THE 47TH ARMORED FIELD ARTILLERY BATTALION was the direct support battalion of Combat Command A.

The 47th was activated as a regiment on 1 June 1941 at Fort Bragg, N. C., with a cadre from the 9th Infantry Division Artillery and the 13th Field Artillery Brigade. On 1 February 1942 the First Battalion of the 47th Regiment was redesignated as the 47th Field Artillery Battalion and moved to Fort Sill where the unit served as school troops until early September.

Arriving at Freda, California, 10 September 1942, during the desert maneuvers the 47th became an organic battalion of the Fifth Armored Division. Lt. Col. H. K. Palmer commanded the battalion until 14 July 1943. On that date at Pine Camp, N. Y., Lt. Col. John B. Rosenzweig assumed command and remained as commanding officer throughout the war.

71st ARMORED FIELD ARTILLERY BATTALION

Lt. Col. Israel B. Washburn

THE 71ST ARMORED FIELD ARTILLERY BATTALION was Combat Command B's direct support battalion.

The 71st was activated 9 January 1941 at Fort Jackson, S. C. It was formed by redesignation of the 3rd battalion of the 83rd Field Artillery Regiment. On 28 May 1941 the battalion was transferred to Fort Sill, Oklahoma and remained as the Field Artillery School troops until September 1942. The battalion joined the Fifth Armored Division in the desert on 10 September 1942 and was redesignated as the 71st Armored Field Artillery Battalion.

Lt. Col. Israel B. Washburn has been the battalion's only commander since 28 July 1942.

95th ARMORED FIELD ARTILLERY BATTALION

Lt. Col. James W. McNeer

THE 95TH ARMORED FIELD ARTILLERY BATTALION was a member of Combat Command R's fighting team.

The 95th Armored Field Artillery Battalion was activated 1 January 1942 at Fort Knox, Kentucky. The cadre came from the 58th Battalion and 65th Field Artillery Regiment (Armd.) The entire Battery "D" of the 65th was transferred and redesignated as Battery "A" of the 95th.

The first commander was Lt. Col. Samuel K. Krauthoff. Other commanding officers were Maj. Malcolm K. Benadum, Maj. LeCount H. Slocum, and Maj. Daniel H. Heyne. Lt. Col. James W. McNeer became CO of the 95th at the end of the desert maneuvers and commanded for the duration of the war.

387th ANTI-AIRCRAFT ARTILLERY BATTALION

Lt. Col. Elmer I. Kenneweg

THE 387TH ANTI-AIRCRAFT ARTILLERY AUTOMATIC WEAPONS BATTALION (Self-Propelled) joined the Fifth Armored Division 1 August in France—just in time for the breakout of Normandy and remained with it until V-E Day.

This battalion's normal mission was to protect the artillery positions and the Division Trains from enemy aircraft, but by war's end the 387th was experienced in all types of warfare. This battalion's record of enemy aircraft is 56 destroyed and 30 probably destroyed.

The 387th was activated at Camp Edwards, Massachusetts, 20 January 1943, as a coast artillery battalion. On 10 April 1943 it was redesignated as an anti-aircraft artillery automatic weapons battalion. The unit trained in Tennessee in February and March of 1944 and was hurried off to England, arriving 17 April. Landing on Utah Beach on 29 June, the 387th moved to Cherbourg where it defended the port until it joined the Fifth Armored.

Lt. Col. Elmer I. Kenneweg commanded the 387th throughout the training and combat periods. Inactivated 30 June 1946.

22nd ARMORED ENGINEER BATTALION

Lt. Col. Fred E. Ressegieu

THE 22ND ARMORED ENGINEER BATTALION was an original Fifth Armored Unit. Maj. Reginald L. Dean was the first battalion commander at Ft. Knox. Commanders at Camp Cooke included Maj. Oliver G. Benson and Lt. Col. Morris M. Bauer. Lt. Col. Ressegieu became the commanding officer in December 1942 and remained with the battalion throughout the war.

In September 1943 the 22nd lost Company E which was redesignated the 989th Engineer Treadway Bridge Company. Company D was also taken away in the reorganization at that time.

The engineers have been called the most versatile troops in the 5th Armored Division. They built bridges, cleared minefields, maintained roads, demolished pillboxes, provided drinking water, and even fought as infantrymen.

In most of the combat a company of engineers was attached to each of the combat commands. Company A worked with CC A, Company B with CC B, and Company C with CC R. During the exploitation in France the engineers spanned many blown bridges, and removed mines and roadblocks to carry the Division to the Seine River. First American troops to reach the Seine were members of a 22nd water point crew. They damaged the locks on the Seine to prevent the movement of supply-laden barges downstream to the retreating Germans.

Appreciated most by the leading tank platoon and doughs was the engineer reconnaissance officer with his expert advice in the removal of charges from culverts and bridges and his knowledge of mines and booby traps.

While Company A was cracking roadblocks in the Compiegne Forest, Company B bridged the Oise River for the Division's sweep to Belgium. Near Conde, Pvt. Thomas E. King alone held off a German motor convoy until he was mortally wounded. He was the first 22nd man to be awarded the Distinguished Service Cross.

Company C built the first bridge across the Meuse River in the First Army sector, one of the three spans the 22nd constructed over that stream. The same company built the bridge at Wallendorf, Germany which carried the first American forces to breach the Siegfried Line.

In the Hurtgen Forest the engineers, in the roughest, most bitter mission they had undertaken, removed mines and filled shell craters under artillery fire to keep the roads open. When enemy fire destroyed the mine detectors they hacked roads with bayonets to locate the buried mines.

Across the Rhine, Capt. Charles Perlman's Company C built a treadway bridge over the Ems canal in record time. Further north Company A, under Capt. Thomas Grose, also bridged the Ems. At the Weser River Capt. Rolf E. Michelson's Company B constructed a 372-foot treadway bridge for the XIII Corps. Bridging of the Elbe River on 13 April was prevented only by orders cancelling the crossing.

127th ORDNANCE MAINTENANCE BATTALION

THE COMMANDER of the 127th Ordnance Maintenance Battalion performed a dual role since he was the Division Ordnance Officer on the special staff.

Whether it was replacing a tank transmission or repairing a delicate watch, it was all in a day's work for the 127th. They had the huge job of keeping the Division's

LT. COL. ROLAND S. BIERSACH

2,400 vehicles in running order. In addition, they repaired and adjusted the 7,100 rifles and carbines, 1,200 machine guns, 221 tank guns, 80 artillery pieces and other assorted weapons. They also repaired gasoline stoves, modified tanks and other vehicles, repaired fire control optical instruments, and ordered, issued, and installed thousands of spare parts.

During the Division's rush across France, Luxembourg, and Germany, the 127th worked under terrible handicaps of time and weather, often setting up in open fields in deep mud and snow. Detachments from A, B, and C Companies were attached to the three combat commands and brought right up to the front to save time.

During the nine months of combat the Ordnance Battalion repaired 1,422 tanks and other combat vehicles and 1,826 general purpose vehicles. During that time more than 1,500 tons of spare parts were handled and issued, all of it in a period when the battalion moved its heavy equipment more than 35 times, or an average of once a week.

The Fifth Armored's first maintenance unit was the 21st Ordnance Battalion (Armored). On 1 January 1942 the 21st was inactivated. For the next 20 months the ordnance supply and repair crews functioned under the title of Maintenance Battalion, Fifth Armored Division. In September 1943 the Battalion was redesignated as the 127th Ordnance Maintenance Battalion. Lt. Col. Roland S. Biersach became commanding officer in January 1944 and remained the 127th director until the end of the war. Previous commanders included Lt. Col. John D. Killgreen, Lt. Col. Chas. R. Pinkerton, and Capt. John P. Sherden.

85th CAVALRY RECONNAISSANCE SQUADRON

LT. COL. KENT FAY

DURING THE FIRST TWO YEARS of training the 85th Armored Reconnaissance Battalion consisted of four line companies. In September 1943 Troops D and E were added with the redesignation and transfer of the Reconnaissance Companies of the 34th and 81st Armored Regiments, respectively. At the same time the title was changed to Cavalry Reconnaissance Squadron and the term "Troop" replaced "Company."

The list of commanders from the beginning included Lt. Col. Frank A. Allen, Jr., Lt. Col. Thomas G. Dobyns, Maj. Wayne J. Dunn, and Lt. Col. Gustavus W. West. Lt. Col. Kent Fay became commanding officer when the unit moved to Tennessee in March 1943.

The 85th reconnoitered routes and front lines 50 miles south of the Division assembly area in Normandy. Troops of the 85th were the first soldiers of the Fifth Armored to contact the enemy – 2 August 1944. Lt. Col. Fay was killed in action as the drive across France approached the Compiegne Forest on 30 August. Maj. John P. Gerald commanded the Squadron through north France and Luxembourg. During the consolidation on the German border Maj. Ger-

MAJ. JOHN P. GERALD

LT. COL. GEORGE C. BENJAMIN

ald was killed in action on 17 October while accompanying one of his reconnaissance patrols. Lt. Col. George C. Benjamin commanded the 85th for the remainder of the fighting.

Trained and equipped as the eyes and ears of the Armored Division the 85th did everything from slugging it out as tanks and infantry to performing rapid road reconnaissance. Across France the troops protected the flanks of the spearheading combat commands, contacted friendly troops across miles of enemy-held area, and kept up the constant flow of enemy information through its many radios.

The Squadron carried its own artillery in Troop E, the assault gun troop. Many times it was the only support for the armored cars and peeps of Troops A, B, C, and D. In the Hurtgen Forest fighting near the Roer River the men from the line Troops fought in the mud as infantry.

Company F, the light tank company, was a burning needle in the flank of many German columns. With other members of the 85th as infantry, these tanks fought through the mud in December to carry supplies and evacuate wounded from Bilstein, Bergheim, and Hill 201 overlooking the Roer River at Winden, Germany.

In the 12-day drive from the Rhine to the Elbe, the 85th came into its own as the peeps and armored cars roamed far and wide over the North German Plain to protect the flanks of the Division's columns.

75th MEDICAL BATTALION ARMORED

GALLANT SOLDIERS were the aid men who followed the tank company in a peep and accompanied the infantry platoon on foot.

Symbolic of the courage and devotion to duty of all Fifth Armored Medical personnel were the actions of S/Sgt. THOMAS A. GREENE. His Distinguished Service Cross citation read: ". . . He was last seen kneeling over a soldier on the side of the road, dressing his wounds."

In the furious fire fights during exploitation across France they used tanks as a shield from machine gun fire as they stopped the bleeding and splinted fractures. After transferring the wounded from peep to ambulance, sometimes it became a rolling hospital as they were evacuated forward. Plasma bottled swung from the tops of the ambulances, pouring life-saving fluid into the veins of the wounded. When the tactical situation permitted, the ambulances would make the long trip to the evacuation hospital.

LT. COL. BENJAMIN H. BADER

At Wallendorf, in the pillbox area, it was "Medics! Medics!" Armored doughboys of CC B and CC R spread the cry as the Germans poured artillery into their positions. Aid men pulled the wounded out of foxholes and surgeons worked miracles in the surgical trucks and tents.

Again in the Hurtgen Forest it was "Medics! Medics!" Artillery was so heavy that frequently the aid men could not crawl to a wounded man's foxhole. Instead they rode in tanks. They pulled the wounded out of their cold, water-filled holes, lifted them into tanks, and took them back to a crude aid station for treatment. Ambulances couldn't make it through the shelling by day, but carried their wounded at night, churning steadily back to the clearing station. Here the men were treated and their pain eased. The men with trench foot had the shoes cut off their purplish, swollen feet. A few minutes later they were moved again, rolling back in ambulances to the comfort of an evacuation hospital.

From July until V-E Day, the 75th Medical Battalion treated 10,346 patients, including many wounded Germans. Members of the battalion won six Silver Star Medals, 43 Bronze Star Medals, 35 Purple Hearts, and a Croix de Guerre.

The 75th was an original unit of the Division. At Ft. Knox and Camp Cooke the commanding officer was Lt. Col. Carlton D. Goodiel. Lt. Col. Benjamin F. Bader took command in the Tennessee Maneuvers and remained until 5 February 1945, when he was returned to the states. Maj. Raymond J. Winkler continued until the end of the war as the battalion commander.

628th TANK DESTROYER BATTALION

LT. COL. WILLIAM J. GALLAGHER

THE 628th TANK DESTROYER BATTALION was attached to the Division 2 August in Normandy and fought with it for the duration except for six weeks in mid-winter—19 December to 28 January. During that period the 628th fought in the Ardennes with the 3rd Armored and 82nd Airborne Divisions.

In offensive action one company of the 628th was attached to each of the combat commands—A Company to CC A, B Company to CC B, and C Company to CC R.

Originally the 28th Infantry Division's Antitank Battalion, it was designated the 628th Tank Destroyer Battalion on 3 January 1942. The battalion trained in Louisiana, Camp Bowie, Texas, and participated in the Tennessee maneuvers in the summer of 1943. It sailed for England on 29 January 1944 and arrived in Normandy on 30 July 1944.

Lt. Col. William M. Hernandez, battalion commander since November 1941, was killed in action in France on 20 August 1944. Lt. Col. William J. Gallagher commanded the battalion for the remainder of the fighting. Inactivated 14 November 1945.

DIVISION TRAINS

LT. COL. KARL L. SCHERER

THE DIVISION TRAINS was organized in January 1942 as the Fifth prepared to move to Camp Cooke, Calif. Col. Gustin M. Nelson commanded the Trains most of the training period and took them to England. Shortly before the move to Normandy Lt. Col. Glenn G. Dickenson was assigned to the Trains and led them until 18 August when Col. Nelson returned. On 7 November Lt. Col. Karl L. Scherer became commanding officer and remained until war's end.

In the exploitation across France the Trains stayed as close as possible to the combat commands for security. When the fighting settled down to the slugging along a line the Trains found it possible to remain well to the rear in order to perform the administrative details required in a division.

The term "Trains" includes all the personnel, vehicles and equipment that make up the rear echelon of the Division. Most

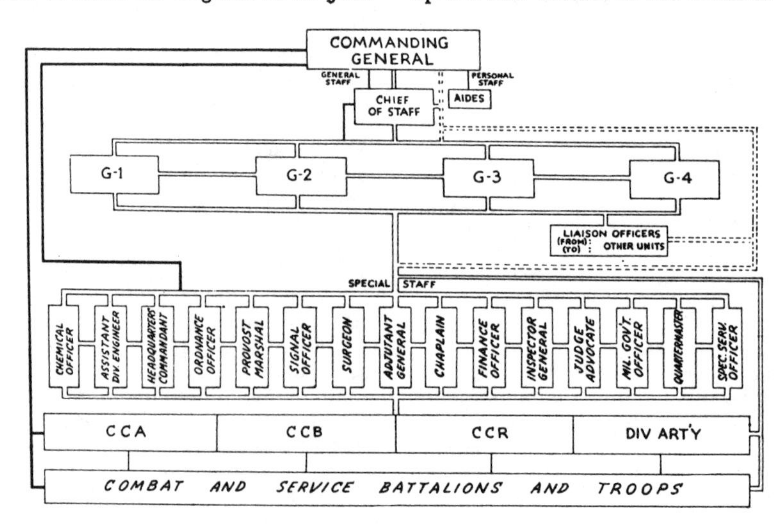

ORGANIZATION CHART

familiar to the combat troops were the Battalion Personnel sections, the Army Post Office, and the finance office. Also located in the Trains area were the Ordnance repair shops, the Signal maintenance and supply sections, the Quartermaster office, the Division Band, the Adjutant General, and the other special staff sections.

Many times the unit personnel officers were required to form patrols from their groups of company clerks and search woods for German paratroopers when the Division was located near the Hurtgen Forest.

Just four days before the Ardennes offensive started the Trains moved from the path of the panzer divisions at Waimes, Belgium. In late December and early January 1944 they assembled at Verviers and Pepinster, Belgium to replace and repair the damages suffered in the Hurtgen.

During the exploitation to the Elbe River in April the Trains played hide and seek with two Infantry divisions in trying to keep up with the rapid advances of the combat commands of the Fifth. The friendly Infantry divisions ordered the Trains off the road several times in an effort to keep up close behind the Victory tankers.

DIVISION HEADQUARTERS

THE FORWARD ECHELON is the tactical headquarters of the Commanding General, his staff, and those directly concerned with the fighting. In the rear echelon are the administrative offices which maintain the vast amount of records and reports. The rear echelon moves with the Division Trains.

Closely behind the fighting combat commands move the halftracks and peeps of the forward echelon. Into this headquarters flow orders from higher headquarters, reports on the progress of the fighting, information of the enemy, reports on strength in personnel and materiel, and the availability of supplies. Here this information forms the basis of the Commanding General's plan of action. Orders covering all phases of the operation go out by radio, liaison officer, wire, and messenger to the units.

During combat Gen. Oliver seldom stayed at the headquarters but was up front with the battalion commanders where he secured first-hand knowledge of the changing situations.

145th ARMORED SIGNAL COMPANY

SIGNAL ACTIVITIES in combat were directed by Capt. Glenn A. Welde, 145th Company Commander, and Lt. Col. Erling J. Foss, Division Signal officer.

The 145th radio operators, repair and supply crews performed the never-ending job of maintaining communications. When on the move, the radio sets were issued on an exchange basis; when the Division stopped, the sets were repaired and wire was used. "No set deadlined more than 24 hours," was the motto of the 145th. A total of 1625 radios were repaired during the fighting period. In addition, all the signal equipment in the replacement vehicles was checked and serviced before it went forward to the combat elements.

The 145th was an original Fifth Armored Unit. Company commanders during the training period were Capt. John S. Gruel Capt. Erling J. Foss, and Capt. Wolf E. Jessen. Succeeded by Lt. Col. Foss in September 1943, Lt. Col. Lee R. Williams was the first Division Signal officer.

QUARTERMASTER TRUCK COMPANIES

THE 3907th Q. M. TRUCK COMPANY was attached on 29th August 1944 and remained with the Fifth for the remainder of the war except for three weeks in December.

The 3912th Q. M. Truck Company was attached on 5 August 1944 and on the very first trip delivered gasoline directly to the tanks in the fields south of the Mayenne River on the route to Le Mans.

Only colored troops to wear the shoulder patch of the Fifth Armored were the men of the 3907th and the 3912th. Their main job was hauling gasoline — the life blood of an armored division. But they also hauled ammunition, food, clothing, and the many other items required by combat troops.

It was a hard, grueling grind, highballing the 2½-ton six-wheeled cargo trucks and their trailers over the rutted, battle-scarred roads of France, Belgium, Luxembourg and Germany, but the truckers can boast they never let the Division want for supplies when they were available. They relate many thrilling stories of rolling through enemy-infested areas and have seen many fire fights.

Eleven 3912th truckers hold the Bronze Star Medal, while five of the 3907th have received that decoration along with five Purple Hearts and eight individual citations.

After joining the Fifth, the 3912th clocked 825,000 truck miles and the 3907th followed closely with 785,000. These truckers claim to be the first colored troops in Belgium, Luxembourg, and Germany, as well as the first Negro soldiers to enter Paris in World War II.

3907th QM TRK Co.
CAPT. CHARLES H. DUDLEY
3912th QM TRK Co.
CAPT. JOSEPH L. ZIOLKOWSKI

THE CHAPLAINS

THE FORWARD OBSERVER was having a tough time trying to keep the artillery fire on the German soldiers, who were appearing on all sides like ants swarming out of an ant hill, when someone tapped him on the shoulder. Turning, he saw that it was the chaplain. "I was just giving you the blessing," said the officer with the cross on his collar. "You keep the shells flying and I'll do the praying."

But the chaplains did more than pray. When all but one of the surgical sections were withdrawn from a particularly hot section of the Siegfried Line, we stayed with the remaining medics, helping to carry litters and evacuate the wounded. He was one of the last to leave when the troops were withdrawn under heavy shelling.

Men at war are always in need of spiritual support. Throughout the Victory Division's rough and stormy career, its chaplains have always been at the side of the fighting men, administering to their spiritual needs and sharing their dangers and hardships.

During the drive across the European continent, all sorts of strange places have served as their churches: beer halls, movie houses and stables. But more often the services were held in open fields, during rain and snow storms, with a portable field organ resting in the mud or an altar on the hood of a peep. Often these services were interrupted by the whine of incoming shells. When the men were too busy to attend services, the chaplains visited them at the foxholes and tanks.

When the fighting was heavy, the chaplains were never far behind the assault troops, at the collecting stations for the wounded, giving aid and comfort to the men, and frequently visiting the forward aid stations.

For their meritorious service in action, nine of the Division's Chaplains have been awarded the Bronze Star Medal and one received the Purple Heart for battle wounds.

Lt. Col. Harold H. Schulz was Division Chaplain and Maj. John H. Callahan was Assistant Division Chaplain.

AMERICAN RED CROSS

John R. Barstow, Sr., *Field Director*
Division Rear (Transferred from Fifth Armored at Malmedy)
Fred Lange Stone, Sr., *Field Director*
Division Rear (Succeeded J. Barstow at Malmedy)
George E. Wright, *Field Director*..........CC B
Harold S. Tinklepaugh, *Field Director,* CC R

MILITARY POLICE

THE MILITARY POLICE PLATOON was activated at Pine Camp in September 1943 and operated under the control of the Provost Marshal, Maj. Alexander T. Nelsen.

The Traffic Section, under 1st Lt. Manuel P. Ashkenas, directed and coordinated the movements of the Division. The Police Section, commanded by 1st Lt. Peter J. O'Neil, collected prisoners of war from each of the combat commands and escorted them to the enclosures.

At Wallendorf, five out of six men at one control point were wounded. As one man was hit, another took his place from the nearby foxholes. In the Hurtgen Forest, 52 control points were set up to control the Division's traffic. After the tank columns crossed the Rhine the prisoner bag became so large that it was not uncommon to see a lone MP in charge of a thousand prisoners.

MILITARY GOVERNMENT

IMMEDIATELY BEHIND, sometimes with, the tankers and infantrymen as they entered the German towns came the Military Government Section (later called the G-5 Section), to assist the fighting troops in controlling the civilians.

Operating as a Civil Affairs Section under Maj. John W. Sampier in friendly countries, this group became the Military Government Section upon entering Germany and was directed by Maj. Alfred E. Baldridge. Its function was to govern the civilians in areas occupied by the Division.

Security was the principal objective during combat. MG men, entering a town, ordered the civilians indoors, the firearms collected, and the soldiers surrendered. They posted regulations and ordered the burgermeister to have the streets cleared of roadblocks.

When the troops stopped long in an area, the MG men regulated the circulation of civilians, selected temporary officials, and listened to many problems of the civilians whose economy had been disrupted by the war.

MAJ. GEN. JACK W. HEARD
COMMANDING GENERAL
October 1941 to February 1943

MAJ. GEN. JACK W. HEARD was the first Commanding General of the Fifth Armored Division.

Following the activation 1 October 1941, the Division trained at Ft. Knox, Ky. until February 1942 when it moved to Camp Cooke, Calif. After completing the basic training for 9,000 soldiers the Division moved to the Desert Training Center for four months of maneuvers in the fall of 1942. Returning to Camp Cooke in December, the troops were in the midst of combat firing when Gen. Heard left the Division. He was transferred to the War Department Manpower Board where he served as chairman and member until May 1946.

Gen. Heard's military career began in 1910 when he graduated from the United States Military Academy with a commission in the Cavalry. In World War I he attained the rank of Lt. Col. He was promoted to Brigadier General in October 1940 and Major General in February 1942.

The list of service schools completed by Gen. Heard includes the Command and General Staff School, the Army Industrial College, the Army War College, and the Naval War College.

Prior to joining the Fifth Armored Division, Gen. Heard commanded the 13th Cavalry and the Armored Force Replacement Training Center at Ft. Knox.

DISTINGUISHED UNIT CITATIONS

COMBAT COMMAND R

TROOP A, 85th CAVALRY RECONNAISSANCE SQUADRON (MECZ)

COMPANY B, 47th ARMORED INFANTRY BATTALION

COMPANY C, 47th ARMORED INFANTRY BATTALION

COMBAT COMMAND R AT KLEINHAU, BRANDENBURG, AND BERGSTEIN

GENERAL ORDERS No. 31

WAR DEPARTMENT
WASHINGTON 25, D. C., 18 March 1947

* * * * *

V.—BATTLE HONORS.—As authorized by Executive Order 9396 (sec. I, WD Bul. 22, 1943), superseding Executive Order 9075 (sec. III, WD Bul. II, 1942), the following units are cited by the War Department under the provisions of section IV, WD Circular 333, 1943, in the name of the President of the United States as public evidence of deserved honor and distinction. The citation reads as follows:

Combat Command R, 5th Armored Division, composed of the following units:
Headquarters Reserve Command, 5th Armored Division;
Detachment A, Headquarters and Headquarters Company, 3d Armored Group;
10th Tank Battalion;
47th Armored Infantry Battalion;
95th Armored Field Artillery Battalion;
Company C, 85th Cavalry Reconnaissance Squadron (Mecz);
Company C, 22d Armored Engineer Battalion;
Company C, 628th Tank Destroyer Battalion (SP);
Company C, 387th Antiaircraft (AW) Battalion (SP);
Company C, 75th Medical Battalion (Armored);
Detachment, Company C, 127th Ordnance Maintenance Battalion,

is cited for outstanding performance of duty in action from 29 November to 8 December 1944 in Germany. During the severe battle of the Hurtgen Forest, this combat command played a heroic and highly essential part in the operation aimed at capturing the vital Roer River dams. *Combat Command R, 5th Armored Division,* spearheaded three important advances during the period, capturing Kleinhau on 29 November, Brandenberg on 3 December, and Bergstein on 5 December. In each instance, the men of *Combat Command R, 5th Armored Division,* were sent out front to capture the fortified town and hold it until friendly infantry could clear the adjacent woods. Under extremely unfavorable weather conditions and over terrain emphatically not suited to armored action, this command gallantly attacked through deadly mine fields against a determined enemy, well-entrenched, fortified, and supported by intense artillery and mortar fire. In conjunction with friendly infantry on the flanks, *Combat Command R, 5th Armored Division,* successfully captured the three important towns and cleared a fortified zone of enemy resistance on the Vossenach Ridge. Since Bergstein was most important to the Germans in connection with the defense of the Roer River dams, they defended it bitterly and made fanatic efforts to recapture it, once it had fallen. However, *Combat Command R, 5th Armored Division,* although reduced to 8 effective tanks and some 20 effective riflemen per company, employed the last available man, and heroically repelled almost continuous combined armored and infantry counterattacks against the heights of Bergstein for a period of 36 hours. In keeping with the highest traditions of the military service, the entire *Combat Command R, 5th Armored Division,* and attached units, by its undaunted determination, outstanding courage, and grim tenacity, captured and held, against the strongest German resistance, the important heights which dominated the Roer River dams.

TROOP A, 85th CAVALRY, AT UNTERMAUBACH

General Orders No. 34 | WAR DEPARTMENT, Washington 25, D. C., 3 May 1945

* * * * *

IV.—BATTLE HONORS.—7. As authorized by Executive Order 9396 (sec. I, WD Bul. 22, 1943), superseding Executive Order 9075 (sec. III, WD Bul. 11, 1942), citation of the following unit in General Orders 12, Headquarters 5th Armored Division, 6 April 1945, as approved by the Commanding General, European Theater of Operations, is confirmed under the provisions of section IV, WD Circular No. 333, 1943, in the name of the President of the United States as public evidence of deserved honor and distinction. The citation reads as follows:

Troop A, 85th Cavalry Reconnaissance Squadron, Mechanized, is cited for outstanding performance of duty in action from 15 to 22 December 1944 near Untermaubach, Germany. During a series of attacks eastward from Kleinhau, Germany, unto high ground north of Untermaubach, *Troop A,* though previously trained and experienced in mounted reconnaissance, exhibited a remarkable adaptability to dismounted infantry tactics and was successful in seizure of its assigned section on Hill 253. Despite a terrific barrage of enemy artillery and mortars and two savage counterattacks, *Troop A* held its sector firmly against overwhelming enemy numbers and fire power for a period of 4 days. On 19 December 1944, having suffered 50 percent losses, the troop was assigned the mission of penetrating to the rear of the enemy outposts and severing the main enemy supply route. The troop, with 50 percent of its fighting strength suffering battle wounds, deftly cut the supply route and established a road block which it held for 3 days, even though the operation planned relief the first day. Although completely surrounded by strong enemy forces, it decisively defeated a concerted tank-infantry attack thrice its strength, using to defeat the enemy weapons no more powerful than antitank grenades. One Mark V tank was destroyed after advancing to within 10 yards of the troop's position, while two others shelled the two houses which the troop occupied, from a distance of 200 yards. Simultaneously, 75 infantrymen charged the houses but were finally repulsed with losses of 60 enemy killed and 6 taken prisoner. This small force of 4 officers and 41 enlisted men was responsible for an effective block which cut off large enemy forces from their base of supply and greatly facilitated the capture of these forces and the sector which they held. The troop held the road block against all odds until finally relieved by other friendly forces. The heroism, fighting determination, and versatility displayed by the members of *Troop A, 85th Cavalry Reconnaissance Squadron, Mechanized,* are worthy of emulation and reflect honor on the armed forces of the United States.

COMPANY B, 47th ARMORED INFANTRY BATTALION, IN CROSSING THE MEUSE RIVER

GENERAL ORDERS No. 45 } WAR DEPARTMENT, WASHINGTON 25, D. C., 12 June 1945

* * * * *

XI.—BATTLE HONORS.—1. As authorized by Executive Order 9396 (sec. I, WD Bul. 22, 1943), superseding Executive Order 9075 (sec. III, WD Bul. 11, 1942), citation of the following unit in General Orders 14, Headquarters 5th Armored Division, 14 April 1945, as approved by the Commanding General, European Theater of Operations, is confirmed under the provisions of section IV, WD Circular 333, 1943, in the name of the President of the United States as public evidence of deserved honor and distinction. The citation reads as follows:

Company B, 47th Armored Infantry Battalion, is cited for outstanding performance of duty in action against the enemy on 4 and 5 September 1944. On the night of 4 September 1944, *Company B* was given the mission of establishing a bridgehead over the Meuse River, east of Charleville, France. In order to do this, a cliff approximately 400 feet high on the north bank of the river had to be taken. Although this company had marched a distance of 96 miles during the period immediately preceding the attack, they dismounted on the south bank of the river, and supported by one battalion of 105-mm howitzers, one company of medium tanks in initial stages, one platoon of engineers, one platoon of heavy machine guns, one platoon of 81-mm mortars, and one platoon of 75-mm assault guns, crossed the river on an improvised footbridge under heavy enemy mortar and artillery fire. Immediately after crossing the river and still under devastating enemy fire, the company re-formed and attacked the cliff where concrete fortifications, underground tunnels, and wire entanglements were manned by approximately one company of a panzer division supported by self-propelled 88 mm guns, antiaircraft guns, mortars, and possibly one battery of 105-mm artillery. This position was formerly part of the French Maginot Line defenses. *Company B* fought grimly for these heights, repulsing numerous enemy counterattacks until 1200, 5 September 1944, when the enemy was defeated and routed from their positions because of the gallantry and determination of this company. Heavy casualties were inflicted on the enemy whereas this unit suffered a total of 1 killed and 12 wounded. The heroic efforts of *Company B, 47th Armored Infantry Battalion,* resulted in the defeat of the enemy, the capture of this height, and the establishment of a bridgehead which enabled an armored combat command to cross the Meuse River and proceed with the attack. Only the will to defeat the enemy in his carefully prepared natural and artificial defenses and the splendid esprit de corps of this company made possible its achievement, which reflects the highest credit on the military forces of the United States.

COMPANY C, 47th ARMORED INFANTRY BATTALION, IN CROSSING THE MEUSE RIVER

GENERAL ORDERS No. 38 } WAR DEPARTMENT, WASHINGTON 25, D. C., 16 May 1945

* * * * *

XIII.—BATTLE HONORS.—2. As authorized by Executive Order 9396 (sec. I, WD Bul. 22, 1943), superseding Executive Order 9075 (sec. III WD Bul. 11, 1942), citation of the following unit in General Orders 14, Headquarters 5th Armored Division, 14 April 1945, as approved by the Commanding General, European Theater of Operations, is confirmed under the provisions of section IV, WD, Circular 333, 1943, in the name of the President of the United States as public evidence of deserved honor and distinction. The citation reads as follows:

Company C, 47th Armored Infantry Battalion, is cited for outstanding performance of duty in action against the enemy on 4 and 5 September 1944. On the night of 4 September 1944, *Company C* was given the mission of establishing a bridgehead over the Meuse River, east of Charleville, France. In order to do this, a cliff approximately 400-feet high on the north bank of the river had to be taken. Although this company had marched a distance of 96 miles during the period immediately preceding the attack, they dismounted on the south bank of the river and, supported by one battalion of 105-mm howitzers, one company of medium tanks in initial stages, one platoon of engineers, one platoon of heavy machine guns, one platoon of 81-mm mortars, and one platoon of 75-mm assault guns, crossed the river on an improvised footbridge under heavy enemy mortar and artillery fire. Immediately after crossing the river and still under devastating enemy fire, the company reformed and attacked the cliff where concrete fortifications, underground tunnels, and wire entanglements were manned by approximately one company of a Panzer division supported by self-propelled 88-mm guns, antiaircraft guns, mortars, and possibly one battery of 105-mm artillery. This position was formerly part of the French Maginot Line defenses. *Company C* fought grimly for these heights, repulsing numerous enemy counterattacks until 1200, 5 September 1944, when the enemy was defeated and routed from their positions because of the gallantry and determination of this company. Heavy casualties were inflicted on the enemy, whereas this unit suffered a total of one killed and seven wounded. The heroic efforts of *Company C, 47th Armored Infantry Battalion,* resulted in the defeat of the enemy, the capture of this height, the establishment of a bridgehead which enabled an armored combat command to cross the Meuse River and proceed with the attack. Only the will to defeat the enemy in his carefully prepared natural and artificial defenses and the splendid esprit de corps of this company made possible its achievement, which reflects the highest credit on the military forces of the United States.

FRENCH GOVERNMENT UNIT CITATION

DECISION NO. 246

On the motion of the Minister of National Defense,
The President of the Provisional Government of the French Republic
Cites to the
ORDER OF THE DIVISION:

Combat Command R, 5th Armored Division, including:
Hq. Detachment Combat Command R
10th Tank Battalion
47th Armored Infantry Battalion
Troop D, 85th Cavalry Reconnaissance Squadron
628th Tank Destroyer Battalion
Company C, 22nd Armored Engineer Battalion

"A group of units inspired by a fierce will to conquer. It especially distinguished itself in the break-through of the Siegfried Line at Wallendorf, Germany. From 14 to 20 September 1944 it threw itself into the attack on the city and drove the enemy from it. It continued its advance and seized a bridge over the river Our. Subject to a counterattack supported by tanks and in spite of heavy losses, *Combat Command R,* nevertheless, continued its advance, penetrating farther and farther into Germany."

* * * * *

"This citation includes the award of the Croix de Guerre with silver star."

General of the Army JUIN
Chief, General Staff of National Defense.
Signed: JUIN
Paris, 15 July 1946.

BELGIAN GOVERNMENT UNIT CITATION

MINISTRY OF THE NATIONAL DEFENSE
Decree of the 20th of November 1945 — No. 1391.
CHARLES, Prince of Belgium, Regent of the Kingdom.

On the proposition of the Ministry of the National Defense.
We decided and decide:

* * * * *

Art. 2. The units mentioned below are cited in a general order of the Belgian Army:

* * * * *

Company A, 47th Armored Infantry Battalion

* * * * *

for the following reasons:

"From 20 December 1944 to 26 January 1945, in the course of the German offensive in the Ardennes, the *9th Infantry Division* of the United States and the attached units received the mission to defend the north flank of the counteroffensive led by the V Corps of the United States Army in the sector of Eupen (Belgium) – Montjoie (Germany). Facing an obstinate defense, it attacked without respite. The enemy counterattacked but was unable to enlarge the breach caused by its break-through. After the enemy attack was unsuccessful, the *9th Infantry Division* and the attached units attacked and forced the German Army to retreat and abandon the Belgian territory in that region."

Given at Bruxelles, on 20 November 1945.

COMMENDATIONS

To the Commanding General, Fifth Armored Division—

14 August 1944

"You have done a fine job. You have whipped the German wherever you have met him. You have strewn the country-side with the wreckage of his equipment. You have captured thousands of prisoners. With the experience gained in this campaign you will handle whatever lies ahead of us with confidence and ease. . . . . ."

5 September 1944

"I desire personally to thank you and every member of your command for the splendid accomplishment of every task assigned. Your achievement as a first-class fighting division is playing a large part in the liquidation of the German Army which is our eventual goal. . . . ."

— MAJ. GEN. WADE H. HAISLIP,
Commanding XV Corps

17 September 1944

". . . . The aggressive courage, unselfish devotion, tenacity of purpose and outstanding leadership of all ranks is evidenced by the fact that the Fifth Armored Division has never failed to capture its assigned objectives and has never lost ground to the enemy.

"I am proud to have had the opportunity of commanding you in battle, and I shall watch your future successes with the greatest of interest, with the knowledge that victory is assured.

— MAJ. GEN. L. T. GEROW,
Commanding V Corps

31 January 1945

"Upon the relief of the Fifth Armored Division from attachment to this corps, I desire to express to you, and through you, to the officers and men of your command, my personal thanks and appreciation for the excellent manner in which they functioned at all times while under this corps.

"With the exception of a comparatively short period of time, the Fifth Armored Division has served with this command since 28 August 1944. It saw considerable action and rendered invaluable service during the pursuit of the enemy through France, Luxembourg and Belgium. Elements of the division were the first Allied troops to enter Germany. . . . .

"I accept this loss to this command with regret. My thanks for the excellent job you did go to each and every one of you."

— MAJ. GEN. C. R. HEUBNER,
Commanding V Corps

15 March 1945

"Prior to its assignment to Ninth U. S. Army, I followed with keen interest the splendid record built up by the Fifth Armored Division during its advance across the continent. Thus it was that the recent assignment of this division to this command afforded me extreme pleasure.

"Likewise it was gratifying to me to know that the division was afforded another opportunity to distinguish itself during the Roer to Rhine Campaign just concluded. That full advantage was taken of this opportunity is conclusively proven in the fine performance by the division during the execution of this operation. . . . ."

— LT. GEN. WILLIAM H. SIMPSON,
Commanding Ninth U. S. Army

13 April 1945

"I wish to convey to you, your staff and your command my commendation and entire satisfaction with your rapid advance from the Rhine River to the Elbe River. Your advance of approximately 100 miles in one and one-half days through hostile country is an outstanding achievement of this war. It exemplifies energetic leadership, skillful employment of armor, and a high order of execution by your troops.

"The Fifth Armored Division by such vigorous execution of all assigned missions has won a high place in the esteem of all ranks of this corps."

— MAJ. GEN. A. C. GILLEM, JR.,
Commanding XIII Corps

7 May 1945

". . . . I wish to convey to you, and through you to the members of your command, my complete satisfaction with the service rendered by the Fifth Armored Division. . . .

"The planning and the energetic and efficient execution of all tactical and technical plans by the Fifth Armored Division during the advance to the Elbe River contributed greatly to the successful accomplishment of all corps missions."

— MAJ. GEN. A. C. GILLEM, JR.,
Commanding XIII Corps

SUMMARY OF AWARDS AND DECORATIONS

Distinguished Service Cross	20
Distinguished Service Medal	1
Legion of Merit	6
Silver Star Medal	312
Distinguished Flying Cross	2
Soldier's Medal	11
Bronze Star Medal	2105
Air Medal	53
Total	2510

CAMPAIGN CREDITS, 5th ARMORED DIVISION

Normandy

Combat zone. European Theater of Operations, exclusive of land areas of United Kingdom and Iceland.

Time limitation. 6 June to 24 July 1944.

Northern France

Combat zone. European Theater of Operations, exclusive of the land areas of the United Kingdom and Iceland.

Time limitation. 25 July to 14 September 1944.

Rhineland

Combat zone. Belgium, Holland, Luxembourg, Germany, and France east of the line: Franco-Belgian frontier to 4 degrees east longitude, thence south along that meridian to 47 degrees north latitude, thence east along that parallel to 5 degrees east longitude, thence south along that meridian to the Mediterranean coast except that the area of the Ardennes-Alsace combat zone is excluded from 16 December 1944 to 25 January 1945.

Time limitation. 15 September 1944 to 21 March 1945.

Ardennes - Alsace

Combat zone. Euskirchen, Eupen (inclusive), Liege (exclusive), east bank of the Meuse River to its intersection with the Franco-Belgian border, thence south and east along this border to the western border of Luxembourg, thence to Metz (inclusive), east bank of the Moselle River to Epinal (inclusive), Strasbourg (exclusive).

Time limitation. 16 December 1944 to 25 January 1945.

Central Europe

Combat zone. The areas occupied by troops assigned to the European Theater of Operations, east of a line 10 miles west of the Rhine River between Switzerland and the Waal River until 28 March 1945, and thereafter east of the east bank of the Rhine.

Time limitation. 22 March to 11 May 1945.

5th ARMORED DIVISION ASSOCIATION

GEN. OLIVER is congratulated by Gen. Jacob L. Devers at the organization of the Fifth Armored Division Association in Washington, D. C., on 11 September 1946. The photo at the activation ceremony includes, left to right: Maj. Gen. Harold W. Blakely, Lt. Gen. Wade H. Haislip, Lt. Col. Maynard N. Levenick, Gen. Devers, Maj. William G. Reynolds, Gen. Oliver, Lt. Col. Harold M. Schultz, and Maj. Henry P. Halsell.

Gen. Oliver was president and Lt. Col Fred E. Ressegieu was secretary-treasurer of the Association for the first year.

The permanent officers were elected at the first annual convention in Chicago in August 1947. Lonsdale P. MacFarland of Columbia, Tenn., succeeded Gen. Oliver as president, and Louis Filas of Lyons, Illinois was the first permanent secretary-treasurer.

ASSIGNMENT AND ATTACHMENT

To Higher Units

Date	Corps	Army		Army Group and Other	
		Asgd	Atchd	Asgd	Atchd
24 Feb 44				ETOUSA	
3 Mar 44		Third			
4 Mar 44	XX	–			
29 Mar 44	XX	Third	SBS Com Z		
17 Jun 44	XII	Third			
31 Jul 44	–	Third			
1 Aug 44	XV	Third		12th	
24 Aug 44	XV	Third	First	12th	
26 Aug 44	XV	First	–	12th	
29 Aug 44	V	First		12th	
29 Nov 44	VII	First		12th	
20 Dec 44	VII	First		12th	Br 21st
23 Dec 44	V	First		12th	Br 21st
18 Jan 45	V	First		12th	–
27 Jan 45	XIX	Ninth		12th	Br 21st
29 Jan 45	XVI	Ninth		12th	Br 21st
1 Feb 45	XIII	Ninth		12th	Br 21st
4 Apr 45	XIII	Ninth		12th	–
4 May 45	XVIII Abn	Ninth		12th	
8 May 45	XIII	Ninth		12th	

(–) Indicates relieved from assignment.

ATTACHMENTS

Unit		Dates
Antiaircraft Artillery		
387th AAA AW Bn (SP)		1 Aug 44 — 25 Mar 45
387th AAA AW Bn (SP)		28 Mar 45 — 9 May 45
Armored		
Sq C Br 1st Lothians & Border Yeo (Br 79th Armd Div)		25 Feb 45 — 4 Mar 45
Cavalry		
4th Cav Gp		1 Dec 44 — 2 Dec 44
4th Cav Gp		11 Dec 44 — 22 Dec 44
Engineer		
996th Engr Treadway Br Co (— 1 plat)		31 Aug 44 — 1 Sep 44
254th Engr C Bn		15 Sep 44 — 22 Sep 44
989th Engr Treadway Br Co		25 Feb 45 — 7 Mar 45
989th Engr Treadway Br Co		7 Apr 45 — 7 Apr 45
Field Artillery		
400th Armd FA Bn		2 Aug 44 — 4 Aug 44
400th Armd FA Bn		5 Aug 44 — 2 Oct 44
208th FA Bn (155 Gun)		17 Aug 44 — 24 Aug 44
975th FA Bn (155 How)		20 Aug 44 — 25 Aug 44
987th FA Bn (155 Gun)		26 Aug 44 — 8 Oct 44
196th FA Bn (105 How)		31 Aug 44 — 7 Sep 44
187th FA Bn (155 How)		11 Sep 44 — 22 Sep 44
Hq 187th FA Gp		11 Sep 44 — 22 Sep 44
953d FA Bn (155 How)		21 Sep 44 — 22 Sep 44
400th Armd FA Bn		23 Oct 44 — 29 Nov 44
987th FA Bn (155 Gun)		28 Oct 44 — 9 Nov 44
987th FA Bn (155 Gun)		20 Nov 44 — 5 Dec 44
400th Armd FA Bn		8 Dec 44 — 18 Dec 44
695th Armd FA Bn		6 Feb 45 — 9 Mar 45
557th FA Bn (155 Gun)		26 Feb 45 — 9 Mar 45
557th FA Bn (155 Gun)		30 Mar 45 — 25 Apr 45
252d FA Bn (105 How)		22 Apr 45 — 23 Apr 45
Infantry		
112th CT (28th Div)		11 Sep 44 — 26 Sep 44
2d Bn 110th Inf (28th Div)		15 Oct 44 — 26 Oct 44
2d Ranger Inf Bn		3 Nov 44 — 14 Nov 44
2d Bn 330th Inf (83d Div)		15 Dec 44 — 22 Dec 44
3d Bn 121st Inf (8th Div)		17 Dec 44 — 21 Dec 44
1st Bn 334th Inf (84th Div)		13 Apr 45 — 16 Apr 45
1st Bn 406th CT (102d Div)		13 Apr 45 — 16 Apr 45
407th CT (— 3d Bn) (102d Div)		17 Apr 45 — 18 Apr 45
1st Bn 335th Inf (84th Div)		17 Apr 45 — 18 Apr 45
Tank Destroyer		
628th TD Bn (SP)		2 Aug 44 — 19 Dec 44
629th TD Bn (SP)		29 Aug 44 — 14 Dec 44
628th TD Bn (SP)		28 Jan 45 — 9 May 45
771st TD Bn (SP)		17 Apr 45 — 24 Apr 45
Armored		
CC A	4th Div	1 Sep 44 — 3 Sep 4
CC A	First Army	14 Oct 44 — 26 Oct 4
CC B	First Army	15 Oct 44 — 28 Oct 4
CC R	VII Corps	9 Nov 44 — 19 Nov 4
CC R	8th Div	19 Nov 44 — 16 Dec 4
CC A	4th Div	30 Nov 44 — 2 Dec 4
CC R	V Corps	16 Dec 44 — 19 Dec 4
Co A 10th Tk Bn	78th Div	19 Dec 44 — 20 Dec 4

DETACHMENTS
(Attached to)

CC R	78th Div	19 Dec 44 – 21 Dec 44
Co A 10th Tk Bn	9th Div	20 Dec 44 – 25 Jan 45
CC R	V Corps	21 Dec 44 – 24 Dec 44
CC A	78th Div	27 Jan 45 – 1 Feb 45
CC B	102d Div	6 Feb 45 – 24 Feb 45
CAVALRY		
85th Cav Rcn Sq.	28th Div	7 Sep 44 – 9 Sep 44
85th Cav Rcn Sq.	102d Cav Gp	23 Sep 44 – 26 Sep 44
85th Cav Rcn Sq.	102d Cav Gp	2 Oct 44 – 24 Oct 44
FIELD ARTILLERY		
5th Div Arty	XIII Corps	7 Mar 45 – 30 Mar 45
INFANTRY		
Co A 47th Armd Inf Bn.	78th Div	19 Dec 44 – 21 Dec 44

COMMAND POSTS

DATE	TOWN	REGION	COUNTRY
1944			
1 Mar	Chiseldon	Wiltshire	England
15 Apr	Ogbourne St-George	Wiltshire	England
15 Jun			
23 Jul	Southampton	Hampshire	England
24 Jul	Utah Beach	Manche	France
25 Jul	St-Sauveur (vic)	Manche	France
2 Aug	Feuillie (vic)	Manche	France
3 Aug	Ganerie (vic)	Manche	France
4 Aug	La Bogerie (vic)	Manche	France
5 Aug	Fougeres (vic)	Ille-et-Vilaine	France
7 Aug	Houssay (vic)	Mayenne	France
9 Aug	Le Mans (vic)	Sarthe	France
10 Aug	Courcement	Sarthe	France
11 Aug	Sure (vic)	Orne	France
12 Aug	Sees (vic)	Orne	France
15 Aug	La Houdiere (vic)	Eure-et-Loir	France
16 Aug	Marville Moutier Brule (vic)	Eure-et-Loir	France
18 Aug	Les Boseus (vic)	Eure-et-Loir	France
19 Aug	Cravent (vic)	Seine-et-Oise	France
24 Aug	Champenard (vic)	Eure	France
25 Aug	Boinville (vic)	Seine-et-Oise	France
30 Aug	Pacy-sur-Eure (vic)	Eure	France
1944			
2 Sep	Noyon (vic)	Oise	France
3 Sep	Maing (vic)	Nord	France
4 Sep	Wasigny (vic)	Ardennes	France
5 Sep	Montigny-sur-Vence (vic)	Ardennes	France
6 Sep	Noyers (vic)	Ardennes	France
8 Sep	La Moncelle (vic)	Ardennes	France
9 Sep			
10 Sep	Bascharage (vic)	Moselle	France
12 Sep	Fels (vic)		Luxembg
18 Sep	Mastroff (vic)		Luxembg
22 Sep	Fels (vic)		Luxembg

COMMAND POSTS (Continued)

Date	Town	Region	Country
5 Oct	Faymonville (vic)	Liege	Belgium
17 Oct	Bambusch (vic)	Liege	Belgium
4 Nov	Neudorf (vic)		
1 Dec	Hahn	Rhineland	Germany
8 Dec	Zweilfall	Rhineland	Germany
24 Dec	Eupen	Liege	Belgium
1945			
28 Jan	Moresnet	Liege	Belgium
5 Feb	Hoensbroek	Limburg	Neth
26 Feb	Ubach	Rhineland	Germany
27 Feb	Hottorf	Rhineland	Germany
1 Mar	Rath	Rhineland	Germany
2 Mar	Hardt	Rhineland	Germany
1945			
4 Mar	Kempen	Rhineland	Germany
10 Mar	Neersen	Rhineland	Germany
31 Mar	Stockum	Westphalia	Germany
1 Apr	Nattuln (vic)	Westphalia	Germany
2 Apr	Everswinkel	Westphalia	Germany
3 Apr	Herford (vic)	Westphalia	Germany
7 Apr	Bad Oeynhausen	Westphalia	Germany
11 Apr	Lessien (vic)	Hannover	Germany
12 Apr	Brunau	Magdeburg	Germany
18 Apr	Neuemuhle (vic)	Magdeburg	Germany
21 Apr	Salzwedel (vic)	Magdeburg	Germany
25 Apr	Neuemuhle (vic)	Magdeburg	Germany